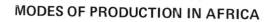
MODES OF PRODUCTION IN AFRICA

VOLUME 5
SAGE SERIES ON AFRICAN MODERNIZATION AND DEVELOPMENT

Modes of Production in Africa

The Precolonial Era

DONALD CRUMMEY and C. C. STEWART
Editors

SAGE PUBLICATIONS   Beverly Hills   London

For information address:

SAGE Publications, Inc.
275 South Beverly Drive
Beverly Hills, California 90212

SAGE Publications Ltd
28 Banner Street
London EC1Y 8QE, England

Printed in the United States of America

Library of Congress Cataloging in Publication Data
Main entry under title:

Modes of Production in Africa.

(Sage series on African modernization and development ; v. 5)
Bibliography: p.
Includes index.
Contents: The poverty of precolonial African historiography / Donald E. Crummey and Charles C. Stewart — In search of the monarch : introduction of the state among the Gamo of Ethiopia / Marc Abeles — Emergent classes and the early state : the Southern Sahara / Charles C. Stewart — [etc.]
1. Africa—Economic conditions—Congresses. 2. Africa—Politics and government—Congresses. I. Crummey, Donald. II. Stewart, Charles Cameron. III. Series.
HC800.M63   338.096   81-1433
ISBN 0-8039-1133-5   AACR2
ISBN 0-8039-1134-3 (pbk.)

FIRST PRINTING

ABOUT THE CONTRIBUTORS

MARC ABÉLÈS is associated with the Centre National de la Recherche Scientifique and attached to the Maison des Sciences de l'Homme in Paris. He has written extensively on aspects of Ethiopian social structure and is the author of *Anthropologie et Marxisme* (Presses Universitaries de France, 1976).

DONALD CRUMMEY is Associate Professor of African Studies and History at the University of Illinois at Urbana-Champaign. His work on 18th- and 19th-century Ethiopian history has appeared in a wide variety of journals and he has published *Priests and Politicians* (Oxford University Press, 1972).

BOGUMIL JEWSIEWICKI teaches in the Department of History at Laval University and has done extensive research on the social and economic history of Zaire. He has published an essay in volume 4 of this series (edited by M. A. Klein), *Peasants in Africa* (Sage, 1980) on peasants in the Belgian Congo and he has written on slavery in the same region.

ROBERTA WALKER KILKENNY is Assistant Lecturer in History at the University of Guyana. She received her B.A. from the City College of New York in 1974 and she has studied at Columbia University.

MICHAEL MASON teaches history at Concordia University and has worked extensively in Nigeria. He has authored numerous studies on aspects of the Nupe political economy, including his recently released *The Foundations of the Bida Kingdom* (Zaria, Ahmadu Bello University Press, 1980).

RICHARD ROBERTS is Assistant Professor of History at Stanford University and previously held a Killam Postdoctoral Fellowship at the Centre of African Studies at Dalhousie University. His Ph.D. at the University of Toronto (1978) rested on field research in Mali. His research interests are precolonial economic and social history.

EDWARD I. STEINHART lectures in history at the University of Zambia and he was formerly associated with the University of Texas. He has written extensively on the lacustrine region on East Africa and is the author of *Conflict and Collaboration* (Princeton University Press, 1977).

C. C. STEWART is Associate Professor of History at the University of Illinois at Urbana-Champaign. He has written on aspects of North and West African history with particular reference to Islam. He is coauthor (with E. K. Stewart) of *Islam and Social Order in Mauritania* (Oxford University Press, 1973).

CONTENTS

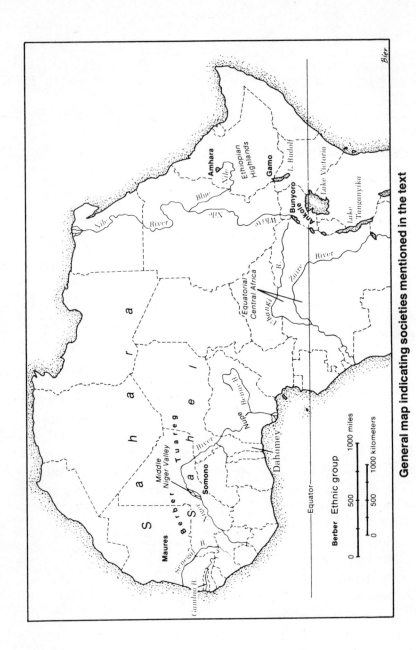

General map indicating societies mentioned in the text

ACKNOWLEDGMENTS

Cultivator and State was the title of the Sixth Annual Symposium of the African Studies Program of the University of Illinois. It was held in the spring of 1977. As organizers of that conference, we owe a great deal to the enthusiasm and encouragement of its participants, which initially launched us on the path which led to this book. Our contributors are evenly divided in number between those who did and those who did not take part in the original symposium. Of the original participants not included here, we would particularly like to acknowledge the stimulation received from Ray Kea. Others have also helped. Contributors Mason and Steinhart, as well as Martin Klein, William Freund, and Robert Shenton, responded to our pleas for criticism of an earlier draft of the introduction and did so in ways which were as collegial and comradely as they were severe. We are indebted to them.

Rene Dramé translated the essay by Abélès; Crummey translated Jewsiewicki's. Jim Bier of the Department of Geography of the University of Illinois assisted in the preparation of maps. The African Studies Program at the University of Illinois underwrote the original symposium and much of the cost of preparing the manuscript. In the latter task it was assisted by the Department of History.

1

THE POVERTY OF PRECOLONIAL AFRICAN HISTORIOGRAPHY

DONALD CRUMMEY
C. C. STEWART
University of Illinois

The purpose of this collection is modest. Its implications are wide. In the essays which follow, we attempt to demonstrate the pertinence, indeed necessity for the application, of the concepts of historical materialism to the precolonial history of Africa. The primary audience to which we address our remarks are the students of African history working in English. The inspiration for this effort has several sources, including the theoretical poverty of the existing historiography of the period and the rewarding applications of Marxian insights to other periods and disciplines within African studies. We will return to these sources of inspiration. But first we should review the origins of our enterprise and suggest its particular rationale within a Marxian frame of thought.

In 1977 we organized a symposium at the University of Illinois on Cultivator and State in Precolonial Africa. In choosing this topic we were seeking a major subject which could link our own very diverse interests and which would have quite broad implications over the whole field of precolonial African history. At one level we were playing on the hoary associations surrounding that old chestnut of African historiography, the state and state formation.[1] At another level we were seeking a subject which would stake out central terrain in the increasingly important field of social history, a subject which would address the question of agricultural production, but do so in such a way as to force a consideration of the interaction of that production with the wider forces in society. And finally, we deliberately structured our questions to raise the challenge of the only body of thought of which we are aware which offers the possibility of an integrated approach to these questions: Marxism. We were extremely gratified by the enthusiasm which developed in the symposium's sessions and by the wider interest which its subject aroused. Our basic judgment on the content of the symposium was that it had, indeed, raised the challenge of Marxian thought to the study of precolonial African history. It is that challenge to which we address ourselves in the pages which follow.

Curiously enough it is from within Marxism itself that we feel the need to offer our initial apologia. Essentially we are arguing in the following pages that the terrain of precolonial African history is the terrain *par excellence* of precapitalist modes of production and that in the voluminous recent literature of precapitalist modes of production this important terrain has been largely ignored.[2] We are not arguing that the study of precolonial African history is a major priority for contemporary Marxism; but we do assert that such a study has integrity within the Marxian tradition; that there is a necessity for it; and that such study would very substantially illuminate major questions of contemporary concern to Marxist theory. If we were to make a major criticism of the vast bulk of Marxian writing about Africa it would be to challenge the reluctance of its authors to cut the umbilical cord which links them to capitalism. Although the central text of the Marxist tradition will always remain Marx's *Capital,* Marxists forget too readily that part of the genius of that work lies in its understanding of capitalism as simply one possible mode of production among many. The study of other modes of production *in their integrity* is one way toward the recovery of the freshness of our understanding of that work.

Marxist scholars, particularly francophone ones, have devoted considerable attention to the study of precapitalist modes of production in Africa. Preeminent here has been Claude Meillassoux, whose *magnum opus* inspired, or was heavily commented on by, much subsequent research (Meillassoux, 1964; Terray, 1972; Rey and Dupre, 1973; Hindess and Hirst, 1975). We will return to a consideration of this tradition of Marxian writing on Africa below. At this point our primary concern is to note that, on the whole, Marxian concern with precapitalist modes of production in Africa has largely directed itself to a consideration of the functioning of those modes within an established colonial, and therefore capitalist, order. Although a few major exceptions do exist (Meillassoux, 1975; Terray, 1975), Marxist scholars have rarely concentrated their attention on the precolonial period. As yet no major scholarly monograph conceived of and executed within the theoretical framework of Marxism has appeared in English dealing wholly with the social history of precapitalist and precolonial Africa.

What do we mean by precolonial, and what is its place in an endeavor of Marxist theory? Precolonial, as such, is a purely chronological, nontheoretical term. Its applicability to the African past is mostly a matter of convenience. From a continental perspective the Scramble of the 1880s marks the end of this era, although it did end earlier in certain localities. Ethiopia never passed through the era at all, in spite of five years of Italian occupation in the latter half of the 1930s. However, the point we wish to underline here is that, again from a continental perspective, by and large the precolonial era is a precapitalist era in Africa. We recognize that the continent's northern and southern peripheries (Tunisia, Egypt, the Cape, Natal, etc.) had been incorporated into the capitalist world at least decades before the 1880s. We also recognize that the continent's relationship with mercantile capitalism is a dominant theme of the history of quite substantial portions of Africa from the 16th century onward. And we are very aware that that relationship had serious implications for relations of production within many African societies of the period. Several of our contributors make this very point (Jewsiewicki, Kilkenny, Mason).[3] Nonetheless, except for the littoral areas already noted above, capitalist relations of production as such did not intrude onto the continent until they did so in hand with colonial rule.

We believe that from the theoretical angle this was a major function of colonial rule: the establishment of capitalist relations of production that came to permeate the entire continent. And the establishment of those relations ought to be the dominant motif of colonial historiography, with due attention paid to the survival of precapitalist modes and to African resistance. Thus it is that the interaction of capitalist and precapitalist modes of production is, and ought to be, a central theme of the history of Africa in the colonial era. The historians of southern Africa in very recent times have been quicker to realize, and develop, this theme than have the historians of other parts of the continent. But the other side of the same coin is that scholars working on the colonial, and generally also those working on the postcolonial, period cannot avoid working within an analytical framework which is dominated by the role of capitalism. Practically speaking, it is very difficult to find societies on the continent which during the colonial era did not come under some quite substantial influence from the capitalist colonial state even if their members were not actually drawn into capitalist relations of production. We reiterate our basic point that the reverse is true for the precolonial period, a period in which precapitalist modes of production prevailed throughout the continent, enjoying a degree of autonomy, even with respect to mercantile capital, that rudely ended with the establishment of colonial rule. Precapitalist modes of production did not die in the 1880s, indeed in many parts of the continent they survive, but their autonomy was profoundly compromised. Thus it is that our precolonial focus allows us to concentrate our study of precapitalist modes of production on the most favorable available terrain.

Finally, within the Marxian tradition we feel it worthwhile to underline the importance of empirical research. The value and need for such research is well-attested both by the works already

cited and by those reviewed below. We believe that the development of African historical scholarship over the past 20 years forms
a challenge to the Marxian tradition. The achievements of African
historical scholarship have been considerable. Since the mid-
1950s an explosion of research and publication about the African
past has occurred. Vast amounts of archival material have been
uncovered, and the testimony of innumerable elders recorded.
Young and vigorous scholars have reported their findings in many
journals and several monograph series,[4] and light has shone in
many an obscure corner of the continent's history. Several of the
field's senior statesmen have enjoyed an influence in the discipline
at large.[5] In Africa itself school and university curricula have been
transformed, lively and vigorous local conferences flourish thanks
to this scholarship, and some major sources of cultural alienation
during the colonial era now safely belong to the past. Judged by the
standards of the profession as a whole, we find African history
reasonably healthy and holding its own. At the empirical level
some good work has been done. The challenge, as we see it, is to
transcend what we can now view as the received tradition of
(mainly) anglophone historical work on Africa by encouraging the
application of historical materialism, which should organize and
direct the humble tools of our historian forebearers with greater
integrity and to new ends.

The plaudits for accomplishments in past African historical
studies aside, and in spite of its impressive volume, we find serious
deficiencies in the historiography of precolonial Africa.[6] Sloppy
and boring work there has been. But the deficiencies we seek to
address are primarily those of conceptualization: the tasks which
historians have set for themselves and the ways in which they have
gone about interpreting their findings (Berstein and Depelchin,
1978–1979). We would summarize our critique under three interrelated heads. The study of precolonial African history has been
far too dominated by the demands and priorities of African nationalism. It has also been dominated by an empiricist ethos. And
where, very occasionally, theory has entered, it has entered largely
in idealist guise.

The connection between the birth of African history as an accepted academic discipline and the rise of African nationalism is close and has long been recognized. African nationalist leaders like Kwame Nkrumah consciously called for the serious study of the African past, used appeals to that past to rally their followers, and enshrined its symbols in their state paraphernalia. Academics began to seek precedents legitimating "African initiatives." This took many forms. The conscious search by scholars at the University of Tanzania for popular origins to the rise of TANU was among the most open (Temu and Kimambo, 1969). Invidious and lasting, however, has been the slightly less overt domination of 20th century ethnicity. In some cases this has meant that scholars have taken as their primary frame of reference units of extremely doubtful historical authenticity. A large part of the study of both the West and the East African past is prone to this accusation. Large amounts of energy went into the study of trade and politics, today largely a dead subject, but one symptomatic of the search for "African initiatives" (Gray and Birmingham, 1970). The motivating belief here was, ultimately, the simple refutation of racist slanders against African passivity and inertia; the subtle effect was the endorsement of African nationalist activity in general and of postcolonial regimes in particular. Research into the state and imperial traditions of Africa was primarily motivated by similar desires to demonstrate that Africans had indeed organized themselves in large units in the past, and presumably were capable of doing so again. Its association with African nationalism thus dictated to African historiography a set of priorities and interpretive motifs from which it has yet to escape. That association also precluded the study of another set of issues and problems, most notably those revolving around inequality, conflict, and division within Africa itself.

Such a confused set of objectives and priorities seems the logical outcome of the essentially empiricist nature of most modern historical research. Empiricism dominates the principal training schools of the English-speaking world, in the United States, England, and Africa. History is taught as a craft, a set of techniques directed toward the discovery of historical sources and their exploitation for ends to be determined by the private researcher. Directors of research sometimes nudge their students toward "significant" themes, but these themes all too often lack coherence or interrelationship. Not only is theory ignored in most programs for the training of professional historians but also the leaders of the profession encourage antitheoretical attitudes. In short, history in the anglophone world presents itself as a pragmatic discipline concerned with the recovery of as much of the everyday world of the past as it can manage. It eschews any higher reaches.

We find "empiricism" a description of the guiding mentality behind the discipline as a whole. The label draws attention to the extreme importance which sources and their factual implications hold in the consciousness of most historians. And it describes the attitude which accompanies this posture, an attitude that holds theory to be dangerous or wayward, or at the least misleading; an attitude which holds that the accumulation of concrete information about the past is the proper path toward discovering the available truth about the past. Most historians, if they allow theory at all, construe it as a form of high-level comparison—the realm of the highest common denominator, as it were.[7] And they believe that the way toward its discovery lies via the accumulation of facts; first facts, then, if ever, theory. The extreme epistemological naiveté which this attitude reveals was unmasked in the great debates about historicism in the 19th century. The failure to respond with a new epistemology, one which incorporates theory, has led contemporary anglophone history to its status as a craft. The extreme hold of empiricism can be seen in the work even of that masterful historical craftsman E. P. Thompson. Thompson has made lasting contributions to English history and to Marxist historiography (Thompson, 1963). His work has been shaped by Marxist theory and priorities; but it is also characterized by an extreme reluctance to make overt or to develop that theory in a dialogue with the findings of his empirical research. Most recently, Thompson has polemicized against the abuses of theory in an onslaught which ends by contradicting in words the practice for which he stands: the marriage of theory and craft in an imaginative exercise of historical reconstruction (Thompson, 1978). In Thompson's case the empiricism has been leavened by Marxist salt. Such cannot be said for most of the discipline's practitioners, much less for the historians of precolonial Africa.

Because of their empiricist biases, most historians of Africa are at the whim of their own interests, or of the interests of the societies in which they live. They find themselves unable to rise to a critical level. Or they find themselves prone to idealist views. One of the most obvious instances of idealist influences is in Fage and Oliver's (1975) celebrated hypothesis about the shaping influence of the concept of divine kingship in the early history of Africa. Most objectionable is simply the notion that ideas work in this way to mold entire societies without the intervention of material factors. However, the hypothesis about divine kingship has a still deeper objection, in that it is an extreme form of diffusionism. Diffusionism in this instance began as an apparently materialist explanation of the origins and spread of agriculture in the Middle East, and subsequently by extension in Africa. Recent work has revealed the extent to which that original hypothesis was itself the product of idealist assumptions about the role of genius in social affairs (Harlan et al., 1976). Or another illustration, in a more contemporary era, is Hopkins's (1973) use of neoclassical economics that is essentially another example of idealism. Hopkins is one of the few historians of Africa to use much theory, so his work is particularly pertinent. We find neoclassical economics inherently idealist in that it entails laws of human behavior which ignore large areas of material interest to which people are prone. In short, it is an idealization of capitalist man: consumer and investor. This position is revealed to be even more misleading when its abstractions are projected back into a precapitalist era, assuming forms of behavior in those eras which have scant applicability to the era from which the theory was derived. Yet another example of the pervasive influence of idealism is revealed in the work of that empiricist par excellence, Philip Curtin. When his work moves beyond data collection to some effort at "interpretative reason," it is chiefly governed by idealism: Islamic reform in West Africa becomes an idea whose time befalls, domino style, successive Sahelian and Sudanic communities (Curtin, 1971); or, where economic theory is woven into his empirical data, it is done in a patchwork manner so that the resultant attempts to explain Senegambian social history effectively lack the coherence of even Hopkins's neoclassical approach (Curtin, 1975).

History in English is thus peculiarly empiricist, but prone to idealist aberrations. Yet there does lie to hand a set of ideas integrated into a body of theory which is most pertinent to the task of the historian and well-suited to the analysis of Africa: dialectical materialism. Scholars in traditions other than that of anglophone history have cogently demonstrated that pertinence and suitability. Indeed, to an increasing degree historians are taking such ideas they use from Marxists or Marxisants. Dependency theory is a case in point, although a somewhat problematic one. Dependency theory as such is not Marxist. However, Marxists have been particularly quick to pick up on and to develop it, even if that phase is now ending. Rodney (1972) was the first writer of whom we are aware to attempt a synthesis of Marxism and dependency theory and to apply that synthesis to the African past. Samir Amin (1973) has gone much further along these lines, both in developing dependency theory and in theorizing its application not simply to Africa's evolving role in a world capitalist economy but also to internal African developments. In the course of the latter enterprise, he outlines the concept of a tributary mode of production which he feels underpins the state formations of the precolonial period, and in so doing addresses a central question: that of the nature of the relations between the governed and the governing in those formations. The answer is too vague and general to be of great local use, although Steinhart, in his essay below, employs the notion to advantage.

French Marxist anthropologists have been much more concrete and detailed in their applications of historical materialism, and in particular their conceptualizing of precapitalist modes of production in Africa, particularly Meillassoux and Terray. Meillassoux (1964) has led the way in demonstrating that the concepts of historical materialism, far from constituting a restrictive straightjacket on the analysis of African field data, rather suggest rich new lines of inquiry and major new sets of questions. He has continued to do this in a very substantial literature, some of which specifically addresses the precolonial past (Meillassoux, 1975). Terray (1972, 1975), while he has yet to produce a magnum opus comparable to that of Meillassoux, has demonstrated an ability to move between history and anthropology, within a Marxian analytical mode, touching on a variety of theoretical and historical points. What we want to underline here is the flexibility and imagination which characterizes the work of these authors, and the way in which their Marxist concerns lead them to new and exciting fields. Of more immediate interest to historians of the precolonial period is Meillassoux's conceptualization, and Terray's subsequent development, of the lineage mode of production. Jewsiewicki in his contribution to this volume makes considerable use of the concept.

Finally, and much closer to the turf on which historians feel at home, the field of political economy has seen stimulating contributions of recent date by Marxian scholars, the full import of which historians have been slow to absorb (Arrighi and Saul, 1973; Cohen, 1974; Mamdani, 1976; Shivji, 1976; Wallerstein and Gutkind, 1976). Perhaps the most impressive of these has been by Colin Leys (1975) in his analysis of independent Kenya. Leys bases his study on an impressive amount of data, and he draws fully on recent theoretical developments in both dependency theory and class analysis.[8] The theoretical framework of the book lies in concepts of neocolonialism and underdevelopment and it demonstrates that these concepts are susceptible to flexible and subtle application. Historians of Africa should be equally attracted to the manner in which Leys applies both the methodology and some of the concepts of Marx's (1852) celebrated *The Eighteenth Brumaire of Louis Bonaparte*. The qualities of the original, which Leys attempts to emulate, include the extreme subtlety with which Marx deploys his concepts of class, the brilliance with which he demonstrates the interaction between economic events and political events and behavior, and the manner in which he bases his political analysis on his understanding of the socioeconomic order. The limitation of Ley's work, for our purposes here, is that he directs his analysis to a capitalist context, thereby blunting the impact of his study for students of Africa's precapitalist past.

This limitation is shared, to a degree, by two other major figures, yet to be mentioned, who have applied the concepts of historical materialism to the African past: J. Suret-Canale and C. Coquery-Vidrovitch. Both have directed their attention primarily to an analysis of European colonialism in Africa and to the African response to that colonialism (Suret-Canale, 1971; Coquery-Vidrovitch, 1972). Both have deftly and cogently demonstrated the interlocking of political and economic forces which constituted the essence of that colonialism, greatly outstripping, in so doing, the vast bulk of English historical writing on the subject. Both have also paid attention to the practical and theoretical questions concerning the precapitalist and precolonial African past.[9] However, in this instance their contributions took place at a level of abstraction comparable to that of Amin. Both Suret-Canale and Coquery-Vidrovitch address the question of precapitalist modes of production in Africa at a very general level. There has been considerable refinement from Suret-Canale's initial attempt in 1964; but Coquery seems still not to have transcended the limitations of the nonmaterialist research on which they based their theorizing.

We should not further belabor the obvious: Precolonial African historiography is theoretically barren. Yet scholars in a wide variety of traditions of African studies have amply demonstrated the pertinence of the concepts of historical materialism to the continent and to its history. We believe that it is also time for the historians of precolonial Africa to seriously come to grips with the challenge of historical materialism. In this exercise they have many potential models to follow. Walter Rodney particularly deserves mention in this regard. Rodney's *A History of the Upper Guinea Coast 1545 to 1800* is primarily directed to the now-fashionable subject of Africa's incorporation into the world capitalist system. It was not conceived as primarily an exercise in African social history. However, in the development of his theme, Rodney cogently analyzes the social development of the upper Guinea coast (Rodney, 1970: 28–38). His comments about the class character of the bulk of the societies in his area have been very largely ignored by his successors, to their detriment.

What, then, are the key concepts of historical materialism pertinent to an analysis of the African past? And what are the principal benefits to be gained by their utilization? In answering these questions, we do not aspire to break new theoretical ground or to resolve current controversies. We believe that the extent of materialist research on the precapitalist history of Africa is as yet too inadequate to allow for serious theorizing at a comparative level. The elaboration of theory must follow the example of the founders of dialectical materialism and proceed in dialectical relationship with research. However, in one respect we would extend, rather than contract, the implications of what follows: The application of the methodology of historical materialism to the precolonial history of Africa is simply one very small part of a far larger enterprise—a fundamental challenge to social thought and analysis in capitalist societies in general, a challenge which seeks the revolutionary reconstitution of those societies.

The basic premise of historical materialism is embodied in Engels's observation:

> The determining factor in history is, in the last resort, the production and reproduction of immediate life . . . . On the one hand, the production of the means of subsistence, of food, clothing and shelter and the tools requisite therefore; on the other, the production of human beings themselves, the production of the species [Engels, 1884].

In short, all history must retain its sense of the everyday material realities which dominate the lives of ordinary people, and the way in which those realities impinge on the affairs of society at large.

The primary analytical tool in historical materialism is that of "mode of production."[10] This concept, which we have already touched on, is the one that links the material realities of everyday life to the wider society within which they occur. The fundamental role of this concept in Marxian thinking appears in the following quotation from *Capital*:

> Each special mode of production and the social relations corresponding to it, in short, . . . the economic structure of society, is the real basis on which juridical and political superstructure is raised, and to which definite social forms of thought correspond [Marx, 1908–1909: I, 93–94, Note 1].

The essential elements of a mode of production are the forces of production and the social relations of production. In the former category lie, for example, human labor, land, and the implements by which it is worked. In the latter lie questions of property and its transfer and distinctive relationships between producers and those who manage or organize production. At its simplest level, the concept of a mode of production is one which fully integrates those forces often separately construed as "social" and "economic." Practitioners of historical materialism have applied the mode of production concept both narrowly and broadly (Godelier, 1977: 18).[11] There is a growing tendency to construe the concept narrowly and to reserve for broader usage the concept of a "social formation." The latter concept allows one to analyze the way in which several modes of production may be essentially and dynamically interconnected (articulated) over a considerable period of time, although Althusser and his followers have used these concepts somewhat differently.

Various factors distinguish one mode of production from another. The development of the forces of production is one extremely important factor.[12] So it is that societies based on plow agriculture take on forms distinctive from those based on hoe agriculture; and the adoption of new crops may substantially affect social development. All modes of production are marked by the generation of surpluses, and the ways in which the surpluses are appropriated and distributed equally distinguish one mode of production from another (Hindess and Hirst, 1975). Variations in the methods of surplus extraction are not solely determined by technical aspects of the forces of production, a fact fully recognized by Marx himself (Marx, 1908–1909: III, 919). However, two implications are worthy of being stressed. On the one hand, it is the relations of production which primarily determine the form of the social superstructure, a superstructure which may take on the form of a state, and not the relations of exchange or circulation, such as trade. This means, quite simply, that a great deal of historical analysis on the origins and nature of African states has been wrong-headed. Second, we would emphasize, in Marx's phrase, that very similar economic bases may exhibit "infinite variations" in the social formations to which they give rise. We find this an apt characterization of much of the terrain of the history of precolonial Africa.

The variety of possible modes of production and social formations and the importance of these in determining the form of the state bring us to another and primary distinction between modes of production: those without classes and those based on class. The latter entail states, the former do not. For historical materialism, the concepts of class and state are interrelated. Neither can be understood independently of the other. From one angle the state is viewed as the necessary coercive instrument for the maintenance of social inequality and for the extraction of surplus. From the other, class is viewed as essential for the maintenance of the state and for the explanation of its behavior. And the concepts of class and the state must be referred back to the primary relations of production. Class is by no means synonymous with inequality. Africa is rich in forms of social inequality which do not take on the character of class: forms of social inequality based on age, sex, kinship, or status. Both Jewsiewicki and Abélès deal with such cases below. Class, in this connection, is a broad concept cutting across the social formation and bringing together in one social group power and prestige and a fundamental relationship to the means of social production which entails the exploitation of another such group which possesses a reciprocal lack of power and prestige. This group must be capable of reproducing itself and the conditions for the reproduction of its opposite class, beyond the lifetimes of its individual components. Essential to the relationship between these two classes is the state. In different ways Steinhart, Mason, and Crummey address the question of class and the state in their essays below. The question is one worthy of still further attention and development.

Historical materialism provides a key to resolve a central problem in African history: periodization. It does so on an objective and indigenous basis, by fixing itself on the modification to or succession of distinctive modes of production and on alterations in the forms and degrees of surplus extraction (Bernstein, 1977). In this periodization the appearance of the state marks a significant stage, as does the appearance of new forces, whether these be metalworking techniques, food crops, forms of the organization of labor, or the demand for new commodities. These forces will be significant insofar as they are disassociated from or incorporated into the preexisting social and economic apparatus, bringing about alterations in the degree of surplus produced, the mode whereby the surplus is extracted, and the formation of, or relations between, classes.

Historical materialism does not require a rigid succession of a fixed and ordered series of modes of production and it does not require that all modes of production fit into a fixed and limited set of categories. Better known texts of Marx and Engels maintained the succession of modes of production first outlined in the Preface to the *Critique of Political Economy:* primitive/communal, slave-based classical, feudal, capitalist, and, standing somewhat to one side, the Asiatic (Marx and Engels, 1966: 183). However, neither Marx nor Engels ever confined himself to this set or to its sequence (Engels, 1884).[13] Already by 1857–1858 Marx had adumbrated far subtler and more sophisticated comments on modes of production and he continued to do so (Marx, 1965). Hobsbawm rightly stresses that historical materialism shares with other historiography of the second half of the 19th century a belief in progress.[14] But this belief is global and secular, it by no means entails the view that progress was universal or unilineal, without retreat. The African data confirm that there are numerous variations in the form and sequence of actual modes of production.

The following essays explore these concepts in different ways and to different effects. We have organized them thematically, not geographically. They run the continuum from stateless, classless societies to fairly developed class formations. All refer to, and base their analyses on, fundamental social relations of production. They posit no new orthodoxy, and open as many, or more, questions as they answer.

Abélès's essay rests on fieldwork among the Gamo people of southwestern Ethiopia, an area practically unknown to the Africanist literature at large. In level of social formation the Gamo are as remote from Crummey's Amhara, with whom they share participation in the modern Ethiopian state, as they are close to the lineage societies of the Congo basin. Abélès skillfully reveals how different forms of inequality and distinct forms of authority can coexist over very considerable periods of time without issuing in class formation. He challenges the predisposition of an earlier literature to interpret central authority as bearing a state character and incidentally touches on the process of class formation which attends the articulation between the Gamo social formation and the wider forces represented by the modern Ethiopian empire. At the heart of his analysis is a depiction of a set of relations of production which guarantee to young Gamo males an autonomous role in the sphere of social production. Abélès, quite correctly, does not characterize this mode of production as a "lineage" mode of production since lineages appear to play very little role in it. The implications are considerable, and we would suggest that at some point in the near future an attempt at broad characterization of the various agrarian modes of production prevalent in Africa would be a valuable exercise.

Stewart raises a rather complex case of the articulation of several distinct modes of production: one predominantly agrarian, the other more pastoral. Lineage organization is much more significant to his case than it is to that of Abélès, but a good deal of his essay is devoted to the question of the extent to which the role of "lineage" in Saharan society is more ideological than material. Such is the burden of his attack on the segmentary concept. Of equal interest is his attempt at analyzing class formation in one of the more unusual African cases, unusual in that some, albeit pre-Marxian, notion of class already exists in the literature. Drawing on Soviet analysis of pastoral societies in central Asia, he suggests a situation of recurrent class formation which hovers on the edge of, but never passes over into fulfillment and the realization of, a state formation. Ecology, and the harsh material environment of Saharan society, is a potent, although not determining factor.

Ecology also enters Jewsiewicki's analysis of the social formations of the Zaire basin. Jewsiewicki, in his dialectical account, draws heavily on the concept of a lineage mode of production and attempts a materialist account of the forces of inequality operating within that mode and the reasons for their continual reproduction. He shows how the elders within such a mode come to enjoy a position analogous to, but short of, that of a class within more evolved formations. He also shows how the states of the area draw heavily on the lineage ideology, but in so doing transform it. He also shows the great resilience of lineage forms of organization during periods of rapid state formation, even when that formation is attended by massive social disruption and demographic unbalance. Jewsiewicki's essay is the most ambitious which we include, covering as it does an enormous territory with a complex and extremely varied array of social formations. It is also the earliest of the essays in the collection to deal directly with the question of the articulation of precapitalist African social formations with mercantile capitalism. He discusses several different stages through which this articulation passed and forcefully shows that the effects of that articulation were many and varied.

Scarcely less ambitious, although in a different way, is Steinhart's account of the origins of states in the lake region of western Uganda. He particularly focuses on the kingdom of Nkore and provides this collection with its only extended account of the transition to state society. In this respect he directly addresses issues raised by Abélès and Stewart as well as by Jewsiewicki. Although his account is informed by, and makes fruitful reference to, the appropriate theoretical issues, we particularly value it for its historical quality. In this sense it is not at all determinist, but fully acknowledges the role of incident and accident in the evolution of societies and polities. In Steinhart's case drought and famine play key roles in precipitating a major historical transition, thus vindicating Hindess and Hirst's point that there can be no theory of the form of transition from one mode of production to another (i.e., no abstract set of laws which will characterize all such transitions), but equally refuting their contention that history is a field without significance to Marxists (Hindess and Hirst, 1975). Like Stewart, Steinhart deals with a situation in which pastoral and agrarian modes of production find themselves in uneasy articulation.

Kilkenny deals with a still more complex situation, in that her case involves the articulation of a number of distinct modes of production into one highly centralized social formation, Dahomey. The case is a well-known one in the historical and anthropological literature, and it raises quite major questions about the relations between mercantile capitalism and the development of African social formations. She joins Jewsiewicki here. And unlike Mason, she argues that we can in fact discern a slave-based mode of production operative within an African social formation. However, unlike some previous analysts of Dahomey, she denies that that particular mode of production was dominant of the formation as a whole. Kilkenny, like Roberts and Mason, addresses the situation in which a very significant proportion of the precolonial population of Africa found itself: subjects of, incorporated into, complex state formations characterized by the articulation of a number of distinct modes of production, only one of which was dominant. None of our contributors finds that capitalism dominated the social formation which they analyze, although in varying ways Jewsiewicki, Kilkenny, and Mason all find it to have been of considerable influence.

Roberts is alone among our contributors in focusing his analysis not upon the social formation as a whole, but on the role of a particular occupational group within a regional political economy. It is a valuable focus, allowing him to discuss the different modes whereby this occupational group was incorporated into a succession of states, which dominated, but did not completely control, the political economy of the middle Niger. In this he joins Steinhart and Mason by making change and development dominant motifs of his account. He thereby escapes the more static and schematized tone which necessarily accompanies some of our other contributions. He also calls attention to the production role played in African social formations by groups other than farmers or herdsmen (or hunters). The Somono exploited the river and used it to provide the wider society with fish. They also played a role in generating social surplus through their transportation activities.

Mason deals with another stretch of the Niger, one dominated in his account by merchant capitalists. His example shows very clearly how the needs and demands of capital could lead to quite extensive changes in the social class relations of precolonial African societies. He shows how the Bida state was very considerably strengthened by its articulation with European traders, but that this strengthening entailed a higher degree of state exploitation of its subjects, the servility of whose status was intensified. Unlike Kilkenny he denies that slavery basically characterizes the mode of production. Rather, he sees the relations between the rulers of Bida and their subjects as mediated by the payment of tribute. His case thus would fit within Amin's broad category of a tributary mode of production, as does Steinhart's.

Crummey, too, sees the payment of tribute as the key to the relations between the peasants of highland Ethiopia and their lords. Alone among the volume's contributors he is willing to

countenance some of the language of feudalism and explores varying notions of property in land in their wider role within the state
formation. In this he goes rather beyond Jewsiewicki who touches
on the issue. Crummey also pays rather more extended attention to
the dialectical relations between the concepts of state and class, at
least at the level of the Abyssinian nobility. He argues against too
simple a notion of the state, one which would sharply separate it
from its class framework. He, too, like Steinhart, Roberts, and
Mason, deals with change, but his change is largely confined to the
political level, the revival of the Solomonic state. However, he
does discuss how the revival of the Ethiopian state led to its expansion, the conquest of southern territories, and the imposition there
of a class system resembling feudalism. In so doing, by bringing
the highland Ethiopian state into the same area as that of Gamo, he
brings the collection full circle.

It is quite clear that we have only begun to explore fundamental
questions concerning the social history of Africa, even in the
precolonial period. It is equally clear that there is massive scope
for the further development and application of the concepts of
historical materialism to the African past. Variations in modes of
production, in particular the viability and further development of
the lineage concept, deserve attention. The origins of states, the
meaning of class, and the development of class-based modes of
production in precolonial Africa are, too, questions deserving
much fuller treatment. A fresh periodization of the history of
particular African societies and social formations—and beyond
them of the regional networks of societies, states, and empires,
through an emphasis on changes in modes of production—is an
urgent task. Finally, the articulation of indigenous modes of production with mercantile capitalism is a major question for substantial parts of precolonial Africa. We hope that in our appeal for the
analysis of precapitalist modes of production in Africa, we will
have provided fresh impetus and a healthier balance to the further
study of that articulation.

NOTES

1. The dominance of which was recognized by the commissioning of Horton's special chapter on stateless peoples in Ajayi and Crowder (1972).

2. See, for example, Hindess and Hirst (1975), Godelier (1977), and Seddon (1978). Meillassoux (1975) is a major exception.

3. See also Ray Kea's (1979) excellent work on the Gold Coast.

4. *Journal of African History, International Journal of African Historical Studies, History in Africa, Cahiers d' études africaines.* See also the Oxford and Ibadan/Longmans series of monographs.

5. Most notably P. Curtin (1969) and J. Vansina (1972, 1973).

6. A historiography enshrined, some would say embalmed, in the formidable *Cambridge History of Africa,* of which Volumes 2 through 5 have appeared at the time of writing.

7. A point on which we agree with Robin Law (1978).

8. Leys (1977) writes that he has reconsidered the dependency theory and would more fully develop his account of class struggle.

9. Coquery-Vidrovitch (1969, 1976) and Suret-Canale (1964).

10. Most highly developed with respect to the capitalist mode of production in Marx's three-volume masterpiece, *Capital,* the concept is widely applied elsewhere. For provocative recent thinking, see: Althusser and Balibar (1970) and Hindess and Hirst (1975, 1977). The last work rejects the concept altogether.

11. In the work of Marx himself, *Capital* is an example of the former and the Preface to *The Critique of Political Economy* an example of the latter (Marx and Engels, 1966).

12. Shaw (1978) has allowed the importance of this factor to lead him into a technicist interpretation of Marx's view of history.

13. See also Engels's footnote to the 1888 English edition of the *Manifesto of the Communist Party* (Marx and Engels, 1966: 35–36).

14. In his introduction to Marx (1965: 12).

REFERENCES

AJAYI, J., and M. CROWDER (1972) History of West Africa (Vol. 1). London: Macmillan.

ALTHUSSER, L., and E. BALIBAR (1970) Reading Capital. London: Macmillan.

AMIN, S. (1973) Le developpement inégal. Paris: Maspero.

ARRIGHI, G., and J. SAUL (1973) Essays on the political economy of Africa. London: Macmillan.

BERNSTEIN, H. (1977) "Marxism and African History—Endre Sik and his Critics." Kenya Historical Review 5: 1–21.

BERNSTEIN, H., and J. DEPELCHIN (1978–1979) "The object of African history: A materialist perspective." History in Africa 5: 1–19.

Cambridge University (n.d.) The Cambridge History of Africa. Cambridge, England: Author.

COHEN, R. (1974) Labour and politics in Nigeria, 1945–71. London: Macmillan.

COQUERY-VIDROVITCH, C. (1969) "Recherches sur un mode de production africain." Pensée: 61–78.

———— (1972) Le Congo au temps des grandes compagnies concessionnaires 1898–1930. Paris: Maspero.

———— (1974) L'Afrique noire de 1800 à nos jours. Paris: Maspero.

———— (1976) "The political economy of the African peasantry and modes of production." In I. Wallerstein and P. Gutkind (eds.) The political economy of contemporary Africa. Beverly Hills, CA: Sage.

CURTIN, P. (1969) The Atlantic slave trade: A census. Madison: University of Wisconsin Press.

———— (1971) "Jihad in West Africa: Early phases and interrelationships in Mauritania and Senegal." Journal of African History 12: 11–24.

———— (1975) Economic change in precolonial Africa. Senegambia in the era of the slave trade. Madison: University of Wisconsin Press.

ENGELS, F. (1884) The origin of the family, private property and the state. London: International Publishers.

FAGE, J., and R. OLIVER (1975) A short history of Africa. Baltimore: Penguin.

GODELIER, M. (1977) Perspectives in Marxist anthropology. Cambridge, England: Cambridge University Press.

GOODY, J. (1976) Production and reproduction. Cambridge, England: Cambridge University Press.

GRAY, R., and D. BIRMINGHAM (1970) Precolonial African trade. London: Macmillan.

HARLAN, J. et al. (1976) Origins of African plant domestication. The Hague, The Netherlands: Mouton.

HINDESS, B., and P. HIRST (1975) Precapitalist modes of production. London: Macmillan.

————— (1977) Mode of production and social formation. London: Macmillan.

HOPKINS, A. (1973) An economic history of West Africa. London: Macmillan.

KEA, R. (1979) "Land, overlords and cultivators in the seventeenth century Gold Coast." (unpublished)

LAW, R. (1978) "In search of a Marxist perspective on precolonial tropical Africa." Journal of African History 19: 441–452.

LEYS, C. (1975) Underdevelopment in Kenya. Berkeley and Los Angeles: University of California Press.

————— (1977) "Underdevelopment and dependency: Critical notes." Journal of Contemporary Asia 7: 92–107.

MAMDANI, M. (1976) Politics and class formation in Uganda. New York: Random House.

MARX, K. (1908–1909) Capital (Vols. 1–3). Chicago: Chicago University Press.

————— (1965) Pecapitalist economic formations. New York: Random House.

————— and F. ENGELS (1966) Selected works in one volume. London: International Publishers.

MEILLASSOUX, C. (1964) Anthropologie économique des Gouros de Côte d'Ivoire. Paris: Maspero.

————— (1975) L'esclavage en Afrique précoloniale. Paris: Maspero.

NKRUMAH, K. (1975) Ghana. The autobiography of Kwame Nkrumah. Edinburgh, Scotland: University of Edinburgh.

REY, P. P. and G. DUPRE (1973) "Reflections on the pertinence of a theory of the history of exchange." Economy and Society 2: 131–163.

RODNEY, W. (1970) A history of the Upper Guinea Coast. London: Macmillan.

————— (1972) How Europe underdeveloped Africa. London and Dar-es-Salaam: n.p.

SEDDON, D. (1978) Relations of production: Marxist approaches to economic anthropology. London: Macmillan.

SHAW, W. (1978) Marx's theory of history. Stanford, CA: Stanford University Press.

SHIVJI, I. (1976) Class struggles in Tanzania. London: Tanistock.

SURET-CANALE, J. (1964) "Les sociétés traditionnelles en Afrique Noire et le concept de mode de production Asiatique." Pensée 117: 19–42.

———— (1971) French colonialism in tropical Africa 1900–1945. London: Tavistock.

TEMU, A., and I. KIMAMBO (1966) A history of Tanzania. Evanston, IL: Northwestern University Press.

TERRAY, E. (1972) Marxism and primitive societies. New York: Random House.

———— (1975) "Classes and class consciousness in the Abron kingdom of Gyaman," pp. 85–135 in M. Bloch (ed.), Marxist analysis and social anthropology. New York: Random House.

THOMPSON, E. P. (1963) The making of the English working class. London: Tavistock.

———— (1978) The poverty of theory and other essays. New York: Random House.

VANSINA, J. (1973) Oral tradition. Harmondsworth, England: Penguin. .

———— (1972) "Once upon a time: Oral traditions as history in Africa," pp. 413–39 in F. Gilbert and S. R. Graubard (eds.) Historical studies today. New York: Random House.

WALLERSTEIN, I., and P. GUTKIND (1976) The political economy of contemporary Africa. Beverly Hills, CA: Sage.

2

IN SEARCH OF THE MONARCH: INTRODUCTION OF THE STATE AMONG THE GAMO OF ETHIOPIA

MARC ABÉLÈS
C.N.R.S., Paris

Classes, exploitation, and state are closely linked in capitalist societies. Did such a link exist in the remote past? What of the precapitalist African societies? First, such writings of Marx as the Preface to Contribution to the Criticism of Political Economies which underlines the relation between mode of production and political-judicial superstructure and, second, Engels's analysis of the origin of the state promoted the view of an unequivocal casuality between infrastructure and superstructure. Engels states, "After reaching a certain level of economic development linked with the division of societies into classes, the state becomes a necessity" (1884: 159). Therefore, the society with a certain degree of internal stratification where it is common practice to extort extra work from producers could not survive without centralization of power.

Such an assumption is questionable, and the study of Gamo history, an Ometo-speaking population of southern Ethiopia, will show the limitations of this interpretation of the relation between exploitation, classes, and state. We shall propose a Marxist analysis of political and economic phenomena which will explain the complexities of relations between superstructure and mode of production. This will attempt to demonstrate that in a society such as the Gamo, without classes, exploitation and inequality may still prevail.

At the end of the 19th century King Menelik II decided to reconquer a number of territories which in the past belonged to the crown. Between 1880 and 1910, this expansionist policy led the Amhara to successfully conquer the Kafa and the Wollayta kingdoms as well as many other territories. Only in 1897 did Menelik's army take over the Gamo land southwest of Wolllayta.

Unlike their northern neighbors, the Gamo did not resist the invaders. However, although the Amhara easily found chiefs among the Kafa and the Wollayta, the situation was quite different with the Gamo. They could find neither a king among them nor a central organization for the whole territory. Today this mountain area is still inhabited by some 40 societies (or *dere*) made up of 5,000 to 35,000 people each. For many centuries these territories (the most literal translation of *dere*) maintained a close relationship. Sometimes they formed federations under a common political body. Until the arrival of Menelik's troops, the *dere* had remained outside the state.

From 1897 on, for the purpose of taxes and the regulation of their affairs, the Amhara officers were to appoint local authorities among those who appeared most influential to them. The search for a monarch failed, but from then on the Gamo became a component of the Ethiopian state. In 1974, the Gamo we talked to, when asked the question, "Who is your king?" replied, "Emperor Haile Selassie." A year later, it had become "Mengistu." However, we shall see that there never existed a term expressing the concept of king. *Ka'o,* the commonly used Ometo term, applies to high priests.[1] Helmut Straube, who was the first to research the Gamo political system, appears to have been misled by this ambiguity (Straube, 1957, 1963). At any rate, his interpretation of the system raises the question: were there monarchical structures in Gamo territories before Menelik's conquest?

Straube indeed makes this interpretation on the premise that the Gamo use two titles: one political and the other ritual. The *ka'o* designates the high priest of the territory and is hereditary, whereas the *halaka,* an elected title, is a representative of the *dere* assembly and as such has to see to it that decisions made by this sovereign authority are carried out. According to Straube, the title of *ka'o* was introduced after that of *halaka.* This *ka'o* institution would appear to be some kind of kingship superimposed over an initially democratic structure. Therefore we are faced once more with a question of the existence of a monarchy before Menelik's conquest.

Thus this problem arises once more because of the very complexity of Gamo history. The erection of altars *(tabot)* dating back to the end of the 15th century in Dorze, Ele, and Kogota proves the Amhara influence at that remote time. The influence of Christianity was to prevail later under Zara-Yakob and Lebne-Dengel to be in turn superseded by Islam with the invasion by Ahmad Gragn. But from 1530 to 1540, the gradual cleavage between northern and southern Ethiopia took place. The Gamo region was to remain apart from the Amhara civilization for more than three centuries, neither penetrated by Islam nor by the successive Oromo invasions.

The first Amhara expansion could not have disappeared without leaving traces behind. Some Amhara priests had settled in the highlands, and to this day beside the churches built during the Amhara invasion, a great number of territories are still inhabited by some clans named *Amara.* These are none other than the offspring of Amhara pioneers.

Straube notes that in Dorze the *ka'o* was a member of these original Amhara clans. His ancestor had been appointed as an administrative officer *(balabbat)* during the 1897 conquest; that *ka'o* held the cross of Dorze. Based on this premise, Straube (1957) posits the thesis that the monarchism characterizing the establishment of the *ka'o* was the result of the first Amhara invasion in the 15th century. Straube also appears to have discovered a royal dynasty in another area: the Ochollo region. But, we happen to have lived in that society for a long time.[2] During our stay we noted that Straube's designated monarch had never been a *ka'o;* he was just a *halaka* who later became a *balabbat*. Facts seem to invalidate this historicist notion: first, the correlation *ka'o/* Amhara is proven only in Dorze; second, one has to wonder whether Straube, in his eagerness to find a "normal" form of evolution in Gamo society as in others, that is, from the absence of a state to the emergence of it, was not misled by his ethnocentrism. In brief, should we really search for a monarch?

These introductory remarks are meant to show the kind of problems that need to be tackled when studying an oral culture. We have sparse chronological data at our disposal, which tempts us to piece together history on very fragile premises. Another difficulty is that we often apply some elaborated categories that are used to understand our own society (monarchy, state, class struggle, etc.) without mentioning implicit notions of human evolution, for example, that societies move from anarchy to gradual centralization.

This is as true of Marxists as of others. But the study of specific cases should permit us to overcome these preconceived notions and difficulties. We shall therefore attempt to describe here the traditional Gamo political structure as well as the infrastructure. Such a description will help us disprove the historicist thesis on the emergence of the state as a result of an outside invasion. On the other hand, we shall note that stratified societies, where it is common practice to extort extra work from dependents, present major obstacles to state centralization. We shall attempt to better define those obstacles in order to question the mechanistic conception concerning the relations of infrastructure/superstructure and classes/state.

The Gamo societies live in a mountainous latitude 6 degrees north and 37.5 degrees east of Lake Abaya and Chamo. These 4,000-meter high mountains cover about 2,500 square kilometers. The area is densely populated, with between 550 and 2,600 inhabitants per square mile. Depending upon the altitude, the crops are greatly varied. The Gamo are primarily farmers. In Ochollo, for example, where we lived, they grew corn and cotton in the lowlands below 2,000 meters and barley on the plateau where false-banana trees *(ensete edulis),* cabbage, and chick peas were also grown. In other high areas such as Dita, Dorze, and Doko one finds potatoes. The Amhara also introduced wheat and teff. Agriculture is therefore the main economic resource for the Gamo. They farm on terraces built around the mountain slopes and in the gardens surrounding their houses. Only the Dorze, who turned into famous weavers all over Ethiopia, prefer handicrafts to farming.

Each community has at least one market where they exchange all sorts of goods. The Gamo travel around easily and take part in the various regional markets. Houses are usually dispersed; Ochollo is the only area where homes are clustered on a rocky peak. The Gamo houses are surrrounded by plantations of false-bananas which shade their gardens. The residents here are strongly attached to their houses and their region. They identify more with their neighbors than with their relatives. Each individual is indeed a member of a clan reckoned by patrilineal descent. But members of the same clan living in different territories scarcely know each other, and the relationship between neighbors is much stronger. People of the same neighborhood *(guta)* gather into assemblies for the purpose of managing public business and settling quarrels between individuals.[3] The *guta* has its own priest and dignitaries.

The *dere,* a higher political unit, is made up of all the various neighborhoods. It is governed by the general assembly of all the inhabitants and is represented by the high priest *(ka'o)* when dealing with other *deres*. Each assembly (of the *guta* and *dere* levels) designates its own dignitaries *(halaka)* from among the citizens. Such a political organization was always based on the distinction between noncitizens and citizens. The former could not own land, unlike the latter upon whom they were dependent. When we arrived in 1974, discrimination between craftsmen and citizens was the norm.

Traditionally, citizens *(mala)* were considered purer than noncitizens *(ts'oma)*. This social class not only included craftsmen such as blacksmiths, potters, and tanners but also slaves. Members of this despised inferior class could not be landowners. Just as slaves changed masters, craftsmen often moved from one area to another. Their settlement in a *dere* was subject to the citizens' approval. They were allotted a piece of land to build their houses on, and the area of the *ts'omas* had to be isolated from that of the citizens. Citizens could drive out craftsmen from the *dere* in which they lived. In Ochollo, the potters and tanners we met were often born in another *dere* before their parents were expelled. Thus craftsmen were a very mobile group; they were prevented from casting their roots anywhere.

Abolition of slavery did not change this situation; the descendents of slaves and craftsmen were still outcasts. In Ochollo, potters and tanners have their own assemblies; potters also named a dignitary who, in the citizens' opinion, was a mere caricature of the *halaka*. He was denied the phallic insignia and his crowning was a poor imitation of that performed for real dignitaries. The *mana halaka* himself made fun of his title and thought of himself as the subject of one of the citizen dignitaries. A very strict endogamous pattern appeared among the *ts'omas* who thus constituted real castes within the society. When castes were abolished in 1975, Ochollo people could not envisage the establishment of equal rights between the *ts'oma* and *mala*. Craftsmen themselves could not imagine mixed marriages between citizens and noncitizens.

In fact, just as craftsmen and slaves were excluded from assemblies, so, too, were women. Gamo societies thus appear to be very stratified formations. The slave was treated as a mere tool unworthy of owning land, and since the craftsman could pollute the soil, he was allowed to till the earth but was kept away from crops. *Ts'omas* were fed by their *mala* protectors; thus dependence, before being political, was first and foremost alimentary.

The Gamo land system was based on individual ownership. Plots were bound by such landmarks as stones, trees, and stakes. It was considered a serious offense to move those landmarks or to farm a neighbor's field, which amounted to breaking a taboo *(gome)*. However, the Gamo land organization did not forbid the temporary or permanent giving up of property, with or without payments for the rights of usage or usufruct over the land. An individual could transfer usufruct of the land to a tenant provided that the latter gave him back half of the crop. It was also possible to sell land. In the 19th century, animals, slaves, and cloth were used as a means of exchange but today money is used as a universal equivalent.

Land inheritance usually involved distribution. Most often a father bequeathed his eldest son with half of his estate and divided the remainder among the younger ones. But he could favor one or another at his own discretion. Private appropriation of land as well as established alienation procedures helped promote inequalities. Some individuals could indeed add to their estate at the expense of others.

Thus two forms of social differentiation in traditional Gamo society can be observed: on the one hand, the stratification between *mala* and *ts'oma*, that is between landowners and nonlandowners and, on the other hand, the cleavage within the citizens' group between rich and poor. The poor could be compelled to farm for the rich as sharecroppers. Unfortunately, it is impossible to measure such disparities in the social economy accurately. However, as indicated by J. Olmstead, "Gamu Highland society, while maintaining a rigid distinction between citizens and noncitizens, encouraged individual achievement among the citizens" (1975: 230). A great social mobility prevailed from one generation to the other because of land transfers. As we shall note below, individual enterprise was strongly stimulated by the ideology of prestige and expenditure.

War played a vital part in the reproduction of relations of dependents and of exploitation which determined social stratification. It was a means to acquire slaves and to rule other territories. Usually antagonism between neighboring *deres* was instigated by issues such as cattle theft or trespassing a neighbor's farm. At the end of the war, in the absence of a clear victory, opponents entered a covenant to secure peace and respect of boundaries. The victorious *dere* in the war ruled over the defeated one. Such a subordination could take many forms: Either the defeated *dere* became a vassal of a victor and had to supply military aid in times of war or it was to work for the victorious *dere*. In the first case, the subject *dere* was considered as *yelo dere*, or "children's territory," and in the second one as *mach' o dere*, or "female territory."

Thus, each citizen of the *mach' o dere* became the subject of one of the members of the expedition of the victors. His task was to perform forced labor in his master's estate while still maintaining the right to live in his own *dere* and farm his own land. This was therefore an advanced form of bondage whereby whole societies were deprived of their political autonomy. The victor's *ka'o* superseded the defeated one when representing the territory. However, the conquered *dere* maintained its assemblies and its dignitaries; it was henceforth an element of a broader political unit. The weakest Gamo societies were absorbed but they still could win back their autonomy by joining an alliance with bigger communities. This is clearly one explanation of the frequency of wars in the past century.

At the end of those wars, victory determined a special kind of dependent relation based on the appropriation of force for *yelo deres* or productive force for *mach'o deres*. In fact, what was appropriated was human labor not the object of labor, land. Why did victorious territories choose this kind of domination? We could agree with Olmstead (1975) that environmental and demographical conditions necessitated a vast labor force. In the densely populated highlands, the poor fertility of soils required the supply of more fertilizer. Animal manure was generally used, but sufficient pasture was necessary to graze animals used in the production of fertilizer. If too many grasslands were turned into farmlands, a cycle of degeneration would start. Therefore, the appropriation of the maximum amount of land was not the ideal, but rather finding enough labor force to feed animals, carry fertilizers, and till and sow seeds. The polygamous landowner usually settled one of his wives away from his own residence on one of his distant lands. She farmed this land and took care of the animals. This was a very widespread practice as was witnessed in Ochollo. It was also to one's advantage to own slaves. Any sudden change in the land structure could greatly harm such a system whereby intensive work and cattle proximity to farmlands were vital to agriculture. It was far better to increase potential production and have whole *deres* work without modifying the organization of the Gamo territories. Thus emerged vast federations which gradually incorporated many dependent territories. The most important we know about were Bonke, west of the Gamo land with about 40,000 people, and Kogo, north of the Gamo mountains covering an even wider area. According to our informants, Ganta, in the southwest area, used to rule over territories, especially Ochollo.

Although largely lacking chronological landmarks concerning the history of relationships between *deres,* we do however hold priceless testimonies. Thus, the anthropological observation of the present may provide us with retrospective information concerning certain aspects of the past. In the case of Bonke, for example, old quarrels have left traces, and relations of dependence established in the past still prevail in the present social structure.[4] Within this federation there exist two categories of very different clans: the Dache and the Gamo clans. The hierarchy is obvious for the Bonke people who explain that Daches were the masters and Gamos the subjects. Intermarriages between both clans were prohibited; the Gamo and Dache statuses were hereditary. The Gamo people farmed the Dache lands, even though they could own their own. Daches always lived in the central area of the Bonke territory. There were built the assembly square as well as the market and the house of the *ka'o*. The latter was of course a member of one of the Dache clans. However, the Gamos lived on the outskirts. Their servitude was maintained by an ideology which associated them with all depreciated values. "Whatever their setbacks in life, Daches remained Daches, that is masters, whereas in the traditional Gamo pattern today's masters would turn into tomorrow's vassals" as Bureau (1978, 1979) pointed out.

There are more Gamo than Dache, but the Bonke population traces the origins of the inequality between Dache and Gamo back to myths referring to divine decision. One day, God visited the Dache and the Gamo brothers clad as a beggar; knowing that they both had milk he asked them for a drink. Only Dache presented God with milk. Therefore, God made him the master and condemned Gamo to slavery (Bureau, 1979: 79).

In their own traditions, Bonke people pass on the story that the Dache were conquerors from the northern areas; whereas others contend that the Dache, neighbors of the Gamo, defeated the latter by resorting to trickery (Bureau, 1979: 81). Thus, in spite of the myths, Gamos were not always subjects. In fact, it appears that the Gamo status was systematically applied to people from all defeated *deres*. It sanctioned dependence and its perenniality. Thus, vassal *deres* could never regain their autonomy. They were merged into a preexisting hierarchy.

Bonke appears to be an extreme example of the conquering dynamics which characterize Gamo territories. In this case the subordination of the *mach'o dere* was transmitted into an immutable differentiation within the federation unit thus formed. Unification became then synonymous with political domination and economic exploitation of long duration.

Within each *dere* we observed the stratification between citizens and noncitizens and the relations of inequality among the citizens themselves. As to the relationship between Gamo territories, another type of dependence was established. Here the extortion of extra work did not apply to individuals only, but to whole structured societies. Defeated political units worked for their masters and even lost their identities, as in the case of regions gathered under the Gamo category in Bonke.

Was this a form of "general slavery," to employ the notion that Marx (1970: 205) applied to eastern populations? We should note that these dominated groups were not slaves per se since their members could not be exchanged on the market. Could they be defined as mere tributaries? It is true that their subordination consisted principally in the obligation to supply their masters with extra labor without pay. In the Bonke case, these tributaries suffered another sociological constraint. They were assimilated with castes and the prevailing ideology prevented them from escaping their inferior status. In other words, the relation of exploitation was legitimated, extended, and reinforced by the hierarchical ideology.

The Bonke case is a possible variant of a more comprehensive relation of collective subordination. Dominated territories often attempted to emancipate themselves by provoking new wars. But in order to maintain their hegemony, the conquerors entered new covenants when they could not meet the threat posed by their dependence. Thus, the federation was preserved but the tribute was abolished. All members of the federation became equal. Such was the case in Kogo, where a similar situation occurred. The *ka'o* representing this area was a member of a group which extended its power over the whole territory. But no social stratification between districts and more generally between citizens could be observed. At Kogo the structural equality between the two groups of districts, Ezo and Zozo which constitute the federation, reflects such tensions. In the 19th century a war was waged between Ezo and Zozo. The Zozo people wanted the federal assembly square transferred to their area. They won, but to this day tensions still prevail between those districts (Bureau, 1979: 204–205).

Thus, the history of relations between Gamo *deres* reveals two contradictory tendencies. First, there is the tendency toward centralization which appears as hegemony and even at times (as with Bonke) as a hierarchy. Second, we have the dynamics of emancipation based on the respect of the basic political unit (the *guta,* the district or group of districts, depending upon the importance of the area involved).

In our opinion, this contradiction which sustains the historical process is but the reverse side of a more profound reality: the interdependence of Gamo societies. This interdependence is linked with a specific mode of exchange and with a mode of production. As far as the mode of exchange is concerned, we should keep in mind that each society had its own market which usually was held once a week. The intensity of exchanges depended upon the variety and complementarity of agricultural products. The relative autonomy of those markets was necessary to circulate the various items from one end of the Gamo mountains to the other. Such an exchange system does not appear quite compatible with centralization measures which would disregard some particular features, notably in agricultural produce, of *deres*.

As we already noted, at the base of the social structure the mode of production necessitates the appropriation of nature under certain ecological constraints. Also the prevailing relations of production defined by private appropriation of land is extended into a relation of exploitation by which social agents extort extra work from direct producers and apply it to their own land. We also noted that such extortion did not prevent subjects from holding on to their own work tool: the land. Quarrels between *deres* resulted of course in the conquerors' monopolization of the work force provided by the defeated. But this force could not be transferred for fear it should upset the very foundations of the productive system. Therefore, although extra work could be concentrated, any reorganization of the farmlands would fail. In spite of the permanent dependence, people of subjected areas continued working their own farms.

The main mode of extortion which involved a form of collective subordination did not result in the destruction of social structures within defeated areas. In fact, these lasted and maintained the unity of defeated *deres*. Even in the most extreme case, in Bonke, where the objective of the hierarchical ideology was to wipe out the autonomy of defeated units by merging them into a single homogeneous class, the boundaries of districts (formerly independent *deres*) remained unchanged and individuals clung to their native soil. The system of dependence had its own limitations: Prohibiting any change in the prewar social relations, it rather encouraged the preexisting groups in their desire to rebel. It was logical for a subordinated *dere* which preserved its internal unity to attempt to shape the role of the conqueror. The very manner in

which extra work was extorted harbored seeds of a counterten-
dency to emancipation. The relations of forces of production (ecological constraints + mode of work)/relations of production
(mode of appropriation + mode of extortion) carried in itself the
very contradiction which pervaded the whole history of relations
between Gamo territories. This contradiction can thus be defined:
It opposes the unifying centralist tendency induced by the relations
of extortion to the centrifugal tendency of territorial autonomy
which resulted mainly from ecological restrictions and the particular mode of appropriation of nature. This explains the relative
instability of relations between *deres:* A radical transformation of
forces of production would have been necessary for one of the two
tendencies to prevail.

After our attempt at studying the "interdependence" of Gamo
territories (or rather their dependence and its limitation), it appears
necessary to return to the paradox which faced the officers of
Menelik II and later Western research workers: In spite of the
stratification and hierarchy in Gamo societies, they reproduced
themselves although without any central authority. Nevertheless,
within each society it was not difficult in 1897 to appoint as effective governor the first dignitary of the country: the *ka'o*. We also
noted that as far as he was concerned, Straube did not hesitate to
regard Gamo territories as real kingdoms. Closer to us, Olmstead
sees *ka'os* as "hereditary kings," although he admits that their
authority was counterbalanced by assemblies (Olmstead, 1975:
224). Sperber, in his research work on the Dorze which depicts the
duality of the *ka'o* and *halaka* titles, states that "both ideologies:
monarchy and democracy, co-exist and have co-existed for a long
time in the Gamo mountains, and that the effective distribution of
power in any specific *dere* tended to waiver from one pole to the
other" (Sperber, 1974: 76).

Thus, just as it was quite difficult to find a monarch, it was
practically impossible to get rid of him. As the proverb states:
"Where there is smoke there is fire." But instead of giving preference to one of the two "poles" much as did Straube and Menelik's

officers (each in his own way and for quite different reasons), we should rather explain this very oscillation between monarchism and democratism.

We shall give a brief description here by way of introducing an analysis which will not only explain the features of each *dere's* internal political system but also the global structure of relations between territories: Obviously, both phenomena are not foreign to each other. There are three components to the political ritual superstructure of each Gamo *dere:* first, the general assembly of citizens *(dulata),* an embodiment of the people's power; second, dignitaries *(halakas),* who are assigned a number of functions and elected by the assembly; third, the high priest *(dere ka'o),* symbol of legitimacy and who holds the highest rank.

Let us start with the latter: In terms of hierarchy the *dere ka'o* is called the eldest *(baira)* of the community. He acquires this status by birth as part of the principle of primogeniture. In some Gamo territories, the *ka'o* is removable but this function is then always transferred to a near relative. The high priest is not only the eldest of his clan he is also *baira* of a territory for which he accomplishes rituals and which he represents in his dealings with the outside world.

The *ka'o* could be easily recognized by the precedence he was given everywhere: In the assembly or in any other meeting he occupied the seat of honor. In some territories he was even isolated from the public by a piece of material. He was entitled to respect in every way and in some *deres* people prostrated themselves before him. The priest was surrounded by taboos and indeed he was considered endowed with a supernatural power *(tema);* it was dangerous for anyone to be cursed by him. *Ka'os* wore special emblems such as rings, necklesses, and bracelets, and their distinctive haircut made them stand out. Part of the privileges enjoyed by priests were such services as having their house built and wood picked by their ritual dependents. They also had the right to first crops, and the right to the best part of animals offered in sacrifices, for example, the right hind leg. Priests also received allowances in kind from dignitaries when they assumed their functions, for example, honey, barley beer, and butter. Having always been indispensable to the community, the *ka'o* without any ambiguity appears as a supreme authority in the hierarchy of the Gamo societies. Indeed, sacrifices played a vital part in public life; in fact, they were closely linked with the economic life.

As in many African societies, symbolic and ritual practices should not be considered an exclusive world isolated from other social practices. For the people, sacrificial rituals guaranteed good crops and good health for human beings. Economic success was not only the fruit of efficient work but also the result of appropriate applications of ritual rules. The *ka'o* was the sole guardian of these rules. Therefore each *ka'o* had his own regulations. He was the only one to know the particular regulations and to be in a position to continue the tradition by carrying out all the necessary operations without failure.

Each priest had his own prescriptions which differed from the others: One recommended killing the consecrated victim by piercing its heart, another by cutting its throat. Some of them used knives, others spears. Thus the community could put their complete trust in these ritual experts who were also endowed with supernatural power *(tema)*. The function of an "expert sacrificer" on behalf of a specific population was sufficient to make the *ka'o* irreplaceable.

Our interviews of a few Gamo people on their native land revealed the prestige enjoyed by the *ka'o*. Those interviewed replied by giving the name of the territory but added that of the priest who was ritually responsible for it. The society without a *ka'o* was unthinkable. By offering sacrifices at the boundaries of a given territory, *ka'os* protected their communities thus circumscribed against any harm (major natural catastrophies, epidemics, wars) or reestablished the broken order.

In Ochollo, the high priest *(ka'o kaza)* offered a sacrifice once a year on behalf of his district *(ke'a)*.[5] He immolated five sheep in five different places, each at the boundary of a district land. Each time he said the same incantations. It was of great importance to perform those rituals during the same day so as not to interrupt the action in its continuity; indeed, this sacrifice could be defined as a survey along which the limits of ke'a territory were established. This was a highly symbolic frontier: The appropriation of land by the community was always established in this way.

It was the same *ka'o kaza* who offered sacrifices in Ochollo's main square, which dominated the *dere* territory. On behalf of the whole community he killed an ox. He thus deserved the title of *dere ka'o*. The animals to be used for the sacrifices were provided by the community. In Ochollo, the various assemblies picked up the required collections and selected the sacrifice dates themselves. These assemblies could refuse supplying the *ka'o* with victims but in so doing they might break the taboo *(gome)* or cause the priest to curse them and threaten them with his *tema*. It was obvious that the power of the assembly over rituals curbed the priest in his innovations.

However, never were the *ka'os* merely officiants. In view of their positions as elders *(baira)* of their community, they were indispensable to guarantee agreements entered with neighboring territories at the end of hostilities with *deres*. They performed specific rituals to consolidate the respective agreements. A distinctive feature of Gamo tradition was that the defeated *deres' ka'o* paid homage to the winner's high priest and the same act was performed by their respective decendants during special ceremonies.

Later in our study we shall come back to the actual power of priests; but let us note that the principle of primogeniture and the hierarchical order could not supersede the assembly, the real basis of the political system. Each political unit, which by definition was also a residential unit, had a place for public meetings *(dubusha)* where current issues were debated. Usually, each district had its own assembly. In order to give a better idea of the role and function of this body, we shall offer the observations we were able to make in Ochollo.

In this society there were three kinds of assemblies because their territory was divided into districts *(bitante)* and subdivided into subdistricts or neighborhood units *(guta)*. Each of these subdistricts sheltered an assembly place. In each district, however, one of those forums was also used as an assembly place for the district citizens. This assembly square always looked down on the other forums. Moreover, in Ochollo, the general assembly square located in the highest area was a huge platform which towered over the whole territory. As we have seen, each territorial group had a particular type of assembly whose location and space clearly indicated its place in the hierarchy: the village assembly was located uphill; the district assemblies downhill.

The assemblies *(dulata)* handled business pertaining to correspondent communities. A great many issues were debated there. *Dulatas* had judicial and management functions. Besides litigations between individuals—concerning the use of wood pipes or boundaries of plots for instance—these meetings also promoted collective initiatives such as the repair of community roads and the organization of sacrifices. Relationships with other *deres* were also discussed: The general assembly *(dere dulata)* was the only qualified body to decide on a war or the negotiation of an agreement with neighboring territories.

How did these assemblies operate? In the subdistrict the assembly was convened by its delegates, the *mura,* at the request of the people. This delegate was appointed by the citizens of the subdistrict to represent the territorial subdivision for life, unless he later ascended to the position of dignitary. Besides convening assemblies, he was responsible for carrying out decisions reached in *dulatas*.

At the district level, however, the dignitaries *(halaka)* were responsible for convening the assembly. When a citizen wished to lay an issue before the *dulta,* he spoke to the main dignitary *(bitane halaka)* who introduced the motion before the "fathers of the land" (the title reserved to elders who had formerly been dignitaries). Subject to their approval, the dignitary convened an assembly of citizens. The *bitane halaka* and his deputy the *aduma halaka* called the assembly to order. The main soldier read the agenda at the end of the ritual performed by the *aduma halaka* to insure prosperity for all the citizens there gathered. The final decision was reached by a motion made by the *bitane halaka*. The latter summed up the wishes of the assembly at the end of very lengthy general meetings, and it devolved upon him to carry out decisions. The *deres'* assembly was characterized by the same organization. The presence of all the dignitaries in Ochollo was necessary. The two most famous *halakas* also belonging to the most ancient clan introduced the issues. The litigations unsettled at the lower levels of subdistricts and districts were laid before the general assembly. Questions concerning all the citizens of Ochollo also fell under its jurisdiction.

In the other Gamo societies, assemblies operated along these general lines, with only a few different points of detail. Opened to citizens only, these assemblies were convened sometimes for days. They passed laws and administered sanctions. Those refusing to abide by the *dulata's* decisions were subject to extreme punishment, including expatriation *(hilo)*. This sanction usually applied to those who refused to pay the fines imposed by the assembly. A short time after our arrival in Ochollo, a man was banned because of his attempt to sell public land to *Amharas*. The Ochollo dignitaries officially closed the doors of his house so he went into exile. He died a short while afterward from an illness which in the Ochollo's opinions was the result of his bad conduct. The people from his district refused to dig his grave because a ban is the equivalent of the social nonexistence of a sanctioned individual.

In assemblies each citizen had the right to express himself freely. Decisions were adopted unanimously; taking a vote and counting the voices, as it is practiced in some societies, is quite foreign to this concept of democracy. Through the interventions, a consensus prevailed and each member finally came around to it. However it was not a purely spontaneous process. The assemblies were prepared long beforehand and decisions were adopted after long negotiations. Members of the assembly did not hesitate to adjourn and take up debates after painful negotiations which would last for weeks.

Dignitaries played a leading role in the preparation and the very proceedings of *dulatas*. However they were forbidden from imposing their choice on other members of the assembly. In Ochollo, where there were given precedents in taking the floor and where they sat in special locations, no other prerogative distinguished dignitaries. They neither presided over the assembly nor ruled it. The presence of *ka'os* was not compulsory during *dulatas*. In this political body we realized that hierarchy is secondary. The principle of primogeniture is not valid in a political debate. The high priest and the assembly were two distinct institutions which, although they complemented each other, also competed. In Ochollo the high priest *(ka'o kaza)* took part in the general assembly of a *dere*. Contrary to other citizens, he could intervene from his seat and not from the assigned place. Moreover, the *ka'o kaza* had no right to keep his opinion and make a motion during the debate. He only intervened when there was trouble within the assembly. He was the guardian of order but he was purely and simply excluded from political debate.

Thus the assembly system made the best of the dual-poled hierarchy: elective and hereditary. Dignitaries symbolized the elective pole: Any married male citizen of a sound mind could become a *halaka*. But he had no right to exceed to this position before his father and his elder brother or before their deaths. Traditionally dignitaries were chosen or "caught" (*halaka aikana:* which means to catch the *halaka*) by their neighborhoods or their district assembly. Once he was nominated by his fellow citizens, the appointee had to organize very expensive festivities which celebrated his change of status.

These festivities were more or less complex, but apart from a few variations from one *dere* to the other, they were all alike. During these festivities the nominee had to give his neighbors, males and females of his *guta* including craftsmen belonging to his *ts'oma* clans, enormous amounts of food. He also offered dignitaries, "fathers of the land" and the high priest, presents in kind and, more recently, in money. The distribution of food was carried on for several days. During these festivities, the *halaka* himself had to eat and drink. He was offered the best dishes for the purpose of making him a different man. The cycle of festivities organized when taking up the title was also seen as a great ritual of transition. At the end of the celebrations, the *halaka* was praised for his new features, his power, vitality, supremacy over the commoners, and the virility of his authority symbolized by the phallic badge.

At the end of this cycle of festivities, the new dignitary was introduced to the *dere* as he made the rounds of the market *(sofe)*. From then on he carried specific emblems such as a stick, sheepskin coat, striped shorts, and the phallic emblem on his forehead. He had to wear his hair long and could no longer shave or work with his right arm. He was surrounded with certain restrictions *(gome)*. The accumulation of a large amount of agriculture produce was necessary to become a dignitary. The prestige of a *halaka* depended upon the expenditures he made during his crowning: Indeed, the guests ate the crops reaped by the dignitary himself. This cycle of festivities, which was a transition period before acquiring the title, can be defined as a process of redistribution of accumulated surplus acquired by a single individual to the rest of the social groups. We are referring here mainly to residential relationships (people of the same neighborhood or district) and also to other links such as familial relation, alliance, and friendship.

Often the future dignitary was named by the assembly years in advance. He had to be given time to store food for his investiture. The transfer of powers from one *halaka* to the next was not in itself cause for litigations. The outgoing dignitary was usually relieved to pass on pressing responsibilities to somebody else. The duration of office varied with societies from a few days to several years. Sometimes the person elected was dismissed because he broke a taboo. But most often the assembly designated a candidate after consultation and approval of the outgoing dignitary. Those who had held the title became "fathers of the land," and they were still called *halaka*. They took an active part in the political life. In Ochollo they formed an exclusive assembly *(koltama dulata)*, together with the incumbent dignitaries, which prepared big general assemblies.

Each *dere* referred to its dignitaries by special titles, *halaka* was just the generic name. For instance, we noted such titles as *aduma* and *bitane* in Ochollo, and *halaka, aduma, huduga, atuma, bitane,* and *keso* in Dorze. Therefore the *halaka* rank itself indicated a hierarchy. Sometimes birth determined the kind of title to which one could aspire. In Dorze, for instance, an individual acquired the title of *huduga* or *atuma* depending upon his particular lineage. Whereas in Ochollo the title depended upon the expenditure. The *aduma halaka* did not give "everything" whereas the *bitane halaka* organized more impressive festivities.

In Ochollo the succession to the position of *bitane halaka* required two ceremonies: at the end of the first one, which included a series of oath takings, the individual became a simple *bitane (mela bitane)*. Later a cycle of longer festivities took place during which the real transition to the new status occurred. This cycle ended with the two ritual rounds of the market *(sofe)*. However, it was possible to directly become a *bitane halaka* under one condition: the nominee should have been formally an *aduma halaka* and should organize the required festivities. There was a tremendous difference in the prestige enjoyed by the *aduma* and the *bitane halaka*. Politically, the *aduma* was the auxiliary of the *bitane* in each of Ochollo's districts. Symbolically the difference emerged during crowning ceremonies. For *adumas* the *sofes* were silent, less spectacular than those of the *bitane halakas*.

Although the characteristics of the title system varied from one *dere* to the other, the elective principle and the ostentatious ideology remained the same; "catching the *halaka*" was a way to point out the individual success of the community in which everybody took advantage of his wealth. We already saw that the Gamo land system and the production organization encouraged private initiative. Also the very root of the difference in wealth lay in the use of *corvée* labor and slaves for manpower. Therefore this extra labor force was the very cause of inequalities between citizens. The mode of accession to titles confirmed these inequalities and established titles for only those who had enough crops to feed their fellow citizens. It was not enough to be generous and to know how to give, one had to be able to give.

But we should also keep in mind that the mode of accession to titles operated as an instrument of regulation, limiting accumulation of private wealth. The dignitary was compelled by the community to give away part of his wealth; of course he gained rank and prestige in return. But the ostentation was a necessity. The community pretended that it took possession of a new *halaka*. In Ochollo a rite symbolized this capture of a selected man: A few young men abducted the dignitary and carried him over to the assembly place of his district and tore off a piece of material which was wrapped around his clothes. This ritual abduction was compared to the kidnapping of a young bride carried to her new home and unclad before her first sexual relationship with her husband. Just like the bride, the dignitary submitted passively to the community. Moreover, the *halaka* was supposed to ruin himself by giving away his wealth to his fellow citizens. Therefore the festivity was really a way of preventing the establishment of a rigid social stratification among the members of the *mala* clans. The mode of accession to titles was not only a means of redistribution. The ostentatious expenditures also resulted in stimulating the circulation of wealth. The introduction of the dignitary to the *dere* in the market place was indeed planned; it was no hazard, for the *halaka* was the ultimate tradesman. As we have already seen, notably in Dita, Dorze, and Ochollo, the dignitaries never really ruined themselves, for each festivity was part of a cycle of loans and restitutions (Halperin and Olmstead, 1976; Abélès, 1976, 1977, 1978). Their kin and neighbors helped the future *halaka* organize the crowning festivities. Therefore, when in turn they had to organize similar festivities, they had a right to expect from him a contribution at least equal to theirs.

In this manner, cycles of exchanges were organized which put new life into the local economy. Many citizens ran for these titles and the capture of a *halaka* was not felt as a negative social constraint or as a sanction against accumulating private wealth. On the contrary, the dignitary's position was a reflection of social success and of accession to a higher social status.[6] It allowed an individual to be entrusted with a political function subject to the assembly's approval. Although the political role of dignitaries appears limited since they were mere agents of the *dulata,* the prestige acquired during the crowning ceremonies as well as their knowledge of business could turn these into real political leaders.

Could a dignitary exceed the assembly's decisions or try to impose his own? We know of such attempts that were quickly checked. In Ochollo, for instance, we heard of a very wealthy *bitane halaka* whose opinions were very respected by the assembly and often acted upon. One day he wanted to order citizens to farm specific lands. The citizens deemed that his initiative was presumptuous. He was finally exiled to Ganta where he spent the rest of his life, and Ochollo people refused to bury him on their territory. This episode, which dates back to the end of the last century before the Amhara conquest, shows clearly that it was not possible to revoke the general consensus and "give orders" to one's fellow citizens. The fact that the dignitary in question was banned with the active support of the prestigious *ka'o* reveals the kind of tensions existing between the various elements of a political-ritual system. Such "structural" tensions tend to neutralize any concentration of power.

The Gamo *deres,* which are societies marked by stratification and inequality, functioned for a long time by maintaining a careful balance between three institutions: the assembly, the priests, and the dignitaries. This balance was often challenged by the opposing ambitions of the representatives of the assemblies and the priests who were the embodiment of the political unit of the *dere.* By definition this system could not stabilize itself around one of the three poles leaving out the others, for the various elements complemented each other in their functions. The assemblies acted as decision-making bodies. *Halakas* were responsible for carrying out decisions reached together: *ka'os* performed the necessary rites for the reproduction of the society.

Dignitaries had their management function; they insured the permanence of political power, for without them the assembly could not govern effectively. Priests, too, were indispensable: Rituals were a determining element in the process of the appropriation of nature. Moreover, *ka' os* were the guardians of the territorial integrity in societies where the political unity was based on the territory. Under the complementary political and ritual functions lay, however, a latent competition between men of various statuses with a real desire to rule. The equilibrium of the political system was the result of tensions exercised by each of these elements.

Each *dere* had its special variation of a general pattern described above. We also note that a given society, depending upon the era, presented diverse versions of this model. These political variations were the result of wars and mainly of the interdependence of *deres*. Indeed, *ka' os* had higher status than other citizens and they were often tempted to turn this hierarchical position into political power. In some Gamo societies, *ka' os* enjoyed an undisputed prestige: Real dynasties of high priests imposed themselves as in Bonke, Kogo, Doko, and Dorze.

In Kogo, after the *ka' os* death, his successor made the ritual tour of the territory when he could appropriate animals, crops, and slaves he wanted. But he had to redistribute them to dignitaries. Another high priest remains famous in this area, *Worka Ka' o* of Ganta. It is said that his ancestor came out of his mother's womb with his hands full of barley. Since then his dynasty has insured the prosperity of the country and in the past century the *Worka Ka' o* (golden *ka' o*) became a local power. Are we dealing, then, with authentic monarchies because of these examples of *deres* and federations dominated by the personality of one high priest? We should give a negative answer to this question for various reasons.

First, in all the cases studied, the assembly maintained a real control over public issues at least until the end of the 19th century; later on, as we shall see, new situations appeared in Kogo, where the *ka' o* levied a tax. He was, however, compelled to redistribute part of the goods he extorted to his fellow citizens.

Second, although the high priest was recognized as the very embodiment of the whole society, he was looked upon however as a member of the community. In the Gamo ideology the *ka'o* is not above the society. The division through which "with time the social function is promoted to domination of the society" (Engels, 1877: 212) did not take place in this case. As we already saw, the assembly took precautions against inappropriate interventions of *ka'os:* Legitimacy and power, hierarchy and government, norm and action were quite separate. Even recently, priests who succeeded in taking over local power by becoming Amhara agents were violently rejected by the assemblies during the revolution of 1975.

We should add to the previous restrictions the fact that the *dere ka'o* was rarely the only priest. In Kogo, besides the high priest are three other people with the title of *ka'o* (Bureau, 1979: 116–120). In several other territories some districts asserted that they had their own *ka'o*. This kind of claim usually reflected former conflicts and resulted in the curbing of the official *ka'o's* claims to exclusive power. This phenomena could be viewed as an expression of an emancipation trend; the *dere ka'o* was challenged as a centralized power.

The existence of many priests was a fact admitted by one *dere* at least: In Ochollo there were 18 priests called *ka'os*. The ritual work was well-divided, in that the priests complemented themselves in their territorial functions. However, there was a hierarchy of *ka'os* with regard to three criteria: the importance of their respective functions, the territorial extension of these functions, and their ancestry. The priest *(Ka'o Kaza)* was preeminent although he was the eldest of the *ka'os* and he had to pay tribute to another priest during his crowning. The interdependence of *ka'os* prevented any monopoly of the sacred.

It would be presumptuous to assert that this society was fully forearmed against the exclusive power of the *ka'o*. However, the Ochollos, just as the other Gamos, always criticized certain aspects of this institution. Heredity by itself could not be used as a basis for power in societies which regarded individual initiative with high esteem. On the other hand, *ka'os* were people who took everything by definition; they were often reproached for not knowing how to give. The following Ochollo tale exemplifies this criticism:

> One day a *ka'o* said, "If I become *halaka* I will be more often invited by my fellow citizens." He submitted his application for this title to the assembly and he was accepted, and ever since the members of this dynasty could claim this status.

This reveals the capacity of the priest. That the Gamo societies, in view of their political structure, could not tolerate the arbitrariness of a single power based on privilege explains this fact. The concentration of extra work in the hands of one individual, whatever his prestige, and the centralization of government would have required a real coup de force. Such a hypothetical event was not inconceivable. But this would have required a devoted, organized military power at the *ka'o's* disposal. On the other hand, the political system was founded on the permanent competition between various elements: Whatever the attempts to take over power, this very structure neutralized them. As a matter of fact, there were many such attempts which determined the political history of *deres* without ever succeeding in establishing monarchies.

Contrary to Straube, we do not think that the first Amhara conquest during the 15th century upset the preexisting democratic system and replaced it by the institution of *ka'os*. Of course we could call the centralizing and hierarchical trends of the system a monarchy. But the establishment of a monarchy would have completely destroyed the assembly system. It seems more likely that Gamo societies borrowed some Amhara notions and used them for their own political organization. With regard to this fact we shall note that *halaka* and not *ka'o* was the term borrowed from Amharic. The contrary would have been more logical had the Gamo really imported the idea of a monarchy from the north.

The absence of a centralized state among the Gamo is not merely the result of the contradictory articulation between productive forces and relations of production, an articulation which as we have shown put restrictions on the federative dynamics which can be seen in the history of relations between *deres*. This resistance to stateship by societies that developed such advanced forms of exploitation can also be explained by the lack of a dominant homogeneous and politically organized class. The process of redistribution of surplus, and the power welded by the collectivity of citizens over the use of surplus production for private wealth, prevented the emergence of a ruling class. Simultaneously, the political superstructure sustained the competition between various institutions under the norm of the assembly system. In such conditions power was divided, even though periodically the agents of the system tried to overtake it. These societies where exploitation was practiced were also societies marked by the division of power.[7] The Gamo monarchism is a retrospective fact: Indeed, it only appeared when the soldiers of Menelik II violated the system by appointing *ka'os* as agents of the central government *(balabbat)*. This initiative had the same effect as a chemical detector: The *ka'os* started behaving as kings. But even this did not fundamentally change the political processes.

The transfer of power to *balabbats* in the Gamo highlands, as in the other regions of southern Ethiopia, indicates the final integration of this province into the Ethiopian state. The prerogatives surrounding the *balabbat* title differed with situations. But everywhere the notion of a local chief to whom the state had given certain rights prevailed. In the Gamo lands the *balabbat* was given the usufruct over the *dere* lands which now belonged to the state.[8] In return the *balabbat* owed the state military assistance and taxes for himself and the community he was in charge of, however, he was exempted from *corvée* labor *(gabbar)*. A middleman between the administration and his *dere,* the *balabbat* was given a highly elevated status as a landowner compared to what it was in the Gamo tradition. Because of his function, he became the owner of a vast estate which he could increase by taking possession of plots, often by doubtful means.

In Ochollo, for instance, the *balabbat* was given plots as "kick-backs" *(gubo)*. Corruption was widespread. *Balabbats* as juridical and revenue officials always attempted to take advantage of their special situation. With the introduction of a state, some Gamo values were destroyed. Land acquisition through work was replaced with ownership by status. The government of citizens by themselves had superimposed an authority upheld by an all-powerful administration. The *balabbat* was in charge of the police work within his *dere;* in Ochollo he used to be the owner of a local jail built next to his house.

Assemblies still existed but *balabbats* could convene them as they wished. Whereas the *ka'o* was excluded from political activities, the *balabbat* function entitled the holder to exercise the real power over his fellow citizens. In fact, for the other Gamos the only advantage to this new institution was to preserve a certain autonomy of *deres* in relation to the central power.

However, the Gamos finally succeeded in curbing the political domination of these new chiefs. Most often, Amharas conferred the title of *balabatt* to *dere ka'os*. The function was to be passed on from father to son. Now, as indicated by the study of genealogies of *balabbats* of different *deres* in 1897, there were many breaks in this system since the holder of a *balabbat* title and the *ka'os* became two separate people. Such is the case when the *ka'o balabbat* has no direct heir. The closest descendant automatically becomes *ka'o* but the functions of *balabbat* can be passed on to a relative. There is another case where the *ka'o* transfers his responsibilities as a *balabbat* to an agent. This disassociation of roles is in keeping with the ruling ideology which tends to restrict the *ka'o* to his symbolic power.

This was a real manipulation of institutional intent which allowed a reverse in the trend of centralization enforced by the Amharas. The successions of *balabbats* promoted litigations in which the *dere* assembly played a vital role of mediator between rival pretenders. When the *ka'o balabbat* and the real *balabbat* were two separate people, their subjects could at leisure oppose the authentic legitimacy of the first to the effective power of the second. The Gamo enjoyed this. The state systems established by force were gradually eroded by the political processes of the preceding era which were still at play behind the new forms.

That the federation of Bonke had the most despotic of *balabbats* was no chance. We already mentioned the social stratification between Dache and Gamo and the pervasive influence of the centralizing trend within this *dere*. Bureau (1979: 130–138) depicts the *balabbat* as a strong character eager of power who uses his many prerogatives without scruples. This person had turned his power into a mode of exploitation. He convened the assembly in his own house and surrounded himself with many clients. But in Gamo, land hegemony has its own limitations: The *balabbat* was challenged, he refused to acknowledge *halakas* who were elected, and, finally, he was banned by his own subjects. He was replaced by the authentic *ka'o;* indeed, the founder of a dynasty had himself separated both titles by passing them on to two different lineages. Therefore, the *balabbat* was just a junior.

This example shows the obstacles met by those who want to rule alone. On the other hand, Ochollo had a more flexible organization. Indeed, the rulers here, more eager to be efficient than establish legitimacy, designated a citizen who knew Amharic as *balabbat*. Thus, Toga Boizo, a slave trader, was the first local chief, but he died without an heir. A brother of his belonging to the same class succeeded him. Later on, the title was transferred by the *dere* itself. The assembly was the only one to appoint *balabbats* according to its own criterion, and it did not hesitate to demote one of them after a year. Thus, this institution was deeply altered: The *balabbat* depended upon the assembly. First, he could not assume the title of *ka'o* and, second, he was not the direct descendant of the first title holder. However, for some 20 years up to the early 1950s, the *dere* was dominated by one figure: Meresho, a former *bitane halaka* who acted as *balabbat*. This man took advantage of the Italian support to consolidate his authority. At that time he openly challenged the *ka'o kaza* who had succeeded in having his preeminence acknowledged by the Italians and in becoming the local power. At the end of the complex intrigue, Meresho succeeded in having the *ka'o kaza* arrested and publicly whipped, thus seriously affecting the prestige of the leading Ochollo high priest.

This episode clearly indicates the limitations of the system imposed by the Amhara. Indeed, although the *balabbat* was the winner in this conflict, the *bitane halaka* was really the one who triumphed over the Amhara chief, thus settling his quarrels with a very presumptuous *ka'o*. This is a typical example of the tension between the elements of the traditional system. Later on, there were other conflicts when Meresho was to be succeeded. Although pretenders sought the support of the central administration, the assembly was still the arbitrator in this competition. In the early 1970s, the incumbent *balabbat* was demoted by his fellow citizens for misuse of power. During our stay in Ochollo, plots were still going on even when the current administration within the Ethiopian state was crumbling.

That Straube thought he had discovered a "monarchical order" precisely in Ochollo is very revealing. The idea of such an institution could cause smiles because of its incompatibility with the social organization of this *dere*. The dynasty mentioned by our author is, in fact, related to Meresho. He himself was never a *ka'o*, and he never belonged to the original *balabbat* clan. Therefore, he could never have passed this title on to his descendants legally. We are citing this era only as an example of retrospective illusion which alters ethnographical observations. When one keeps searching for the monarch, one finally finds him.

If the Amhara never succeeded in really altering a system which is ultimately antimonarchical, the anthropologist and the historian should take note of the persistence of the superstructure. We have tried to show how the contradiction between forces of production/relations of production explains the articulation of antagonistic tendencies (centralism/autonomism) which prevented any unification effort of Gamo *deres* under centralized power. But the analysis of the political system reveals that none of the Gamo societies—societies of exploitation and caste, but not societies of class—has been able to establish a state. The lack of a politically structured ruling class is not only the result of the relations of production. It also appears as the result of the superstructure: First, the specific mode of accession to titles and, second, the permanent conflict between the *halakas* and *ka'os* inherent to the political-ritual system stood in the way of the emergence of a homogeneous ruling class which usually is the instrument for political transformation. Also, as a result of the superstructure, the *balabbat,* in spite of their extensive privileges, were unable to deeply change the former forms of exploitation. In other words, if the nature of infrastructure explains the essential characteristics of a political system, it should be added that this system played a decisive part in assuring that the reproduction of traditional relations of production remained unchanged. It should be concluded that the state could never be introduced by a decree: Any centralism imposed from outside should necessarily rest upon preexisting forms which could considerably restrict its real efficiency. It falls upon the historian and the anthropologist to unveil these forms, provided that they stay away from retrospective ethnocentric illusions which pervade our research work.

NOTES

1. The functionary known as *ka'o* in Gamo society has been translated here and below as "priest" and, for the principal *ka'o,* "high priest." Literally, "sacrificer" and "chief sacrificer" might be more accurate.

2. We lived in Ochollo from 1974 to 1975. The fieldwork was carried out through funds allocated by C.N.R.S. to the Laboratoire d'Antropologie Sociale, Collège de France. This research work was the subject of a Ph.D. dissertation in ethnology defended in 1977 and directed by Claude Lévi-Strauss, see M. Abélès (1976).

3. See the discussion of the political system below.

4. Cf. Bureau's (1978, 1979) analysis. He himself lived in Bonke where he was able to compare various Gamo *dere's* political systems.

5. *Ka'o Kaza* was both his district's high priest (see definition below of the district in Ochollo) and the priest of the *deres*.

6. On the ideology regarding the functions of *halaka,* see Sperber (1974). As Meillassoux stated on ostentation: "Equalization of wealth is possible only in an economic framework which promotes discriminating wealth" (1977: 163).

7. Let us note that Gamo societies characterized by exploitation and a stratification into castes were not class societies however. This information is vital to understanding why no other form of centralized state appeared in the Highlands.

8. Concerning the definition and the role of *balabbats,* see Berhanou Abebe (1971) and Markakis (1974); compare Bureau's (1979) indications, too.

REFERENCES

ABELES, M. (1976) Le lieu du politique. Contribution à l'étude de l'organization de l'espace, du pouvoir et des rites dans une population Ometo d'Ethiopie méridionale: Les Otchollo. Thèse de 3e cycle. Paris. (mimeo).

_____ (1977) La grande bouffe, Dialectiques 21: 7–22.

_____ (1978) Pouvoir et société chez les Otchollo d'Ethiopie méridionale. Cahiers d'Etudes Africaines 18: 293–310.

BERHANOUTH, A. (1971) Evolution de la propriété foncière au Choa (Ethiopie), du règne de Ménélik à la constitution de 1931: Paris: n.p.

BUREAU, J. (1978) "Etude diachronique de deux titres gamo." Cahiers d'Etudes Africaines 18: 279–291.

_____ (1979). Introduction aux systèmes politiques gamo. Thèse de 3e cycle. Paris. (mimeo)

ENGELS, F. (1877) Anti Duehring (trad. fçse, 1968). Paris: n.p.

_____ (1884) L'origine de la famille, de la propriété et de l'Etat (trad. fçse, 1954). Paris: n.p.

HALPERIN, R., and J. OLMSTEAD (1976) "To catch a feast-giver. Redistribution among the Dorze of Ethiopia." Africa 46: 146–166.

MARKAKIS, J. (1973) Ethiopia, anatomy of a traditional policy. London: Oxford University Press.

MARX, K. (1970) Sur les sociétés précapitalistes. Paris: n.p.

MEILLASSOUX, C. (1977) Terrains et théories. Paris: n.p.

OLMSTEAD, J. (1975) "Agricultural land and social stratification in the Gamu highlands of southern Ethiopia," pp. 223–224 in H. Marcus (ed.), Proceedings of the first (1973) United States conference on Ethiopian studies.

SPERBER, D. (1974) "La notion d'aînesse et ses paradoxes chez les Dorzé d'Ethiopie méridionale." Cahiers internationaux de sociologie 51: 63–78.

STRAUBE, H. (1957) "Das dualsystem: Und die Halaka-Verfassung der Dorze als alte Gesellschaftsordnung der Ometo-Voelker Sued-Athiopiens." Paideuma mitteilungen sur Kultukunde 6: 342–353.

———— (1963) West Kuschitische Voelker Sued-Athiopiens. Stuttgart, Federal Republic of Germany: n.p.

3

EMERGENT CLASSES
AND THE EARLY STATE:
The Southern Sahara

C. C. STEWART
University of Illinois

Underlying the preoccupation of scholars who delve into describing, defining, and deifying the significance of various modes of production in the precolonial African setting is the heuristic value such an analytical method holds for understanding the nature and growth of the state and the impact of Western capitalism. Both concerns are reflected in the essays in this volume as is the tantalizing chicken-and-egg problem implicit in these concerns as they relate to the mechanisms of state formation, perhaps most directly addressed by Steinhart and Jewsiewicki in the following two chapters. In each of these essays, the punch line seems to be the emergence of a class system and state apparatus which correspond at the same time to shifts in the mode of production and increasingly sophisticated methods of surplus extraction. Abélès, on the other hand, meets head on the problem of exploitation and inequality in Gamo society, outside a class structure and in a context where the collective control over the redistribution of surplus effectively blocks the formation of classes. Somewhere on the spectrum that links the Gamo with these other societies that emerged as states lies the social formations found in the southern Sahara.[1]

The region with which we will be concerned in this essay stretches from the Atlantic to the Chad Basin. The peoples living in this belt of semiarid and arid land are most frequently described in the ethnographic literature as organized by tribal units that are hierarchically arranged just as those units are internally characterized by seemingly rigid social strata. Thus the notion of class has wide frequency in descriptive literature about these societies, yet state apparatuses in this region do not dominate historical accounts. To come to terms with the contradiction this presents will necessitate, first, a critical examination of the received literature on these societies and, in particular, a circumvention of standard segmentary lineage models that permeate most analyses of these societies. Second, an assessment of the applicability of notions of a lineage mode of production to these societies will allow us to examine the concept of class in the southern Sahara (and similar formations in Sahelian societies to the south). And finally, with this theoretical baggage thus packed, we shall reexamine the historical significance of two stages of development in these societies: their foundation myths that generally are attached to events in the 17th century and the intrusion of peripheral Western capitalism during the 19th century.

The received literature on the social and political structures of southern Saharan societies exhibits a remarkable homogeneity. Whether indigenous accounts of these societies written prior to colonial occupation, descriptions set down by colonial administrators, or recent postindependence historical accounts, this literature seems to tally on most important features (al-Shinqiti, 465 et seq.; Poulet, 5 et seq.; Norris, 13 et seq.).[2] In brief, these societies were made up of a complex hierarchy of social groups and identified with each social group were specific economic functions, rights, or prohibitions. The social categories and the hierarchy of social groups in these societies are explained and legitimated by sometimes elaborate ideologies based on the origins of the groups and their sequence of arrival in the southern Sahara. Where adequate documentation exists on the divisions within individual groups as well as the social hierarchy within a given area, these divisions and hierarchies are explained in terms of "class." In this context class is used with reference to descent groups holding unequal statuses by virtue of their length of residence in a particular area. Class, in a Marxian sense—groups demonstrating differential relations of production, private ownership, and class antagonism—will be argued below to be a concept of considerable analytical value in examining events in southern Saharan society during the late 19th century. But at this stage of our discussion these two notions of class should be distinguished. The question of class aside, most social anthropologists would agree that these societies correspond closely to models of segmentary lineage structures, and so it is that they have been described, including in work of my own (Stewart, 1973). We will return to these notions of "segmentarity," to use Bonte's useful shorthand for segmentary lineage structures, and the ideology that supports them (Bonte, 1975, 1979), and the pitfalls of these notions in historical writing. But it would be appropriate, first, to establish the universe with which we are dealing when speaking of "southern Saharan societies."

The broadly similar ecological environment inhabited by the peoples on the Saharan fringe and Sahel of West Africa dictates a common economy based upon livestock husbandry and supplemented by agricultural activities in those low lands where adequate if not always predictable water resources will permit. The population density is light and the majority of inhabitants in precolonial times adhered to nomadic patterns along fairly well-defined north/south corridors, demarcated by family or clan cemeteries, wells, and pasturage areas. Scarce resources in this harsh ecological setting heightened competition over pasture lands and wells as well as the sparse and diffuse agricultural tracts. Cereal markets to the south were defined by four main areas, notably along the Senegal River valley, the Niger Bend, Rima Valley and points northeast toward Zinder, and the Chad Basin.[3] But it is not only the ecology of this belt of land that warrants our treatment of its inhabitants as a homogeneous grouping.

I have argued elsewhere that broad similarities in variously described Arab, Moorish, Berber, and Tuareg societies in the southern Sahara support their consideration as a composite group, namely,

> the societies' class systems, which maintain a political, social and occupational hierarchy; their similar social charters; their economic organization; and their mechanisms for the resolution of conflict [Stewart, 1976a: 74–75].

What appears in the standard ethnographic literature on these societies is an explanation of their social structures that is invariably founded in events that took place during the last half of the 17th century. This, too, is the explanation offered by historians from within these societies. At that time, we learn, conflicts or migrations brought to loggerheads indigenous peoples with others, more recently arrived in the southern Sahara. The outcome of these confrontations provides at once a foundation myth and a set of social, political, ideological, and economic roles which are used to explain the hierarchical stratification of societies inhabiting the terrain from Shinqit to Ahir.

> The social classes, which are also portrayed as political classes and occupational groupings, generally follow a model, carefully preserved by the "nobles," in which society is politically dominated by a group of temporal leaders ("warriors") who are led in each region by a single lineage. Politically subordinate to the "warriors" are other classes of absorbed or conquered people, some of whom are regarded by the society as being of "noble" stock themselves. Beneath these are classes of freed slaves, slaves and artisans. In Shinqit the subordinate classes of nobles are recognized as tribes and they maintain a carefully guarded separate identity from the temporal powers, even though they may be in tributary relationship to them. Eastwards from Tagant these subordinate classes of nobles

tend to be more closely integrated into specific "drum groups" . . . .
However, aside from this minor variation the political and social
hierarchy of these classes in southern Saharan society is remarkably similar [Stewart, 1976a: 75–76].

At base this model is the Saharans' own view of their social structure in precolonial times. One deviation from the model of which
we should take note is one derived from extensive fieldwork in
southwestern Mauritania. There, it is evident that in the 19th century the dominant lineages in any one region tended to be associated with *either* a raiding economy (the "warriors" of the model)
or a pastoral and agricultural means of livelihood. These latter
lineages tended to be identified with Islamic learning and scholarship and thus with mediation activities between bellicose groups
(Stewart, 1973). The important political function such groups
served in the maintenance of the ideology of the society's hierarchy
and the origins of the social stratification described above, much
less adjudication, would seem to extend well beyond southwestern
Mauritania. Throughout the southern Sahara, and despite the standard description of class hierarchies topped off by warrior groups,
the noble lineages that dominated individual regions appear to
have represented either "warrior" or nonwarrior ("maraboutic" in
the French literature) divisions of Saharan nobles. The main conclusion to be drawn from this relates to the importance of (and
misleading assumptions that may be drawn from) the ideology,
discussed below, that supports the structures of southern Saharan
society.

Parallels between this hierarchy of social and occupational
groupings in southern Saharan societies and comparable structures
in Sahelian societies to the south should not be ignored. Similar
notions of social stratification, comparable foundation myths
among the Hausa and Wolof, and Roberts's description of the
Somono social formation in this volume all point to the fact that we
are dealing with a set of phenomena that stretch well beyond the
confines of the southern Sahara. The reason that little has been
made of the parallels between the social structures of these south-

ern Saharan societies and their Sahelian neighbors lies in the analytical tools with which the respective regions have been described. In the west-central Sudan and Senegambia the political units which make up the basis of historical accounts have been variously labelled "state systems," "micro-states," "kingships," and "city-states" (Curtin, 1975: 29–37). In the southern Sahara the anthropological model of segmentary lineage structures has most frequently sufficed to explain political organization in the absence of any clearly defined system or structure of government. The guiding principle behind the segmentary lineage model is the theoretically balanced set of kin units within larger clan structures and clan or tribal units within regions; the opposition and complementarity of these units at lesser and greater levels of social organization is said to account for the equilibrium of these societies over time and to explain their absence of any formal structure of government. The use of this model has made it possible to identify these Saharan societies within an established colonial literature on nomadic societies while still making allowance for various dominant lineages in particular regions (the "Amirates" in Shinqit; the "Sultanate" in Ahir) at specific points in time. The problem remains over the extent to which these particular political institutions are more the product of a colonial administrative understanding of past political structures than an accurate description of functional units. But even in granting such units a transitory importance in the political history of particular regions, descriptions of southern Saharan segmentary lineage societies have not been compromised. It is to this concept of segmentarity that we should next turn, for if it can be set aside, then the analytical equipment that takes its place can be tested against comparable social stratification in the Sahel as well as the southern Sahara.

Much might be said about the shortcomings of the concept of segmentarity, its particular utility and function in colonial anthropology, and its inherently ahistorical bias. Bonte has offered one critique of the concept in his analysis of functionalism in British anthropology concluding with, in my judgment, a broadly correct attack on my own work (Bonte, 1975, 1979). Speaking of descriptions of segmentary lineage societies as neatly "fixed . . . and removed from time and history" (Bonte, 1975: 51), he points to the inadequacy of the model to account for any dynamic external to the society.

> This view [of segmentary lineage systems] becomes a caricature when the analysis turns to societies governed by classes and where the State exists, particularly in the case of Saharan or Maghrebian societies. It ends up by eliminating the real problem: the existence of class relations and their dynamics, subsituting instead the utopian vision of societies which are in initial equilibrium thanks to specific institutions (judicial, religious, and political [Bonte, 1975: 51].

With particular reference to *Islam and Social Order in Mauritania,* he points up:

> Such an analysis results in denying the reality of the political and economic power exerted by a dominant class, the centrally organized warrior aristocrats (emirate), [sic] which benefited the great marabouts who acted as mediators [Bonte, 1975: 66].

I will take issue with Bonte's understanding of "the centrally organized warrior aristocrats" and with his preoccupation with external dynamics which would lead him to underestimate the internal developments within these societies. But I embrace his skepticism that the concept of segmentarity can serve any useful purpose in the portrayal of historical process, and I will admit to preparing that study with primary reference to the world-view held by nobles from within southern Saharan society. Thus the emphasis upon "social order" rather than the mechanisms of "change" about which the study revolves, for example, Chapter V, "Economic Power and Religious Influence" (Stewart, 1973: 109–130). In brief, the concept of segmentarity served well the interests of the noble classes in many of these societies just as it did the functionalist anthropologist/administrators.

This brings us to the second problem set out for discussion in this essay: If segmentarity as an analytical tool is misleading and ahistorical, can its replacement by analyses based in historical materialism, particularly with reference to specific modes of production, aid in an understanding of historical process in southern Saharan societies? Can it be demonstrated that segmentarity is but an aspect of the ideology, following Bonte (1979), of those groups that dominate the forces of production? Work by Meillassoux (1964) on the Guro and Terray's (1972: 95–186) critique on "Historical materialism and segmentary societies" points to the problems that arise when lineage-based modes of production are simply substituted in the place of segmentary lineage systems. Such an exercise alone, no more than Bonte's (misleading) discovery of centrally organized political units in Moorish society, does not resolve the problem of describing the dynamics of historical development in southern Saharan society. The one recent effort to do this suffers from both its brevity and thin data base. Mahfoud Bennoune has described the political economy of precapitalist Moorish society as one based on a class structure and "small segmentary [sic] 'city-states'" in a formation he sees dominated by tributary and pastoral nomadic modes of production (Bennoune, 1978: 33–34). Tidy as such conceptual schema may be, they have yet to provide any concrete insights into historical process in southern Saharan society. Indeed, efforts to find the state hidden within the proliferation of social stratification in the southern Sahara has done much to obscure even the advantages to be gained from the application of historical materialism.

At this point it would be well to return to a description of southern Saharan society that avoids both the analytical baggage associated with concepts of segmentarity and the heady reaches of Marxian theorizing about precapitalist political economies. My object shall be to identify a dominant mode of production and, to avoid confusion between that mode of production and a general description of the economy, I shall follow Terray's criteria for determining a mode of production: that it encompass an economic base, a juridico-political superstructure, and an ideological superstructure (Terray, 1972: 145). First, we shall examine those basic economic and social units that account for production and reproduction in the society, then the relationship between those units, and, finally, the regional structure of corporate groups of these units. With this foundation laid, it should be possible to return to questions posed at the outset about class and political structure in these societies. Our primary focus shall be upon the societies of southwestern Mauritania and the historical period from which data will be drawn is the mid-19th century.

The most fundamental economic, juridical, and ideological unit in southern Saharan society was that of the lineage. For descriptive purposes I will define this lineage unit as a group of families that expressed their relation to one another in terms of kinship and that ranged from three to five generations in depth. These families might have included dependents or clients who were attached to them temporarily or who were in the process of being absorbed into them as fictive kin into the family. Or such dependents may have been in a servile relationship to the lineage families. The economic activities of the lineage might have been wholly nomadic, pastoral ones, or wholly sedentary, agricultural in focus in the setting of an oasis or in southern semiarid lands bordering on riverain or lowland terrain. Then, again, especially among those lineages that dominated others, the lineage might include families that were engaged in both pastoral and agricultural activities. A typical lineage unit that was among the dominant ones in a corporate tribal or subtribal (fraction) group—those claiming a common putitive ancestor—might have led a relatively settled life, alternating their residence sites between two or three pasturage areas according to the seasons. Attached families that looked after the actual herding or stock breeding activities would move with the lineage; others would be settled on agricultural lands and make periodic visits to the lineage heads for the purpose of construction work or transporting cereal or date harvests. In addition, leading lineages might also have attached to them smiths or musicians or Arabic scholars whose labors were supported by the lineage unit. It was lineages capable of supporting such a range of specialists, particularly those that managed to integrate in their services both pastoral and agricultural activities, that were the most likely to accumulate the wealth within their families that was necessary to arrange for advantageous (endogamous) marriages, to attract clients who would provide labor in return for security, to develop expertise in animal husbandry, for example, in camel breeding, and thus to engage in major commercial ventures, be it the construction of granaries, well digging, long-distance caravan traffic, or the requisition of slaves or booty through raiding parties. With the advent of European markets on the Senegal River for gum arabic, these were the lineages most advantageously placed to direct the harvesting, transportation, and marketing of gum.

Lest this description suggest something of an elementary monopoly with little restraint upon a lineage that successfully branched out into major entrepreneurial activities, it should be pointed up that the successful lineage was its own worst enemy. Competition between families in the lineage, as the lineage grew and the genealogical span encompassed by the lineage stretched, brought a hiving off of new groups, new lineage units that now competed alongside the original but truncated "core" lineage. In this way the process of building clients, incorporating fictive kin, and eventually entering into entrepreneurial activities over and above the subsistence necessities of the lineage led to the reproduction of the basic unit.[4]

But even this, too, oversimplifies the process, for a wide range of internal ecological and demographic determinants frequently interrupted or reversed this model of endless fission. And external stimuli from within the southern Sahara and from without the region promoted or retarded the competition between would-be "successful" lineage units. Indeed, few were the lineages that completed the course; the vast majority remained as poor cousins to a relatively better off lineage or simply attached themselves as tributaries to a wealthy unit. Under such circumstances they tended to provide labor resources in return for security and economic assistance in times of need. This might include the loan of livestock for building a decimated herd, assistance in arranging a marriage alliance, mediation in instances of blood-money disputes or other major litigation, or rights to burial at sites of notable ancestors in the lineage. The labor and resources that these poor cousins and clients might contribute to the dominant lineage could include joining forces for the purpose of a raiding campaign, participation in a seasonal salt or gum arabic caravan, construction projects (wells, tombs, granaries), or technical expertise (smithing, camel breeding, special competence in the Islamic sciences). The best way to describe relations between dominant lineages and their clients and/or poor cousins is in terms of their reciprocal obligations and rights, for even lineages of the lowest social status— smiths and *haratine* (freed slaves)—could and did change alliances, seeking out lineages better able to serve their interests when this became necessary.

One of the most striking features of this lineage competition was the elaborate ideology that defined and supported it. The chief guardians of genealogical lore which demarcated the noblesse of the noble lineages and, one may assume, the chief manipulators who established fictive kinship, were one and the same as the leading personalities in the principal families of the dominant lineages. Their authority tended to be legitimated by their literacy in Arabic or their Arab pedigree, and in instances where they were learned in the Islamic sciences as well, the full weight of that training lent special credence to their juridical and cultural activities. But authority in the dominant lineage was not always defined by Islamic learning; more often it derived from an Arab pedigree and reputation for military prowess. Few were the major lineages reputed for either their holy men or their bellicose leaders that did not seek and enjoy some relationship with a lineage of the opposite persuasion, generally in a form of tributary relation. We will return to the ideological superstructure which bears remarkable similarity throughout the southern Sahara; suffice to note that it rested in the hands (and books) of the dominant lineages and permeated—indeed, played an important role in forming—the social stratification system to which we have referred.

How does this description relate to the hierarchical and stratis-
fied nature of southern Saharan society? Material from the 19th
century suggests that in any one region of the Sahel and southern
Sahara, there were a number of potentially dominant, competing
lineages, each replete with attached "poor cousins," tributary lineages, and clients. These potentially dominant lineages were distinguished from others chiefly by their capacity and effect in the
accumulation of surplus and its redistribution. To these potentially
dominant lineages was attributed a noble status which was, in turn,
legitimated by various complex readings and value systems placed
on their pedigrees. This noble status and its legitimation was at the
center of the ideological superstructure to which we have referred,
and it tended to be associated with particular facets of economic
activity. Lineages distinguished for their raiding and tribute exactions, for example, were associated with Arab (Hassani) origins in
Shinqit. In the same region, pastoralism and trading activities
corresponded with lineages that claimed a pacific (maraboutic)
lifestyle. Clients and "poor cousin" tributaries, too, were generally
identified with one or another of these types of economic activity,
and other, lower social stratum such as praise singers or smiths also
were made up of lineages distinguished for their economic specialization. The ideology of social stratification, inclusive of the notion of segmentarity, was thus an expression of occupational activities while at the same time it served to define and legitimate the
noble lineages and to reinforce their dominant role in political and
juridical matters.

Lest this view of the function of ideology in southern Saharan
society be taken as something rather abstract, two examples of
important lineages that rose to noble status should be cited. The
most famous of these is that of the Kunta confederation which, by
the early 19th century, was dominating the political economy of
the upper Niger Bend and adjacent Azaouad region (Batran, 1972,
1979; Marty, 1918–1919). Historical research into the origins of
the Kunta influence has been clouded, first, by a near-exclusive
preoccupation by researchers with the religious activities and copi-
ous texts written by learned men from within the dominant Kunta

lineage. And second, virtually all the manuscript sources that relate to Kunta origins (and their noblesse of old) seem to have been authored by Kunta scholars themselves. However, it would appear that the Kunta emerged out of a "poor cousin" and/or tributary status, originally of Berber descent, and that the branch of the tribe that settled in the Timbuctu region rose to importance only from the late 17th century onward. Since that time, and especially under the direction of their most famous saint, Sidi al-Mukhtar al-Kunti (1729–1811), it would seem safe to suggest that their history has been literally rewritten. As Batran has described, they have become of Arab origin, descendant from the conqueror of the Maghrib under the Umayyids, and more or less since that time they have dominated the religious life of the central and southern Sahara (Batran, 1979: 114–124). A parallel but somewhat better documented story comes from the N'tishait lineage within the tribe of the Walad Ibiri in southwestern Mauritania during the 19th century. There, a lineage that appears to have been of "warrior" persuasion in its own accounts of ancestors' activities in the late 17th century can be traced through metamorphoses of first tributary, then "poor cousin" status with a maraboutic group, and finally to a dominant position within the tribe and eventually within the entire region of Trarza. There, too, efforts seem to have been made to actually rewrite accounts of their origins (Stewart, 1969), and there can be no doubt about their firm establishment among the noble lineages of the region by the mid-19th century.

These two examples should serve to illustrate the not very profound point encapsulated in Plumb's (1969) dictum: "authority once achieved needs a secure and usable past." With reference to southern Saharan society this involved a constant reshuffling of the hierarchy of social status for particular lineages reflecting the shifting fortunes of competing, potentially dominant lineages. The dynamics of this competition over the forces of production within this geographical terrain was such that one lineage might replace another as the dominant lineage within a region in a relatively short period of time. In the documented instance of the N'tishait, mentioned above, approximately 30 years sufficed for an inconsequential lineage to rise to a position of economic, political, and juridical dominance in Trarza. It was the leaders of these dominant lineages, variously called shaikhs, amirs, and sultans by French intelligence officers during the 19th century, who tended to become identified (and fixed) as temporal authorities for specific regions in the European accounts. These, too, are the "centrally organized warrior aristocrats" noted by Bonte (1975: 66).

If the social hierarchy in southern Saharan society can thus be described in terms of an ideology supporting those lineages that dominate the forces of production, can we employ Marxian notions of class to explain the relations of production? There clearly existed differential relations of production between the noble lineages and substrata of tributaries and slaves, but private ownership does not appear to have entered into this distinction, and class antagonism does not emerge as a central feature of southern Saharan political history. On the contrary, primary identities from top to bottom of the horizontal divisions in these societies seem to have been with the "vertical" associations of lineages within tribes. What these societies then seem to demonstrate is a stage of "emergent classes" or, in Khazanov's (1978: 124) description of communities on the Eurasian steppes, "early class relations." In Khazanov's view, population density, dependence upon nomadism, and the specific features of cattle breeding account for "the virtual economic impasse [nomadic societies] invariably reach, . . . [whereby they] enter periods of class formation, reach the early class stage of development, conquer agricultural areas and evolve a state formation, and then, that state having disintegrated, find themselves thrown back to the early class or even some lower stage of development" (Khazanov, 1978: 125). This vision of a Eurasian evolutionary treadmill may be overschematized, but it does point to analogies between class in southern Saharan society and other stratified nomadic societies, and it also suggests an explanation for the periods of state formation which can be demonstrated by the amirates and sultanates that fleetingly dot the history of the southern Sahara.

There can be little question that centralized types of polities did emerge within the southern Sahara at various points in time and for varying duration. And we need not reckon to medieval times to note the real, if transitory political influence such polities demonstrated. During the 19th century the Amirate of Trarza in southwestern Mauritania sought to extend suzerain rights over the Walo region of modern-day Senegal both by conquest and through marriage alliance (Stewart, 1973: 92). Similiar efforts to gain control over agricultural lands in the Fittuga region of the Niger Bend may be attributed to the Kunta during the first half of the 19th century (Stewart, 1976b: 500–502), and the better-known Sultanate of Ahir periodically surfaces in historical accounts of the west-central Sahel as a polity of temporary significance (Hunwick, 1971). Kubbel (1974), writing of an earlier period about Songhay, allows for a society that "may possess elements of separate administrative-political institutions, characteristic of emerging government, and yet have no government, i.e., no fully formed apparatus of class domination." The point Kubbel is arguing is that none of the western Sudanese empires rightly deserves the appellation "state," although Songhay came closest, because none developed an enduring apparatus of class domination; in this light these formations bear close similarity to the stage of statehood which Steinhart (in this volume) has christened the "dyna-state" in western Uganda. The early state, thus, in a southern Saharan setting may be interpreted as a state formation in correspondence with the early class stage of development which these societies exhibit. At such points in time when the early state made an appearance, no true government generally emerged, and the relations of production, founded upon the lineage, were not fundamentally restructured. As a result, the early state was a transitory phenomenon in the southern Saharan setting. This was due, in the main, to the demographic and ecological limitations imposed upon these societies, for in societies exhibiting similar class structures to the south, we have ample evidence that adequate labor supplies and relatively plentiful agricultural land gave rise to a series of state structures throughout the history of the Sahel and Sudan.

A great deal of further work is called for if we are to refine the notion of class formation in Saharan contexts and to effectively distinguish historical reality in these societies from their ideological superstructure. Historical materialism does allow us to move beyond analyses based upon that ideology and permits a sober and critical look at the historiography in this region which has largely been developed both by and for the noble classes. But how can this new conceptual baggage be applied to specific historical developments in the Saharan past? We will briefly examine two phases of southern Saharan history in an effort to bring this discussion down to ground: the late 17th century (to which period most foundation myths are attributed) and the mid-19th century in Moorish society (when the impact of European merchant capital can first be most graphically illustrated).

I have noted above that one of the common features of the southern Saharan societies is their common attribution of social charters to events that took place in the late 17th century. The foundation myths or social charters to which I refer have been summarized elsewhere; in brief:

> Although tradition records a multiplicity of origin myths which distinguish the ancestry of tribes or groups of tribes prior to [the last half of the 17th century], the social status and political functions of noble lineages . . . seem to be regarded as the outcome of a number of battles or migrations dated to the period 1650–1700. . . . The causes of these conflicts and re-organizations [of the social hierarchy] may differ in the various traditions, but they seem to agree upon . . . the period from which modern history is reckoned in the southern Sahara . . . [which is also] the period in which the social charters that . . . thereafter regulate relationships between noble classes and subordinates . . . [were] established [Stewart, 1976a: 76–78].

Several explanations may be set out for external forces acting upon these societies which may have precipitated events that find their expression in the social charters. Repercussions of the demise of the Saadian dynasty in Morocco, for example, the loss of Saadian control over the important central Saharan commercial *entrepôt* of Touat by midcentury, may have contributed to a restructuring of social relations. The decreasing ability of the middle Niger Pasha-lik to weld effective control over that region may also have been a factor, as might have been the effects of a mid-17th century drought (Stewart, 1976a: 78).

But none of these events adequately accounts for the internal dynamics of social and political change associated with this pe-riod. And such explanations do not further our understanding of the contradictions between the received traditions about these so-cial charters and the documented history of these societies. For instance, one chief ingredient in these social charters is the two-fold division of noble lineages into "warriors" and "marabouts." Yet we know that bellicose marabouts were not uncommon, and instances such as the N'tishait—noted above, of lineages said to be of "warrior" persuasion that became pacifists—can be cited. Fur-ther, in regions such as Shinqit where adequate documentation is at hand, it would seem that these divisions between warrior and holy lineages predated the event (Shurr Bubba) to which is attributed this very distinction. We have established above that the emergent class system and ideology of social hierarchy in southern Saharan society were props for those lineages that dominated forces of production; by the same logic the foundation myths under consid-eration here should relate to the social relations of production in the last half of the 17th century.

If we may accept the general validity of a lineage mode of production as dominating these societies in the 17th century, and the presence of an emergent class structure, the events of the last half of the 17th century may most easily be explained in terms of early state formation. The uniformity of these social charters sug-gests a common influence upon these societies which may be found in demographic pressures and consequent competition over the means of production in an ecological and technological setting that imposed finite limits upon the forces of production. The eclipse of the Kel Gres and Kel Ferwan in Ahir and rise of the Kel Owi, the emergence of Kunta influence north of the Niger Bend, and the confrontations known as Shurr Bubba in Shinqit are among the better documented results of this process.

What happened in the aftermath was the emergence of a tributary mode of production which coexisted with lineage modes but which provided the dominant lineages in particular regions with a control over the forces of production that was far more effective than had previously been possible. In Shinqit dominant lineages were thus able to extract hospitality rights from their tributaries, use their wells and religious services, and call upon them for raiding parties, for agricultural produce, and for livestock. To the east, in Ahir, a "proto-" or "dyna-" or "early" state actually emerged with its base at Agades, temporarily, and although its influence rapidly waned after the end of the 17th century, a tributary mode of production served to reinforce the domination of the Kel Owi. The social relations of production under the tributary mode in southern Saharan societies tended to overlap lineage modes and greatly expand the means of production for dominant lineages.[5] Surplus accumulation accentuated the occupational specialization of dominant lineages: Its investment was in the trappings of finery imported from the Maghrib and Europe, Arabic books or the patronage of Arabic scholarship in the Islamic sciences, cattle and camels, and raiding material. That no sustained state formation, save the equivocal evidence from Ahir, resulted from the introduction of this tributary mode of production would seem to point to the continued preponderate influence of a lineage mode in the political economy of the southern Sahara. But the contradictions between the roles assigned to particular lineages in the late 17th century social charters and their actual practice in the following two centuries are largely resolved by taking into account the contradictions between the tributary mode and lineage mode of production. In short, the foundation myths in southern Saharan society and the tenacity with which these social charters are held by those societies suggest the introduction or heightened importance in the last half of the 17th century of a mode of production based on tribute; it was this mode that differentiated noble from subordinate, emergent classes. We may look to demographic or ecological pressures behind this process or to shifting economic fortunes of Maghribi dynasties; during the next two centuries, however, the intrusion of European merchant capital on the African littoral did much to fortify this new social formation.

One of the common themes to the essays in this volume is the extent to which European merchant capital undermined or consolidated African social formations in precolonial times; the relative importance of this theme obviously bears most directly upon those societies that were the guardians of markets or products that were highly valued by that merchant capital. In this respect the southern Saharan societies with which we have been concerned here ought not to come off as center stage in the unfolding drama of the peregrinations of merchant capital. Aside from the gum arabic industry in the Senegal Valley, contact between these southern Saharan societies and European traders prior to colonial occupation was limited to a handful of 19th-century European travelers. But, like the gum trade in the Senegal Valley, the impact of Maghribi trade with West Africa as a result of European activity in Tripoli did much to consolidate the emergent class structure and the dominant lineages within the southern Sahara.

Here I will be concerned only with a brief sketch of the history of regions affected by the gum trade, adjacent to the Senegal River basin, for it was in this area that the most dramatic impact of merchant capital can be traced. The Senegal basin story of gum arabic marketing from 1779 onward has been told elsewhere (Stewart, 1973: 91–93) and need only be summarized here. Although English merchants frequented the Senegal River in search of gum from 1779 to 1815 and, thereafter, traded along the Atlantic coast occasionally until 1857, the main European traders on the Senegal were French after 1815. French gum trade with the right bank of the Senegal accounted for 75% of the exports of the Colony of Senegal and Dependencies by 1842 (Stewart, 1973: 161). This single-commodity focus for French trade was typical for another two decades in Senegal after which time that colony's groundnut exports took over in importance with a corresponding shift of French interest to the hinterland of Dakar (Klein, 1968: 37). Not only was the production of gum arabic thus of primary importance to the maintenance of the French colony from 1815 to the 1860s but also, as this suggests, French orchestration of politically dominant lineages on the right bank of the Senegal was repeatedly attempted in this period also. Efforts to undermine the dominant lineage of the region of Trarza (the extreme southwest of modern day Mauritania), which the French took to be a state or amirate, and to fortify the dominant lineage of Brakna (the region immediately to the east), also called an "amirate," in effect led to the strengthening of the former and weakening of the latter. But more important than either of these results of French policy was the growth during this period of yet another noble lineage, the N'tishait, which came to dominate the politics of both regions by the 1860s through their control over the forces of production in the gum arabic industry (Stewart, 1973: 91; 93; 119–121). It was this same lineage that, two generations later, helped to usher in the formal occupation of Mauritania by the French and in 1960 took on the main offices of government in the newly created Islamic Republic of Mauritania. Such a gloss hardly does justice to the complexities of competiton among dominant lineages in the southwestern Sahara from the early nineteenth century onward or to the complex mechanisms used either to build or to legitimate the clients, "poor cousins," and servile labor that eventually led to the preeminent position of this lineage and its tribe in Mauritanian politics. But it does point up the significance of European merchant capital in the consolidation of the social formations in one area of the southern Sahara during the 19th century, as well as the vitality of the lineage mode of production in the growth of the N'tishait.

In effect, the intrusion of merchant capital served to consolidate the emergent-class role occupied by certain noble lineages that were able to demonstrate most of the trappings of class, in a Marxian sense, by the early colonial period. What remained, however, were the pervasive ideologies of segmentarity and social stratification which underpined the lineage mode of production, a mode that remained vigorous throughout the colonial occupation.

In sum, these data drawn from the southern Sahara offer to our study of precolonial modes of production in Africa both a perspective and a note of caution in dealing with social stratification. Social class in southern Saharan societies, as the term has been employed in much descriptive literature, needs to be carefully distinguished from class as an analytical tool in historical materialism. In the Saharan setting, as in similar nomadic societies, a pervasive ideology of social stratification (and segmentarity) has largely masked the reality of emergent classes. Historical processes in which these emergent classes gained control over new forces of production generally point to phases of state formation— sometimes transitory, occasionally of some lasting impact. Such a process appears also to account for the foundation myths or social charters in many of these societies, and it was quite definitely the outcome of the intrusion of merchant capital in southern Mauritania.

NOTES

1. By "southern Sahara" I am including a broad sweep of the Sahel belt, inclusive of nomads, seminomads, and agriculturalists who are economically interdependent. As such, the area includes those groups and dependents to which the ethnic labels "Moor," "Berber," and "Tuareg" are generally applied.

2. Much of the following description of southern Saharan society shall be set in an "ethnographic past," referring to social structures that were observed or idealized in the 19th century; at the conclusion of the essay these social relations will be placed into a historical context.

3. This is a very schematic presentation, but it does underline the main Sahelian societies that were in relationship with the Saharan social formations and, incidentally, the main geographic areas in the Sahel that seem to have been most dramatically affected by Saharan social ideology.

4. No reference has been made to the larger entity of the "tribe" which was composed of multiple lineages that traced descent from a common putative ancestor. For our purposes in analyzing the political economy of these societies, the tribe makes up a part of the ideology that supported

and defined the economic activities of lineages, but it cannot be considered a functional economic unit.

5. The most obvious examples of tributary relations come from accounts of the "warrior" lineages which exacted protection money from their subordinates in the form of livestock and/or agricultural produce, but "maraboutic" lineages, too, were built upon the donation of tithes offered by subordinates that were scarcely less exacting (Stewart, 1973: 110).

REFERENCES

BATRAN, A. A. (1972) "Sidi al-Mukhtar al-Kunti and the recrudescence of Islam in the middle Niger region." Ph.D. dissertation, University of Birmingham.

———— (1979) "The Kunta, Sidi al-Mukhtar al-Kunti, and the office of Shaykh al-Tariq al-Qadiriyya," in J. R. Willis (ed.), Studies in West African Islamic history: The cultivators of Islam. London: Cass.

BENNOUNE, M. (1978) "The political economy of Mauritania." Review of African Political Economy 12: 31–52.

BONTE, P. (1975) "From ethnology to anthropology." Critique of Anthropology 3(Spring): 1–26.

———— (1979) "Segmentarité et pouvior chez les éleveurs nomades sahariens," pp. 171–200 in Pastoral production and society. Cambridge, England: Cambridge University Press.

CURTIN, P. (1975) Economic change in precolonial Africa: Senegambia in the era of the slave trade. Madison: University of Wisconsin Press.

HUNWICK, J. O. (1971) "Songhay, Bornu and Hausaland in the sixteenth century," in J. F. A. Ajayi and Michael Crowder (eds.), History of West Africa (Vol. 1). New York: Longman.

KHAZANOV, A. M. (1978) "Characteristic features of nomadic communities in the Eurasian steppes," pp. 119–126 in W. Weissleder (ed.), The nomadic alternative. The Hague, The Netherlands: Mouton.

KLEIN, M. (1968) Islam and imperialism in Senegal. Stanford, CA: Stanford University Press.

KUBBEL, L. E. (1974) Songaiskaia Derzhava. Moscow: Nauka Publishing House. Cited in E. Gelner, "State before class, the Soviet treatment of African feudalism," in W. A. Shack and P. S. Cohen (eds.), Politics in Leadership. Oxford, England: Clarendon Press, 1979.

MARTY, P. (1918–1919) Etudes sur l'Islam et les tribus du Soudan (Vol. 1). Les Kounta de l'Est. Paris:

MEILLASSOUX, C. (1964) L'Anthropologie ecnomique des Gouro de Côte d'Ivoire. Paris:

NORRIS, H. T. (1968) Shinqiti folk literature and song. Oxford, England: Oxford University Press.

PLUMB, (1969) The death of the past. Harmondsworth, England: Penguin.

POULET, G. (1904) Les Maures de l'Afrique occidentale française. Paris: Challanel (extrait de la Revue Coloniale).

SHINQITI, A. A. (1961) al-Wasit fi tarajim udaba' Shinqit. Cairo: n.p.

STEWART, C. C. (1969) "A new document concerning the origins of the Awlad Ibiri and the N'tishait." Bulletin de l'Institut Fondamental d'Afrique Noire 31, series B, no. 1.

———— with E. K. STEWART (1973) Islam and social order in Mauritania. Oxford, England: Oxford University Press.

———— (1976a) "Southern Saharan scholarship and the Bilad al-Sudan." Journal of African History, 17: 73–93.

———— (1976b) "Frontier disputes and problems of legitimation." Journal of African History 17: 497–514.

TERRAY, E. (1972) Marxism and "Primitive" Societies: Two Studies. New York: Monthly Review Press.

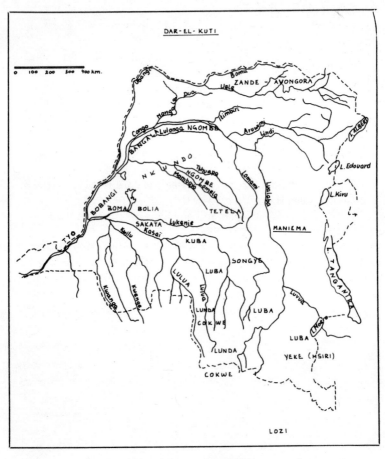

Equatorial Central Africa:
ethnic groups mentioned in the text

4

LINEAGE MODE OF PRODUCTION: SOCIAL INEQUALITIES IN EQUATORIAL CENTRAL AFRICA

BOGUMIL JEWSIEWICKI
Laval University

The crystallization of material realities and ideologies of inequality into a structure of social classes is a complex and nonlineal historical process. It is as much a matter of the elaboration of the material conditions of the existence of the classes as it is a matter of the "production" of the culture proper to each class and hence of that of the society as a whole. The culminating point of the formation of the specific culture of a class is the elaboration of class consciousness. The acquisition of the latter guarantees the passage from a class in itself (an economic category) to a class for itself (a political category). The production of the specific culture is a dialectical process of assimilation, rejection, and adaptation of

Author's Note: Part of the documentation used in preparing this work was made available thanks to a grant from the Social Science Research Council of Canada. I must equally thank J. L. Vellut for his comments which I have used in revising my first draft. My thanks are also due to the editors of this volume.

This text is rather more theoretical and methodological in focus than it is a statement of empirical research. I am aware that many of my hypotheses are more illustrated than proven by the citations. However, nothing stimulates research more than a group of hypotheses which arouse discussion, or even hostility.

the ideological principles of the dominant and dominated modes of production, of cultural heritages, and of innovations (Thompson, 1968; Roche, 1973; Konstan, 1979; Mészaros, 1971; Carchedi, 1977; Bourdieu, 1966; Markovitz, 1977; Terray, 1975; Gramsci, 1975: 693–698).

Before proposing some analytical principles for the analysis of the evolution of the forms of inequality in the lineage societies of central Africa, I think it is necessary to point up the implicit ethnocentrism in the search for wholly formed social classes and the utilization of such concepts as private property of the means of production, the hereditary transmission of social position through the family, and so on. Without wishing to adopt an extreme historicism, or a reductionist evolutionism, we must certainly admit that the formation of social classes takes place along many different lines of historical development and does not necessarily result, in each case, in the formation of a bipolar society of antagonistic classes (Jewsiewicki, 1980a, 1980b; Schwarz, 1979). The analytical principles I suggest are:

(1) A dominant group, en route to consolidation as a class, can arrest the formation of other classes and, to this end, make use of such tools as an ideology of kinship.[1]

(2) The absence of a juridical notion of private property in the means of production hardly precludes the legitimation of an unequal appropriation of surplus production. Such legitimation thus does not precede the formation of classes but historically accompanies it.

(3) A general market in goods and services is not required for the maintenance of social inequality and the crystallization of that inequality in a structure of social classes. However, such a market is required in order that economic constraint can generally replace noneconomic constraint in social relations.[2]

The dominant ideology in central Africa in the 18th, 19th, and 20th centuries was a lineage ideology based on the notion of seniority. This ideology was attached to the political control of a territory of which the perpetual "property" was symbolically held by the ancestors, and in reality by their representatives, the elders.

Serious economic consequences ensued. Beyond the level of the basic production group and of the lineage, the ideology of seniority operated in two main ways: First, there was an extension of kinship relations to the "elders" of groups associated in a political system, for example, the Luba-Lunda political culture, as well as to groups and individuals dominated and incorporated under the rubric of cadets, for example, the Kuba, or Avongara-Zande, political culture. Second, there were alliance relations, such as exchanges of blood, spouses, or fellowship, which guaranteed the circulation of people and goods. A political system thus embraced a system for circulating surplus from one group to another.

Kinship expressed and gave a "natural" form to the ideology of the relations of production and reproduction (Labica, 1974). Normally the appropriation of surplus followed the apparent structure. Surplus was given over to the elders for motives which were not at all immediately economic. We should also note that when a loss of producers/reproducers occurred by means of marriage exchanges, it was accompanied by the acquisition of the means for compensating for it (most frequently deferred) by a direct equivalent. The mediatory role played by goods was sometimes seen so directly that a relationship of seniority was established between the woman who quit the group in return for a dowry and the one who entered it thanks to the same dowry. Such was the case among the Mongo (Hulstaert, 1938, 1961). Rights of appropriating surplus followed rules of kinship, not of residence. This was essential for maintaining the logic of the political and ideological system. Only a dependent of servile status, who had no kin beyond his master, knew no other obligations than those to his master (Jewsiewicki, 1980c).

Political rights followed along from rights to surplus labor and superimposed themselves on rights of control over access to the resources of the "ancestors'" territory. For full enjoyment of political rights, it was necessary to found one or more of the units of production/reproduction which gave rights to the appropriation of the surplus labor of "biological" or "social" cadets, that is to say, one had to found a family. The power to do this was social and even not really biological. First, it was necessary to have a political right to the exploitation of all the resources in order to temporarily be able to alienate some of them. This right came from being physically and socially a potential elder.

Thus it was necessary to be a fully fledged male member of society, which habitually excluded recently assimilated men. Only this route allowed one to aspire toward cooptation to the elders. This cooptation was real in small groups, but purely ideological in large ones.

In social and political practice, and in ideology, only the "elders" established alliance relations or practiced "kinship politics." Cadets were transferred materially, via matrimonial exchanges, but not socially. They kept their kin status in their group. However, other transferees fell, at least temporarily, to the bottom of the social scale. Each cadet thus had a profound interest in remaining in his basic group of production/reproduction, which he viewed as a kin group, on pain of losing his recognized status. By contrast, the elder was encouraged to widen his external relations by playing the alliance game.[3]

A territory was the sum of the natural resources available to and exploitable by a social group. It constituted the setting for the kinship social group (lineage, maximum clan) which bore the forces of property relations. Property was thus a relationship between men and things destined for consumption. The only condition for the permanence of property relations was their constant reproduction. Property in a means of production thus lay in the capacity to appropriate the goods created by its productive utilization and not in its private control. By controlling the conditions of assimilation to the basic group, the elders controlled access to the productive utilization of resources. Certainly, the appropriation of surplus labor took the form of controlling the circulation of men. Still, the "production" of men resulted, in the long run, from the "material" production of the basic cells and from their social reproduction. Property is a continuous process of appropriating things and, not as the juridical concept would have it, a passing moment in the subject-object relationship of wills.[4]

Territory formed the basis, at one and the same time, of the political and economic autonomy of the kinship group. Only specific resources were ever ceded to foreign groups. By contrast, the forced cession of all the resources of a territory led to the formation of an economically and politically distinct group, whether this was the result of an internal political split or of a military conquest. Participation in the political control of a territory was conditioned by the immediate, or deferred, control of a unit of production and reproduction. Economic exploitation of this territory was identified by the granting of a status related to the kinship/alliance structure. Surplus and the need to organize its circulation appeared when the whole society, or some of its components, was able to produce more than what was necessary to satisfy its vital needs, needs which were as much biological as cultural. In the long run an increase in productivity, even if limited to one sector, was indispensable for the reproduction of a political system.

Overexploitation of vital needs could provide a surplus only in the short run. One may ask to what extent the sale of persons, reproduced outside the central political system, took care of this difficulty. Extensive exploitation of uncultivated resources through hunting and gathering were economic activities, often accompanied by the slave trade, which allowed the extraction of a surplus often sizable, but always risky. States, which were as vast as they were ephemeral in their centralizing attempts, rested on control of the circulation of such surpluses. Nevertheless, since vital needs are a function of social status, an increase in subordination, whether through domestic slavery, the incorporation of dependent groups as cadet-clients, or the like could lead to an increase in, or to a freeing of, surplus (Decaillot et al., 1977; Heller, 1978).

It is obvious that even though it is possible to talk of the formation of the elders as the potential embryo of a "class," there was simply no comparable process at the level of the cadets, beyond the area of preferential matrimonial exhanges. In spite of the circulation of women and of slaves, social mechanism favored rapid integration into basic groups, while nonintegrated slaves were rapidly removed from social space by the slave trade. Such integration was the only possible way of inserting oneself into the ideological rotation which led from cadet to elder, and this rotation was the basic mechanism for legitimating social integration. A posteriori legitimation of economic and political realities was universal, but was nowhere the rule.

In lineage societies, surplus was derived immediately from two sources: (1) appropriation of the production of direct dependents such as wives, cadets, slaves, and clients, who had been integrated into the extended family or lineage, and (2) appropriation from other extended families and from temporary units of production such as hunting or fishing groups. This fact was the basis for the initial hierarchization between family heads. The first relations of social differentiation manifested themselves in unequal participation in consumption of the social product, which reserved for the "elders." In extreme cases, the latter enlarged the circle of their direct dependents, held back the economic autonomy which the cadets achieved through marriage, and got underway an increasingly private accumulation of specific prestige goods. Nevertheless, the rules of succession restricted the enjoyment of these goods to "elders" of the group who were often not members of the immediate family of the late elder.[5] Individual enjoyment was temporary, but appropriation by a distinct group of "elders" tended to become permanent. From this angle the creation of distinct consumption codes justified social differentiation and unequal participation in the redistribution of the social product (Décaillot et al., 1977).

Although the market was not the source of the exploitation of the cadets by the "elders," or of the inequality between them, it did permit a gradual transformation from inequality of function to inequality of position.[6] Solidarity among the elders of different territorial groups appeared in economico-political exchanges and led to the formation of an intergroup political and ideological culture.[7] By opening up wide possibilities of competition for the surplus labor extracted from the different basic groups, the market favored a diversification of exploitation, the formation of regional "political cultures," and a social concentration of surplus labor. Through opportunities for competition over the distribution of local surpluses, commercial exchanges stimulated the creation of an "elite" of elders with ideological solidarity at the regional level.

The cadets' position became more dependent and more permanent when ideology and dominant social practices were taken into account.[8] The slave trade offered new possibilities for political autonomy on the part of the elders. But, even though social reproduction and the legitimation of enslavement were rooted in lineage society, slave societies never appeared in black Africa (Létourneau, 1980). Lineage ideology in this way formed the ideological apparatus of the mode of production (Robin, 1973, 1977). It allowed control of access to the means of production of the territory "appropriated by the ancestors" and expressed the solidarity of the "elders," whose seniority was based on (1) genealogy, (2) symbolic political position such as the order of migration, rights of occupation, and the like, or (3) simply on such facts as conquest or the control of an important group of dependents.

In the historical process of class formation, the transformation of differences of fact into significant distinctions occupies an important place. Among other ways, it takes place through the social code of consumption. If directly observable consumption behavior corresponds to the society's own system of norms and values, it reflects and legitimates social stratification as that stratification relates to the processes and relations of production (Godard, 1975; Baudrillard, 1970).

Here I am essentially concerned with the conditions of social differentiation which result from the evolution of the social capacities of production, accumulation, and appropriation of surplus. Throughout central Africa, seniority seems to have formed the main principle justifying an unequal division of those goods which for various reasons fell within the common domain. "All our ancestors' laws . . . distinguish between an elder's share and that of a cadet" says a Bolia (Mune, 1959: 44). The same principle of centralization and appropriation based on seniority was found, applied via different mechanisms, among the riverine peoples of the Zaire River and among the Chokwe in the light forest south of the Equator.[9] Authority and power were regularly transmitted according to the principle of seniority. They were justified and legitimated by it. Nevertheless, this principle—which legitimated the right to control men and resources of high productivity, such as hunting (especially when it was collective), also often collective fishing, the exploitation of saline areas, and so on—was universally the fruit of "accumulating" people, in the form of dependents and of goods, and was rivalled in political practice by the individual's personal position. Oral traditions are rich in accounts of confrontations between these two principles, conflicts which resulted in compromises adjusting seniority to real power. In this way both ideological principle and political reality remained safeguarded (Mpase, 1974; Mune, 1959; Hulstaert, 1965, 1959, 1958; Mumbanza, 1980b; Philippe, 1959).

One complex tangles between (1) the three principles of affiliation which locate individuals in kinship groups which are matrilineal, patrilineal, and/or by acquisition (hostages, purchases, indemnities) and (2) the kinship of alliance, which is proof of the search for an equilibrium between, on the one hand, ideology, which founded the legitimation of power on seniority, and, on the other hand, practice, which based it on wealth (Harms, 1978; Mumbanza, 1980b; Vansina, 1973; Reefe, 1975; Ndua, 1978). Paraphrasing Orwell, one might say that all an ancestor's descendants were equal, but that the elders were generally more equal than the others. I say normally since a rich and powerful man could always found a new group living around his extended family; and, either by force or the threat of force, he would acquire territory. Nevertheless, the Nkundo say that "men die, but power remains" (Hulstaert, 1958: 236). Whatever its real origins, power belonged to the "elders" and was legitimated and transmitted via real or ideological seniority. A "parvenu" often invented by "supernatural" means a seniority based on adoption or alliance and official traditions retained this claim for his descendants, even if everyone knew that it referred to a former slave, and thus a man without kin, who, because of this fact was "legally" outside the group's circles of seniority.[10]

This reflection allows us to isolate four important elements for the analysis of the dynamic of the political systems of central Africa during the 19th century: first, is the formation and transformation of local political systems under the impact of the changes which took place in the 19th century and which was not necessarily an evolution toward the state. The existence of the state seemed to depend on the relations between the specific ecological milieu, the productive activity from which the surplus was derived in a direct line, taking into account the means by which it was realized, and the density and dynamic of human occupation which allowed the permanent removal of producers from lineage groups and their deployment in a productive manner on the spot.

A second element in the dynamic of these systems was, by contrast, the internal evolution of the structures of inequality of the production/reproduction groups which was a continuous, but not at all linear, process and which tended toward the formation of conscious, formalized stratification, at least at the level of the "elders." This process seems to me to have been directly articulated on an intensive exploitation of resources, on the control of the circulation and of the appropriation and consumption of surplus, and finally on the mechanisms of circulation and accumulation of men. The intensification of the exploitation of resources allowed the expanded reproduction of the relations of production and this led to an increasing ascendance over the utilization of, or access to, these resources through the control of the group's social reproduction. The first regional political cultures began with the mechanism of matrimonial exchanges, that is, with the circulation of men and of prestige goods. These cultures formed the basis for the permanence of the political ideologies of kinship which reinforced the elders' position insofar as this formed a permanent and universal social structure. Yet the formation of groups of personal dependents during the 19th century also started concurrent structures of inequality and of surplus control. It signalled the formation, within lineage societies, of bipolar societies of groups which tended toward a social status which was ideologically and practically hereditary. The crisis of certain lineage societies took place to the profit of this new structure of inequality where the control of firearms and of land became the instruments of domination (Cordell, 1977; Lohaka, 1972; Ntambwe, 1971; Vellut, 1973).

A third element demonstrated by these systems is that the formation of the state rested on, but did not necessarily result from, the parallel evolution of, on the one hand, the organization and allocation of labor and, on the other, of changes in technology. Only this double change allowed political organization to acquire the necessary autonomy with respect to the kinship structures and to the lineage mode of production. A comparison between the Lunda "empire" on one side and the Kuba kingdom on the other is significant in this regard. From the 18th century the two passed through a long period of hesitation between the autonomous structure of a political power which rested on the various functions of the capital and the ideological function of legitimation of lineage structures and on a structure dedicated to the organization of the circulation of surplus (Vellut, 1979b). The remarkable capacity of lineage structures for assimilation and neutralization of change and the impact of the Atlantic slave trade prevented the formation of an autonomous central political structure among the Lunda. By contrast, at the same time the ecological situation of the Kuba allowed them a more intensive exploitation of an environment on the border between the forest and the savanna. The reduced scale of the society as a whole, and its marginal but not wholly isolated position with respect to Atlantic exchange, explains the formation of the Kuba state. The capital ensured its increasing autonomy to the detriment of that of the lineage structures of the incorporated societies, but at the peripheries the tributary relations between the capital and local societies prevailed (Vansina, 1978).

In the 19th century we witness the multiplication of two political models. On one side there were states whose autonomy was ensured by the economic and demographic importance of their capitals, by the quasi-individual control of an important number of firearms, and by the formation at the center of a new mode of production whose extension was accompanied by the progressive destruction of the lineage mode of production. This new mode of production was based on the massive utilization of personal dependents and on the personal control of cultivable lands at the center (Cordell, 1977; Lloyd, 1977). On the other side we witness the extension of "decentralized" political cultures based on the extraction and trade of wild products by basic production/reproduction units. Lineage ideology formed the ideological apparatus of these political cultures. These political cultures were distinguished from

the lineage societies of the 18th century by the massive assimilation of slaves coming from neighboring societies and the increasing importance of personal wealth, which nonetheless was con-
stantly integrated by the lineage structure. Multiple and complex
alliances between the elders, many of whom were "self-made
men," guaranteed not only the conditions of the wide circulation of
men and goods but also allowed the birth of a new dominant social
layer which ideologically remained that of the elders (Mumbanza,
1980b; Harms, 1978; Miller, 1969, 1976). A fourth element in
these systems was the regrouping of basic units within political
systems that responded to two imperatives at once contradictory
but with convergent effects: competition between residential units
to control the circulation of surplus and producers and the elders'
fundamental solidarity of "interests." These two factors worked in
a socio-cultural environment which was the result of the historical
action of the relations of economic and social complementarity,
that is, of exchanges, and particularly of matrimonial exchanges,
and of the cultural contacts which arose from those relations. At
the level of the elders as a group, and not as individuals, the
relations of alliance and competition were forged; and these led to
the creation of a network of more or less stable links (a field for
political forces), links which were structured by fictional kinship
relations. The stabilization and reinforcement of these relations
between the elders led to the creation of an elders' subculture which
had specific consumption codes and which entailed the exercise of
certain ideological and juridical functions and so on. The relations
of competition created a hierarchy among the elders and the groups
which they represented. The permanence deriving from economic
and from socio-political contacts reinforced the unity of regional
cultures, which in the majority of cases remained weak at the level
of the cadets as great linguistic diversity proves.

By contrast, states were formed by opposition to this "system"
and were based on the simultaneous political and economic autonomy which ensured them control over the natural and human resources of the capital. The latter's expansion took place at the
expense of the lineage mode of production.

To conclude, let us stop at the permanence of the kinship structures, which is so striking to researchers. Sometimes some go so far as to affirm the changelessness of the basic structures. Yet they forget that this "changelessness" of the basic rural structures was just as striking in Europe prior to the industrial revolution, before primitive capitalist or socialist accumulation destroyed village communities.[11] The phenomenon is probably more spectacular in central Africa than it is elsewhere. It seems to me possible to explain it within the following framework of analysis.

The permanence of the lineage mode of production was a basic fact. Taking account of the ecological conditions and demographic dynamic, the contradictions built up within each basic group were able to resolve themselves by the splitting of the group and thus by simple reproduction of the social system. The subsistence economy, which was mainly based on nonagricultural activities, allowed not only a pronounced mobility of production/reproduction groups but also the abandonment of one territory for another. Besides, within the context of shifting agriculture, any productive investment in the land was rendered void after a fairly short period of time. The appropriation of collective surplus in the form of men, both by the elders and by the political structures, weakened potential demographic pressures and limited the internal dynamic of the mode of production, thus ensuring a greater stability of the basic structures. During the period of the slave trade, by the very nature of the articulation with the world economy, commerce was reinforced in its apparent character of a political activity, since merchandise could not be acquired, preserved, and transported except as a function of the social capacity to the exclusion of the group. Only in the second half of the 19th century did the capacity to accumulate goods become an individual one, linked to the possession of firearms and based on external raids. Yet even then the mode of production/reproduction, which was organized according to the kinship structure and integrated into the larger group as a function of that same ideology, permitted the integration of dependents and the control of their surplus.

A political territory defined the entirety of the resources to which the group had potential access, and which was appropriated by the group by virtue of descent from the territory's first proprietor or conqueror. The first foundation of the elders' functions and rights was established at this level. Genealogically closest to the ancestor, the elders were the depositories of the social and ritual rights of access to this territory, rights which meant exclusion from or inclusion into the group. On the other hand, the units of production/reproduction needed free access to these resources taking into account their basic subsistence activities, of gathering, small hunting and fishing, and shifting agriculture. Thus this group, although it was a residential one in the sense of possessing a common residence but not a long-term permanent one, could only be based on the principle of kinship, and this all the more so since so far as possible the functions of reproduction prevailed over those of production so far as the society was concerned. Production served the primary object which was the expanded demographic reproduction of the group. Finally, also in this way the collection of surplus was realized, which, given both the fragility of biological reproduction and low productivity, could only be realized by pooling different surpluses of the various units. Matrimonial circulation was the main mechanism for this and its control allowed unequal participation in the appropriation of the surplus which came from the various units. Another way of appropriating surplus came from the units' collective effort and was based on social force or on politics. The latter came through the attraction exercised by the powerful leader of a prosperous unit; social violence meant the enslavement of a unit's members and military conflict.

Nevertheless, neither the lineage mode of production nor its corresponding infrastructure was at all changeless. The first signs of this were the appropriation of certain high-yielding natural resources, such as copper mines, fields of saline grasses, and the like, by the holders of political power; other signs were the appropriation by families of intensive fisheries or the artificial construction of territorial holdings. Another proof was the creation of plantations thanks to the concentration of servile manpower and to the possibilities of disposing of their produce. Toward the end of the 19th century some residential groups, which were engaged in commerce and fishing, seemed to evolve toward associations, and individualism began to prevail wherever a generalized market in goods had been solidly planted.

The events of the second half of the 19th century showed that the internal assimilation of slaves along with an external market for products allowed the expansion of regional political cultures, and these progressively diverged from the lineage structures. Chokwe migrations, the migrations of Bangala language and "culture," and Avongara-Zande expansion all led to a profound assimilation at the regional level, an assimilation which was not even egalitarian in appearance. On the contrary, social as well as economic differences between the members of the group were accentuated. Linguistic and cultural unification within a regional society might have constituted the basis for the eventual formation of a dominant class "for itself," one which lay outside the kinship system and which might start the process of evolution toward structures of a national type. European political colonialism cut short these tendencies as much in the economic sphere through paralyzing African commerce, as in the social and political spheres. Withdrawal and defensive conservatism best characterize the social reaction of the colonized societies of central Africa. Many researchers deduce changelessness from this, but in so doing they lose sight of the second half of the 19th century and mistake the tightening of social structures in the 20th century for a "traditional" condition.

NOTES

1. The works of Heusch (1972; cf. Hoover, 1978) are particularly useful in reflecting on the role of symbolic codes in social control. The recent French discussion on the state, to which Augé (1975, 1977) has made the most recent and enjoyable contribution, also contributes important elements to this discussion (see the fine critical insight into Augé by J. Muller, 1978). A comparison of the works of Heusch and Augé is very stimulating and my thoughts have been inspired by it.

2. Many Marxist historians are inspired by this thought which comes from Marx among others and according to which economic constraint is the fundamental instrument for surplus extraction only in the capitalist mode of production. See, for example, Lémarchand (1971: 87).

3. To avoid many tiresome references, I confine myself to the special number of *Dialectiques,* 21, 1978.

4. Here I follow Sik (1978: 191–197) and Godelier (1978a).

5. Vansina (1973, 1977) and Miller (1976) contain much interesting material without following the same reasoning. Van Leynseele (1979) and Mumbanza mwa Bawele (1980) confirm this analysis for the area of the Zaire River. It clearly differs from the analysis of Rey (1971).

6. In this connection it seems worthwhile to cite Touraine (1965: 26): "The social significance of an action is not to be confused with the meaning which the actor gives to it. To try to establish this meaning at the most superficial level is to condemn oneself to fall back on mechanical explanations every time some divergence appears between opinions and conduct. On the contrary it is necessary to attain a collective social consciousness which does not coincide with the consciousness of individuals and which thus appears as unconscious."

7. In this connection see the analyses of Vellut (1978, 1979a), Miller (1976), Heusch (1972), N'dua Solol (1978), Musasa Samal (1974), Kayamba Badye (1975) and Reefe (1975, 1978). The following quote from Vellut (1979b: 7) gives a good idea of the process of formation of the solidarities in question: "The agent of this movement might be a prestigious territorial chief who is trying to integrate himself into the dominant political hierarchy, or again it might be a lord who 'is looking for a land,' i.e. who is trying to establish a connection at one and the same time with a territorial chief, and with a superior political power. In the Lunda world it is this relationship which unites a *chilol* with a major political title represented in the capital *(mussumba)*. Their relationship with the state results in the dissolution and recombination of certain aspects of the local communities, but these communities remain a basic support in a structure of exploitation."

8. Rosdolski affirms, following Marx, "that one cannot appropriate foreign merchandise . . . without also alienating one's own" and consequently that "property in merchandise precedes exchange." Exchange organized into a tributary system consequently witnesses the existence of social differentiation since it follows the appropriation of a local product (surplus labor) by a socially distinct group.

9. This very curt summary is intended to avoid too long an argument and many references which would be out of place in this chapter. It is a question of widespread, but by no means isolated, examples. Vansina is preparing a book on the historical evolution of the societies of the central basin. His book will either confirm or decisively refute this summary and many of the other hypotheses put forth in this chapter.

10. This claim is essentially based on an analysis of the administrative inquiries which preceded the creation of chiefdoms and sectors in the central basin. The records of these inquiries are deposited in the administrative archives of Equatorial Province and in the capitals of the subregions. See also the De Ryck Papers on deposit at the University of Wisconsin—Madison; they are available on microfilm. See also Van der Kerken (1920, 1944), Hulstaert (1972), De Jonghe (1949), and Jewsiewicki (1980d).

11. I think many Africanists will find this quotation illuminating: "The system resists because the entire social edifice rests on it, and because the cadets, with few exceptions, themselves make use of it to maintain that inequality of which they are victims, but against which they never dream of rising up, because they are too convinced by the reigning ideology of the absolute necessity of their exclusion, even of their sacrifice," and "Those who are excluded, what do they have? Nothing, unless they marry, or if their family is too poor to provide them with a dowry that allows them to establish themselves. Unless they succeed in getting it for themselves, all or in part. But everyone cannot work outside the group, because it takes manpower for it to survive" (Lamaison, 1979: 725–726; 724).

REFERENCES

AUGE, M. (1977) Pouvoirs de vie, pouvoirs de mort. Introduction à une anthropologie de la repression. Paris: Flammarion.

Anthropologie tous terrains. Dialectiques 21 (1977), special number.

BAUDRILLARD, J. (1968) Le système des objets. Paris: Gallimard.

_____ (1970) La société de consommation, ses mythes, ses structures. Paris: S.G.P.P.

Besoins et consommation. Pensée 180 (1975), special number.

BISHIKWABO CHUBAKA (1979) Notes sur l'origine de l'institution du "bwami" et fondements de pouvoir politique au Kivu oriental. Cahiers du CEDAF 8.

BOELAERT, A. (n.d.) Untitled research. n.p.

BOURDIEU, P. (1966) "Condition de classe et position de classe." Archives européennes de sociologie 2: 201–214.

BURAHIMU-MUKAYA (1973) "Les structures socio-économiques et le commerce swahili à Kasongo vers la fin du XIXe siècle," M.A. thesis, UNAZA, Lubumbashi.

BYLIN, E. (1966) Basakata: Le peuple du pays de l'entre fleuves Lukenie Kasai. Lund: Studia Ethnographica Upsaliensis.

CARCHEDI, G. (1977) On the economic identification of social classes. London: Routledge and Kegan Paul.

CLARENCE-SMITH, W. G. (1979) "Slaves, commoners and landlords in Bulozi c.1875–1906." Journal of African History 20: 318–338.

CORDELL, D. (1976) "Dar-al-Kuti: A history of the slave trade and state formation on the Islamic front . . ." Ph.D. dissertation, University of Wisconsin—Madison.

DECAILLOT, M et. al. (1977) Besoins et mode de production. Paris: Editions sociales.

DE JONGHE, E. (1949) Les formes d'asservissement dans les sociétés indigènes du Congo belge. Brussels: IRCB.

DENIS, J. (1935) "L'organisation d'un people primitif." Congo 1: 923–947.

——— (1940–1941) "Notes sur l'organisation de quelques tribus aux environs du lac Leopold II." Anthropos 35–36: 815–829.

DE PLAEN, G. (1974) Les structures d'autorité des Bayanzi. Paris: Maspero.

DE RYCK, M. (1937) "Les Lalia-Ngolu." Trait-d'Union 6: 93–244.

FRIEDMAN, J. (1975) "Tribes, states and transformations." in M. Block (ed.) Marxist analyses and social anthropology. London: Malaby.

GODARD, F. (1975) "Classes sociales et modes de consommation." Pensée 180: 140–164.

GODELIER, M. (1978a) "Territory and property in primitive society." Information sur les sciences sociales 17: 399–422.

——— (1978b) "Infrastructures, societies and history." Current Anthropology 4: 763–771.

GRAMSCI (1975) Gramsci dans le texte. Paris: Editions Sociales.

GREVISSE, F. (1937–1938) "Les Bayeke." Bulletin des Juridictions indigènes et du droit coutumier congolais 5: 1–16; 29–40; 65–74; 97–113; 125–140; 165–175; & 6: 200–216.

HARMS, R. W. (1978) "Competition and capitalism: The Bobangi role in Equatorial Africa's trade revolution." Ph.D. dissertation, University of Wisconsin—Madison.

HELLER, A. (1978) La théorie des besoins chez Marx. Paris: Union Générale d'Edition.

HEUSCH, L. de (1972) Le roi ivre ou l'origine de l'Etat. Paris: Gallimard.

——— (1975) "What shall we do with the drunken king." Africa 45: 367–372.

HOOVER, J. (1978) "Mythe et remous historiques: A Lunda response to de Heusch." History in Africa 5: 63–80.

HULSTAERT, G. (1938) Le mariage des Nkundo. Brussels: ARSC.

———— (1958) Proverbes Mongo. Tervuren: MRCB.

———— (1959) Losako. La salutation solonelles des Nkundo. Brussels: ARSC.

———— (1961) Les Mongo. Apperçu général. Tervuren: MRAC.

———— (1965) Contes Mongo. Brussels: ARSOM.

———— (1972) "Une critique de L'ethnie mongo de G. Van der Kerken." Etudes d'histoire africaine 3: 27–60.

HUTERAU, A. (n.d.) Histoire des peuples de l'Uele et de l'Ubangi. Brussels: Goemaere.

JEWSIEWICKI, B. (1980a) "La production de l'histoire et la conscience sociale: 'Civiliser' l'Autre." Conférence: "Philosophie de l'histoire et la pratique l'historienne d'aujourd'hui." Ottawa, April 18–20.

———— (1980b) "L'histoire en Afrique ou le commerce des idées usa- gées," in A. Schwarz (ed.) Les faux prophètes de l'Afrique ou l'afr(eu)-canisme. Québec: PUL.

———— (1980c) "Le contexte de l'esclavage en Afrique centrale équato- riale." Conference on the Ideology of Slavery in Africa. Toronto, April 3–4.

———— (1980d) "Les archives administratives zairoises de l'époque col- oniales." Annales Aequatoria. Mélanges Hulstaert 1.

KAYAMBA BADYE (1975) "Les Bena Ngoma de la Lufira: Histoire d'une société lignagère pré-coloniale des origines à 1980." M.A. thesis, UNAZA, Lubumbashi.

KONSTAN, D. (1979) "Class and labor in ancient society." Marxist Perspectives 5: 124–131.

LABICA, G. (1974) "De l'égalité." Dialectiques 1–2: 3–29.

LAMAISON, P. (1979) "Les stratégies matrimoniales dans un système complexe de parentée: Ribennes en Gévauden (1650–1830)." Annales ESC. 24: 721–743.

LEMARCHAND, G. (1971) "Féodalisme et société rurale dans la France moderne," in CEREM: Sur le féeodalisme. Paris: Editions sociales.

LETOURNEAU, J. (1980) "Mode de reproduction et mode de dèpen- dance de la formation sociale ashanti aux XVIIIe et XIXe siècles: Nouvelles évidences à la théorie de l'articulation des modes de pro- duction." Xe Conference annuelle de l'ACEA. Guelph, May 6–9.

LLOYD, D. (1977) "The Precolonial Economic History of the Avongara-Zande c.1750–1916." Ph.D. dissertation, University of California, Berkeley.

LOHAKA (1972) "Ngngo Leteta, pénétration arabe chez les Tetela du Sankuru." M.A. thesis, UNAZA, Lubumbashi.

MATEMBONI AKPAKALA (1974) "Les traditions orales de la cuvette." M.A. thesis, UNAZA, Lubumbashi.

MARKOVITZ, I. L. (1977) Power and class in Africa. Englewood Cliffs, NJ: Prentice-Hall.

MEILLASSOUX, C. (1971) "Adaptation et réaction des sociétés ouest-africaines aux transformations de la traite," in C. Meillassoux (ed.) The development of indigenous trade and markets in West Africa. Oxford, England: Oxford University Press.

MESZAROS, I. [ed.] (1971) Aspects of history and class consciousness. London: Routledge and Kegan Paul.

MILLER, J. C. (1969) Cokwe expansion 1850–1900. Madison: African Studies Program, University of Wisconsin.

———— (1976) Kings and kinsmen. Oxford, England: Clarendon Press.

MOELLER, A. (1936) Les grandes lignes des migrations des Bantous de la Province Orientale du Congo belge. Brussels: IRCB.

MPASE NSENGELE (1974) L'evolution de la solidarité traditionnelle en milieu rural et urbain au Zaire. Kinshasa: Presses de l'UNAZA.

MUELLER, E. (1958) "L'organisation sociale des Ekonda et la terminologie-sociologique." Aequatoria 21: 41–59.

———— (1959) "L'application de la terminologie de Murdock à la structure sociale des Ekonda." Aequatoria 22: 8–15.

MULLER, J. C. (1978) "Vers une anthropologie des pouvoirs." Revue canadienne des études africaines 12: 429–448.

MULYUMBA WA MAMBA (1978) "Aperçu sur la structure politique des Belege-Basile." Cahiers du CEDAF 1.

MUMBANZA MWA BAWELE (1977) "Fondements économiques de l'évolution des systèmes de filiation dans les sociétés de la Haute Ngiri et de la Moeko du XIXe siècle à nos jours." Enquêtes et documents d'histoire africaine 2:1–30.

———— (1980a) "L'éevolution de l'organisation socio-politique des groupes riverains de l'entre Zaire-Ubangi: Rôle des facteurs endogènes et exogènes dans l'articulation au système mondial du XVIIIe au XXe siècle." Xe Conférence annuelle de l'ACEA, Guelph, May 6–9.

_____ (1980b) "L'histoire des peuples de l'entre Zaire-Ubangi." Ph.D. dissertation, UNAZA, Lubumbashi.

MUNE, P. (1959) Le groupement de Petit-Ekonda. Brussels: ARSC.

MUSASA SAMAL (1974) "Histoire des Kanintshin: Quelques perspectives sur l'histoire ancienne des Etats Lunda." M.A. thesis, UNAZA, Lubumbashi.

MUTUZA, K. and NGINDU, M. (1978) "La superstructure de la société lega, frein ou moteur du développement." Presence africaine 105/106: 10–11.

NALDER, L. F. (1937) A tribal survey of Mongala Province by members of the province staff and Church Missionary Society. Oxford, England: Oxford University Press.

NDAYWELL E NZIEM (1973) "Organisation sociale et histoire: Les Ngwili et les Ding." Ph.D. dissertation, Université de Paris.

N'DUA SOLOL (1978) "Histoire ancienne des populations Luba et Lunda du plateau du Haut-Lubilash." Ph.D. dissertation, UNAZA, Lubumbashi.

NKIERE BOKUNA (1975) "L'organisation politique traditionnelle des Basakata en Republique de Zaire." Cahiers du CEDAF 7–8.

NTAMBWE, C. A. (1971) "Les Luluwa et le commerce luso-africain dans la deuxième moitié du XIXe siècle (1870–1895)." M.A. thesis, Université Lovanium.

PHILIPPE, R. (1959) "Les modes de propriété chez le Mongo: Essai d'étude comparée." Kongo-Overzee 25: 17–72.

REEFE, T. (1975) "A history of the Luba Empire to c.1885." Ph.D. dissertation, University of California, Berkeley.

_____ (1978) "The Luba political culture c.1500–1800." Etudes et documents histoire africaine 3: 105; 116.

REY, P. (1971) Colonialisme, néo-colonialisme et transition au capitalisme. Paris: Maspero.

ROBIN, R. (1973) Histoire et linguistique. Paris: Colin.

_____ (1974) "De la nature de l'Etat à la fin de l'ancien régime: Formation sociale, Etat et transition." Dialectiques 1–2: 31–54.

_____ & DE CERTEAU, M. (1976) "Débat." Dialectiques 11: 42–64.

ROCHE, D. [ed.] (1973) Ordres et classes: Colloque d'histoire sociale. Saint-Cloud, May 24–25, 1967. Paris: Mouton.

ROMBAUTS, H. (1945) "Les Ekonda." Aequatoria 8: 123–128.

ROSDOLSKY, R. (1976) La genèse du "Capital" chez Karl Marx. Paris: Maspero.

SCHWARZ, A. (1979) Colonialistes, africanistes et Africains. Montréal: Nouvelle Optique.

STAS, J. B. (1939) "Les Nkumu chez les Ntomba de Kitoro." Aequatoria 2: 109–123.

SIK, O. (1978) Pour une troisième voie. Paris: PUF.

TERRAY, E. (1975) "Classes and class consciousness in the Abron Kingdom of Gyaman" in M. Bloch (ed.) Marxist analysis and social anthropology. London: Malaby.

———— (1977) "De l'exploitation." Dialectiques 21: 87–96.

THOMPSON, E. P. (1968) The making of the English working class. Harmondsworth, England: Penguin.

TOURAINE, A. (1970) Sociologie de l'action. Paris: Seuil.

VAN DER KERKEN, G. (1920) Les sociétés bantoues du Congo belge. Brussels: Goemaere.

———— (1944) Ethnie Mongo (vol. I, livres 1–3). Brussels: IRCB.

VAN EVERBROECK, N. (1961) Mpomb'Ipoku: Le seigneur de l'abîme. Tervuren: MRAC.

VAN LEYNSEELE, P. (1978) "The incidence of colonial occupation on traditional society in Equatorial Africa." Leiden. (unpublished)

———— (1979) "Les Libinza de la Ngiri: L'anthropologie d'un peuple des marais du confluent Congo-Ubangi." Ph.D. dissertation, University of Leiden.

VANSINA, J. (1973) The Tio Kingdom of the Middle Congo 1880–1892. London: IAI.

———— (1978) The children of Woot: A history of the Kuba peoples. Madison: University of Wisconsin Press.

VELLUT, J. L. (1973) Questions spéciales d'histoire de l'Afrique. Lubumbashi: UNAZA. (mimeo)

———— (1978) Histoire de l'Afrique centrale. Louvain: UCL. (mimeo)

———— (1979a) "A l'est du Kwanza, c.1800–1925: De l'économie de traite à la nouvelle définition des espaces économiques." (unpublished)

———— (1979b) "Afrique centrale de l'Ouest (histoire precoloniale)." (unpublished)

VERBEKEN, A. (1956) Msiri, roi du Garenganze. Brussels: Cuypers.

WOLFE, A. W. (1961) The Ngombe tradition: Continuity and change in the Congo. Chicago: Northwestern University Press.

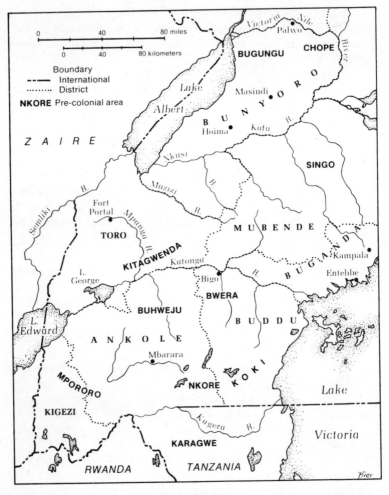

Western Uganda

5

HERDERS AND FARMERS:
The Tributary Mode of Production in Western Uganda

EDWARD I. STEINHART
University of Zambia

In recent years, historians of western Uganda have lain the once-fashionable conquest theory of state formation in the dustbin of history. This theory credited the origins of the state and virtually all major cultural developments to a superior race of light-skinned, cattle-owning, warlike "Hamitic" invaders. Although the racist interpretation has been abandoned, as yet no satisfactory explanation for the emergence of the state, rooted in either Marxian or conventional anthropological theory, has been devised to fill the gap.

In this chapter an attempt will be made to utilize a theory of state formation based on an analysis of the changing modes of production within the western lacustrine region of Uganda between the 14th and 19th centuries. The state in this view is an abstract creation of objective conditions and relations of production which, like all social relations of production, did not appear until "the material conditions of their existence . . . matured in the womb of the old society" (Marx, cited in Avineri, 1969: 37). The process of intensification and transformation of the forces and relations of production in the "classless societies" of western Uganda's social formations led to the emergence of early class society which manifested a tributary mode of production (Amin, 1976: 13– 58). The state was thrown up by society only when a class society had developed, and within which the dominant class became conscious of itself as a ruling class and asserted itself as such.

The kingdoms of Bunyoro-Kitara and Nkore (Ankole) offer both advantages and disadvantages to this kind of analysis. The region developed its historical social formations in almost complete isolation from societies at higher stages in the development of production as were found in Europe and the Middle East. It was therefore free from contaminants to autonomous internal evolution such as the diffusion, imposition, or influence of externally developed modes of production, at least until the last century. On the other hand, isolation has meant the virtual absence of independent and documentary evidence until a similarly recent era. We must rely upon the extensive and welcome accounts of recorded oral traditions, a highly developed historical form among the lacustrine kingdoms. But these sources, deriving from the ruling class and its direct courtly dependents, reflect a bias toward dynastic history which is consistently self-serving and shows little concern with social and economic life. The historian is confronted with many obstacles in discovering the pattern of economic change or the principles of social evolution manifested in the "infinite variations and gradations due to innumerable different empirical circumstances" (Marx, 1967: 762). It is to obtain a deeper knowledge of these principles of change that we analyze the traditional histories and the empirical circumstances that they purport to record.

The earliest period in the recorded history of the kingdoms of the Kitaran region is spoken of as "the reign of the gods" or Batembuzi. Recent scholarship (Buchanan, 1974) has identified the Batembuzi with early Nilo-Saharan-speaking immigrants to western Uganda between the 11th and 13th centuries. This settlement appears to have consisted of localized "clan groups" of common totemic identification and nominal common descent. Prior to the Batembuzi era, the area was settled by loosely organized groups of Bantu speakers

(Webster, 1979b), who possessed knowledge of seed agriculture and iron working but no political centralization beyond the village or clan. The encounter of Sudanic Batembuzi with Bantu cultivators is supposed to have created "a level of political centralization" (Buchanan, 1974: 45) and the emergence of the earliest states of the Kitara complex (Webster, 1979c: 126).

In what sense can we speak of states at this stage of lacustrine history? Such usage would reduce the meaning of state to any supra-familial authority in society, making "some sort of state a universal feature of human culture" (Lowie, 1927: 44). This essay will reserve the term *state* to mean a particular kind of social organization and institution: the instruments of control consisting of the means of coercion and ideological hegemony, the apparatus of administration and extraction of surplus value wielded by a ruling class. As such, the small groups of mixed farmers under the leadership of clan heads, elders, personal leadership of strong men, or heroes does not warrant the application of the term *state*. Nor does the later veneration of these leaders, their deification as gods or ennoblement as kings, justify our acceptance of these descriptions of men who were, in fact, neither (Buchanan, 1969; Cohen, 1968: 651–657). The grant of royal title to the Batembuzi involves the anachronistic application of later royal titles and concepts "to ancestors who were politically prominent" (Buchanan, 1974: 60). I would rather see the Batembuzi era as a predynastic period of clan-based village agriculture with some hunting and craft specialization, one in which political leadership was largely restricted to kin group and ritual authorities. It was not marked by an "early state" of any sort (Claessen and Skalnik, 1978: 3–24).

Claims to statehood made on behalf of the Bacwezi, the successors of the Batembuzi, are not so easily discounted. Royal and popular traditions over a wide area have made these demigods the founders of a vast empire of considerable power, innovation, and impact, if of relatively short duration. The Bacwezi era of perhaps 100 to 150 years is attested to by ethnological and archeological evidence of a more developed mode of production. But did this mode of production produce a social formation of early class society in which the state was an instrument of ruling class hegemony? To answer this we must reexamine the question of the Bacwezi and the nature of their "empire." That they were real people rather than spirits is agreed by all but the hardiest of skeptics (Wrigley, 1959). And the bulk of evidence identifies them with the first migration of "pastoral folk" who today constitute the Bahuma (and Bahima) of western Uganda's kingdoms (Karugire, 1971: 118–121; Posnansky, 1966: 5–7).

Between the 14th and 15th centuries, western Uganda underwent a profound transformation at the hand of those people now venerated as the Bacwezi. An intrusive population[1] entered the region with their herds and built a distinctive pastoral economy in the dry land corridor centering on the Mubende district (Nyakatura, 1973: 47–48; Gray, 1935: 226–233). Was this extensive domain of the herders a state or empire as claimed? The traditions of the entire region are unequivocal in naming the leading Cwezi heroes as kings (Nyakatura, 1973: 17–31; Katate and Kamugungunu, 1967: 11–25). There is much to suggest that this is either the anachronistic description of former leaders in terms which became familiar at a later date or efforts by the royal chroniclers to claim exalted status and ancient forbears for subsequent monarchs. It appears that rather than sweep previous rulers under a mythic rug, an effort has been made to capitalize on prior traditions of leadership and elevate, even deify, past rulers (Buchanan, 1969: 19–21).

The capital of the Cwezi "empire" has been located at the great earthworks at Bigo on a tributary of the Katonga River (Posnansky, 1966). Bigo is the largest of a group of cognate sites stretching southward from the Bugoma forest in Bunyoro to the south of the Katonga in Masaka District, Buganda (Lanning, 1960: 184). The connection between these sites and the pastoral intruders is not questioned here. Only the interpretation of these remains as requiring a high level of political centralization and coercive labor control, that is, a state organization of society, is seen as conjectural. To argue that only surplus labor, extracted forcibly by a centrally directed bureaucratic state, is capable of such extensive public works is certainly common. That such earthworks and trenches as described for Uganda *may* have been constructed by voluntary labor, communally organized, seems possible. I believe the herders themselves, working seasonally under the direction of lineage or tribal leaders, organized in age groups or the like were capable of constructing such enclosures as places of safety and sociability, without requiring forced labor of dependent farmers, who had no need for such structures.[2] The picture of newly arrived herdsmen adapting their cattle-oriented economy to a new land under pioneer conditions accords better with the circumstances of the 14th century than the contrasting scenario of a large subject population of agriculturalists forced to build these extensive cattle enclosures as monuments to a powerful imperial ruling class of conquering herdsmen. The sparseness of the agricultural population of the semiarid pastoral regions in which the earthworks appear seems to me to accord with the idea that they were built by the herdsmen themselves.

> When these people first entered the plains with their large herds of cattle, there can have been no cause of friction between themselves and the original inhabitants. The inhabitants remained attached to their small plots of land which they cultivated to yield their yearly supply of grains and vegetables, while the invaders required the large grassy plains unsuited for agricultural purposes. The two sets of people could thus live in the same district without danger of falling foul of each other [Roscoe, 1924: 14].

This description by a missionary-ethnographer both simplifies and encapsulates the essential relationship produced by the ecological and economic situation of the two autonomous groups of farmers and herders. Some exchange of the products of the different economies certainly existed from an early period with iron implements and weapons, millet beer, and salt forming the staple agricultural items exchanged for meat and milk. But such exchanges are unlikely to have formed the basis for pastoral hegemony or state formation.

One further argument for the early development of state forms must be considered. Both traditional and scholarly sources (Nyakatura, 1973: 8–9; Buchanan, 1974: 122–124) assert that the modern kingdoms inherited their provincial structure from early days. The last Batembuzi ruler, Isaza, is credited with the division of his territories into counties and their distribution to elders in gratitude for their sagacity in saving his life. Isaza "himself lived in Kitara county, but would visit the other counties to inspect his cattle" (Nyakatura, 1973: 9). It is believed that the division and distribution of counties *(amasaza)* instituted an administrative structure of empire and thus provides substantial evidence for state formation. I would point out that Isaza, as one of the Batembuzi rather than Bacwezi, would put state formation back even earlier than the era for which it is commonly accepted. And the division of territory among old people and kinsmen would appear to reflect a distribution of herds and pasturage areas rather than the delegation of administrative responsibilities over subject people. Last, in this tradition, Isaza is seen as the owner of extensive herds of cattle, with a keen, even obsessive, preoccupation with their welfare (Nyakatura, 1973: 13). But, the imputation of cattle as symbols of wealth and power and pastoral attitudes and values to the Batembuzi again suggest an anachronism—the attribution to an earlier era of items and ideas which become manifest only after the Bacwezi invasion had transformed the Kitaran region.

After three generations of undisputed dominance, the era of the Bacwezi mysteriously ended. The last Mucwezi, Wamara, led his kinsmen out of Kitara, where they had lost the respect of their followers and begun to suffer strange misfortunes. The mandate of heaven was lost and Wamara was told by prophecy that "the throne of Kitara would be taken over by black men who did not resemble the Bacwezi" (Nyakatura, 1973: 40). Thus without invasion or revolution, a period which had witnessed an unestimable transformation was ended.

The introduction of pastoral economies made possible a significant increase in the productive capacity of the dry regions of western Uganda. The growth of a herding economy was achieved by both the transmigration of exotic men and their long-horned cattle *(en-shagara)* and the incorporation of some preCwezi population and their short-horned cattle *(endora)* into the clans and herds of the early Huma community (Buchanan, 1974: 149– 161; Mushanga, 1972). Despite periodic setbacks due to drought and disease, herding became a central feature of every subsequent social formation, often politically dominant if always economically secondary to the production of grains within the agricultural economy of the wider region.

The political legacy of the Cwezi "empire" is supposed to be "a system of administrative officialdom accustomed to ruling small districts as the local representatives of a centralized monarchy" (Oliver, 1953: 135). However, both the rapid disappearance of Cwezi power and the circumstances of suicidal despondency over the death of favorite cows and obsessive fears and loss of confidence caused by bovine disease (Nyakatura, 1973: 34– 44) "raise questions concerning the heralded administrative system and sizeable state" attributed to the Bacwezi (Buchanan, 1974: 193). It rather strongly suggests that the Bacwezi were identical with the early Bahuma herdsmen, whose relationship to territory was more in terms of pasturage and water sources than administrative districts and governmental responsibilities. The difficulties which the Bahima chiefs of the early colonial era had in adapting to the political and administrative roles thrust upon them by the colonial state is further testimony to the incompatibility of pastoralism with the administration of a state (Steinhart, 1977: 151– 154; 199– 204).

With the Bacwezi gone, the political field was open to newcomers. In general, the succession fell to two different dynastic groups. One, the Babito, succeeded in the north central segment of the Kitaran region and the other, the Bahinda, on the southern marches. The political systems established by both Babito and Bahinda shared certain common features during the period of their emergence (c. 1450– 1650). These features I have termed a "dyna-state" (Steinhart, 1978), by which is meant a proto-state form lacking in the social relations of class antagonism and consciousness and the political relations of domination and ideological hegemony.

Instead, a dyna-state is structured by a lineage or clan segment which is *primus inter pares* among like groups and claims leadership and authority on a hereditary basis. This dynastic authority is unsupported by a state apparatus of administration or other institutions of government. One is tempted to refer to such a formation as transitional but for the fact that all historical social formations are in the process of becoming or disintegrating and so are all transitional (cf. Stewart, in this volume).

Turning first to the Babito, two things emerge clearly from the oral traditions. First, they were strangers who entered Kitara from the Luo-speaking areas north of the Nile. Second, they created a dynasty—a genealogically related series of figures succeeding each other from father to son or occasionally brother to brother. With the Babito the framework of remembered history for the Kitaran region becomes the Babito king list or succession sequence.

The idea that the Bito or Luo-speakers brought the state with them and imposed it on the Bantu-speaking peoples of Kitara has little support in their own traditions or modern historical research.[3] Bito claims to supremacy were reinforced by the assertion that they were the heirs of the Bacwezi, who in turn were elevated to a new pantheon in a Bito-supported cult movement which survives as a popular religion until today (Buchanan, 1969; Webster, n.d.). The claim of genealogical relationship to the Cwezi did not impress the Bahuma who held aloof from the cult and tended to view the Babito as little better than upstart Bairu farmers (Nyakatura, 1973: 48). Similarly, the idea of Bito military superiority and "strong military leadership" (Buchanan, 1974: 212) is not supported by tradition, leaving few reasons to believe the Luo were more advanced in military technology or organization than the Bacwezi or their Bantu-speaking subjects. How are we to account for their ability to dominate?

First, we must reexamine the evidence for Luo settlement in Kitara. Prior to the arrival of the Babito, other Luo speakers called Palwo had begun to settle on the south bank of the Nile on the northern fringe of Kitara (Adefuye, 1973: 1–11; 1976: 232–250).

This settlement, part of the general migration of the Luo from the southern Sudan to as far south as the Nyanza Province of western Kenya (Ogot, 1967), provided a staging area for the subsequent Bito "invasion" of Kitara. A period of one generation is usually allowed between the end of Cwezi hegemony, dated by Webster (1974) by "Wamara's Famine" at c.1382–1409, and the arrival of Isingoma Mpuga Rukidi, the first Bito dynast (gen.1436–1463)[4] again dated by aid of a famine referred to as "Rukidi's." Rukidi's arrival is not only dated by reference to famine but also famine is seen by tradition to be central to the transfer of power. The most important item of Cwezi regalia, the royal drums, were allegedly exchanged with the Bito for foodstuffs, in this case, millet porridge, a highly regarded food among the Banyoro farmers (Nyakatura, 1973: 55–56; Adefuye, 1974: 13–14; Buchanan, 1979: 108). Not only does this suggest something about the transfer of power but also it is a clue to a profound revolution transforming the economic basis of the Kitaran social formation.

Rukidi is alleged to have established his capitals in the pastoral counties of Bwere and Bugangaizi (Nyakatura, 1973: 53–57; 61–63), although his burial site and those of the next three Bito dynasts have been located in the Palwo district on Kitara's northern fringe. Adefuye (1973: 30–34) has used the burial sites to argue for an early period of Palwo domination of Kitara, but the same fact might indicate a far longer interregnum between Wamara and Rukidi, perhaps four or five generations. The Bito may have first settled among their Palwo kinsmen and the culturally and economically less developed agriculturalists identified by Onyango-ku-Odongo (1976: 124–130) as Ludumi. In the Palwo region the mixed farming practices of the Luo had the economic advantage of the Nile valley in which to promote their leading crop, millet. The advantage of millet in times of pastoral crisis such as Wamara's and Rukidi's famines may explain the basis of Bito dominance. By the reign of Olimi I (gen.1517–1544), Bito ascendancy seems to have been secured in the Kitaran heartlands (Steinhart, 1978b). The likely key to this ascendance was the development of a mixed, or rather compound, economy of millet cultivation in the wetter regions and cattle-keeping in the dry zones. Thus, the Bito dynasts came to mediate between Iru farmers, Huma herders, and their own Luo supporters.

Under Olimi I the capital of Kitara was relocated in the pastoral Mubende district, which became and remained the burial place of Kitara's Bito rulers through the 19th century (Ingham, 1953: 138–145). Olimi began a series of expansionist campaigns from Mubende to the south and east against pastoral districts including Singo and Buddu of what later became the Buganda kingdom. With the exception of Nyabongo (gen.1544–1571), who redirected Kitaran expansion against the Sudanic-speaking Madi people to the north, Olimi's successors became increasingly involved in southern campaigns, culminating in the invasions of Nkore and Rwanda by Chwa I (gen.1626–1652; Nyakatura, 1973: 67–74; Rennie, 1973; Adefuye, 1973: 30–31; 226).

These invasions coincided with a cycle of droughts and famines which caused enormous dislocation across much of northern Uganda during the 1580s (Nyarubanga) and 1620s (The Great Famine) identified by Webster (1979). The dislocation affected both farmers and herders, but it did so differentially. The pastoralists appear to have become more aggressive, undertaking raids to replenish their herds and expanding into areas of higher rainfall or permanent water sources. The farmers, stricken by poor harvests, were reduced to extremes of scavenging and often permanently uprooted.[5] Livestock became a reserve, a kind of famine insurance, called upon during the worst periods. Paradoxically, the death of cattle during drought could lead to increasing meat consumption among the herders.[6] The drought/famine cycle appears to have produced an important shift in the balance of economic power from the stricken farmers to the increasingly aggressive herders.

The shift of power continued through the Nyamdere Famine of the early 18th century, which was a small-scale repetition of the 17th century crises (Webster, 1979). By this time the Bito dynasty had become thoroughly identified with the Huma pastoral group. The adoption of Bantu language and the frequent intermarriage of

Babito with Huma women accelerated the acceptance of pastoral values and culture. This process was marked by a rejection of the Palwo connection of the dynasty in the reign of Winyi II (gen:1652–1679). The reign of Olimi III (gen.1733–1760) was the culmination of the Humaization of the kingdom. The exodus of the Palwo from Kitara between 1680 and 1760 was the result of both drought-induced crises and of the persecutions brought about by the proHuma and antiLuo policies of Kitara's "Banbu" dynasts.

We turn now to the emergence of the Hinda dyna-state of Nkore after the end of the Cwezi era. Groups of herdsmen fled the Kitaran heartland in the wake of the Cwezi "disappearance," probably driven by the same drought/famine cycle which accompanied the collapse of the Cwezi dominion. One such group under the leadership of the warrior-herdsman Ruhinda, who like the Bito has been given a genealogy connecting him to the Cwezi, arrived south of the Kagera River. There, according to the traditions of Karagwe and other kingdoms of northwest Tanzania, Ruhinda began to conquer and dispossess the rulers of the Bantu societies which he found (Katoke, 1971: 524–529; 1975). After establishing a new regime in Karagwe, he led his pastoral followers north of the Kagera, dispersed the Bantu population, and established his second "kingdom" in Kaaro-Kirungi or Nkore. After a brief stay, the restless conqueror returned south for further conquests and the establishment of new regimes. Ruhinda's son, Nkuba, was left to rule in Nkore on his father's behalf and a new dynasty was created (Karugire, 1971: 137–146; 1972: 7–9).

The evidence from a variety of local traditions is that Ruhinda was the leader of a cluster of Huma herdsmen, who subsequently took his name and became the Bahinda ruling dynasty of Nkore and several other pastoral societies. The question remains whether this movement was the flight and resettlement of refugees or the invasion of militant pastoral conquerors. Did they impose a pastoral kingdom on helpless Bantu farmers or take over a well-organized set of Bantu principalities from their previous agricultural rulers (Katoke, 1971a: 512–514; 1971: 518–521)? Speaking for Nkore, at least, neither of these views appears satisfactory. The original site of Nkore, the present county of Isingiro in the southeast of Ankole District, has always been a dry, hilly plain, thinly populated and virtually uncultivated. While the Hima successfully discouraged cultivation in their pasturelands down to this century, the environment was an even more persuasive discouragement to the intense agricultural settlement typical of the areas west of Nkore in Igara, Buhweju, and Shema counties. If Isingiro supported a farming population in the 15th century, it was on a marginal basis unlikely to have been capable of supporting a political hierarchy beyond the village or lineage level. What, then, was the significance of Ruhinda's "invasion" and "conquest" of the farmers of Nkore recorded in pastoral traditions?

The answer seems to lie in the original cause of the Hinda "invasion," the drought and famine of the last Cwezi days. Ruhinda appears as a leader of a band of refugees and their weakened herds, looking for fresh pasturage and water resources. Led by the young warriors guarding the herds, such a cluster of pastoral lineages would almost certainly include the cattleless Hima victims of drought and some nonHima victims of famine attracted to the movable resources of the pastoralists and attached to the cluster by ties of personal dependence. Moving into the dry and nonarable short grasslands between the settlements of the Bantu farmers, the claim to pasture and water would have required little force and no need to assert authority over the scattered farmers, who may have dispersed or been incorporated as personal dependants. Thus, the "band" of herdsmen surrounding Ruhinda and his family would hardly constitute a state. The inheritance of Nkuba upon Ruhinda's departure for greener pastures was his position as leader of a core lineage of this seminomadic band of herdsmen. It was these who set about multiplying themselves and their herds as the uncertainties of climate and disease permitted (Steinhart, 1978a: 133–134).

Within Nkore, those who continued to cultivate were certainly dominated by the herders, whose monopoly over cattle ownership and exclusive and obsessive concern with their cattle's welfare gave short shrift to the interests of the despised farmers. Relations between the two populations were minimal and characterized more by "segregation and avoidance" than by political domination or control (Elam, 1974: 159–162; Karugire, 1970: 22–33). Organized around extended lineages and cattle kraals, the herders must have been then, as in the 19th century, very close to self-sufficient in their food and labor requirements. Beer from millet was the only vegetable item of consequence in the Hima diet, and this along with a few craft items like milk pots and iron blades were in all likelihood obtained in exchange with the farmers for clarified butter (ghee) and unproductive cows. A strict prohibition on losing control of productive cows was in force but hardly necessary, given the pastoralists' valuation of cows and calves. In addition, the tasks of herding and animal husbandry were exclusively the charge of Hima males. They would no more allow a Mwiru to attend their cattle than the women of the kraal. Even the odious and menial tasks of cleaning the kraal and collecting dung were done by the herdsmen. There is little need or place in such an economy for servile labor (Oberg, 1943: Taylor, 1962; 103–107; Williams, 1938: 17–42).

Meanwhile, in the areas of western Ankole District which supported relatively intense cultivation of millet, yams, and pulses, the denser population of farmers existed in autonomous village and lineage communities probably much like those of the neighboring agricultural societies of the Bakiga, Baamba, or Bakonjo (Edel, 1957; Taylor, 1962; 82–85; 93–94). In such villages, subsistence production by each family unit left little economic surplus for exchange outside the family or village community and agricultural life followed its own seasonal routine, regulated by religious belief and practice unmarked by pastoral influence (Oberg, 1938: 129–159; Williams, 1936: 203–219). Iron-working, basketry and manufacture of wooden and gourd vessels which were exchanged with the herders was done on a parttime basis which neither created a distinct artisan class nor led to extensive networks of trade among the farmers or between them and the herders (Kamuhangire, 1972).[7] In brief, agriculture was an independent pursuit outside the purview of the herders and unconnected with the servile status attributed to it by the Bahima and their European observers of a latter date (Roscoe, 1915: 102–103; 1923).

The traditions of Nkore bear a curious mute testimony to the autonomy of the two communities. They are silent on agricultural life and for 200 years, from the founding of the "kingdom" by Nkuba, virtually silent on all domestic matters. "One of the chief problems of Nkore history in this period is the yawning gaps during which nothing of importance seems to have taken place" (Karugire, 1971: 159). Problems of forgetfulness do not satisfactorily explain this dearth of information. It is clear we know more of Ruhinda's movements and Nkuba's suppression of "clan rebellions" (Karugire, 1971: 142ff) which are further back in the time than the gaps in memory from *Mugabe* Nyaika (1475–1503±39) to *Mugabe* Mirindi (1671–1699±28). The exploits and innovations of Ntare IV Kitabanyoro (1699–1727±26) seem to have revived the memories of Nkore's historians.[8] It appears that until then little or nothing that happened constituted history to those charged with remembering the past. They were only concerned with recording events which bore on the kingship and its place in the redistributive or tributary economy (Polanyi, 1971: 139–158). Thus, we find the selective memory of wars of conquest and events which enhances the status of the Hinda regime and is silent on the mundane affairs of common herdsmen and certainly of farmers, whose economies of reciprocity were beneath the purview of royal memorialists.

Virtually all of the traditions of this long "period of incubation" (Steinhart, 1978a: 136) beyond the names of the Hinda dynasts refer to developments in the reign of Ntare I Nyabugaro. It is he who is credited with the consolidation of dynastic control by the introduction of titled offices and honors given to members of various clans (Karugire, 1971: 148–152; Katate and Kamugungunu, 1967: 56–63). The gift of honors served to institutionalize the kingship by attaching the clans to the *mugabe* since each had a representative attending the court and fulfilling some (generally menial) function such as milking the king's cows or making the royal beds. At this stage the bond between the *mugabe* and the rest of the population remained that between a dominant lineage head and the other lineages and clan groups (Steinhart, 1978a: 136–137). By distributing patronage and establishing ties of personal service between the dynasty and the associated clans, the *mugabe* became the center of a network of mutual obligations, the main "giver of gifts," the literal meaning of *mugabe*. The institution of clientage *(okutoizha)*—the gift of cattle from the patron in exchange for personal and political support and occasional labor service by the client—certainly existed by this time. The *mugabe* as titular owner of all cattle was the fount of all clientage contracts and thus "liege lord" of the entire pastoral population, which was at this time the only population involved in clientage institutions. By adding the gift of honors to that of cattle, the Hinda rulers after Nyabugaro established their dominion over pastoral society only.

An incidental effect of Nyabugaro's gift of offices was the creation of something of a "court life" (Karugire, 1971: 161) among the titled and honored clan representative who attended him at his peripatetic kraal. Added to the special relationship between the nonHima Bayangwe clan, whose members were personally tied to the Bahinda by a mythic shared ancestry and ties of dependence (Karugire, 1971: 86–88; 96–97; 137–149), the Hinda ruler began to claim distinctions and privileges beyond those of any clan elder and thus appears increasingly a monarch and less *primus inter pares*.

Another indication of the growing importance of the dynasty during this period of incubation is the tradition referring to the first disputed succession which ended the reign of Kitera (1643–1671±30) cited by Karugire (1971: 152). The intervention in the dispute of the rival maternal kin of the reigning monarch and the successful pretender, Rumongye, while the Bahinda remained divided or neutral has been cited as evidence of the security of the dynasty which, after nine generations, could afford an internal power struggle. It also might indicate that the question of succession by the mid-17th century remained largely a matter of family concern between the dynasty and the clans of maternal kin of the sitting monarch. While the title of *mugabe* may have grown to be worth the fight, the range of contestants was still a local and family matter within the pastoral clans close to the dynasty. No army, bureaucracy, or judicial or territorial administration took part in this dispute as no army or administration existed with an interest in the affairs of the Nkore "dyna-state" until after the close of the 17th century.

Scattered and incomplete evidence from the late 17th to 19th century suggests that the economic base of the western lacustrine region underwent a transformation from local autonomous village and kraal economies. From a reciprocal and essentially classless "communal mode of production" the area developed a redistributive economy based on a dominant class of nonproducing "rulers" of the state apparatus who claimed and appropriated the surplus value created by a large majority of direct producers. The form of surplus appropriation was tribute paid to the state as the ultimate "owner" of the means of production, principally land and cattle. Described illusively by Marx (1967: I, 357–358, III, 790–792; Avineri, 1969: 88–95) as the Asiatic mode of production, the system is one in which surplus is appropriated by means of a "tax/rent couple" or tribute. To avoid the unfortunate overtones of geographical specificity, I prefer to use the phrase "tributary mode of production" (Amin, 1976) as focusing properly on the mode of appropriation of surplus value characteristic of the objective relations of production. Whereas, under the feudal mode, which is characterized by private ownership of land and the appropriation of surplus by means of feudal rents paid to private landlords, under the tributary mode presentations by the state are demanded of the direct producers, who are "held in a relationship of political/legal subordination" (Hindess and Hirst, 1975: 192). Tribute in labor or in kind (cattle or agricultural produce) was paid to political officials or state agents who were thus provided with the resources to support them as a nonlaboring, ruling class of state officials. This class was the reciprocal of the producing class who were excluded from ownership of the means of production although they continued to live in village and lineage communities. Their former "extra labor" on communal efforts and in voluntary relationships was now converted to "surplus labor" and was appropriated as tribute (Godelier, 1977: 188–195; Avineri, 1969: 5–30; cf. Hindess and Hirst, 1975: 178–220).

This transformation of autonomous owner-producers into subjects and producers of "surplus value" took place without major destruction of villages or kraals. And it did not replace the dynastic or ethnic framework of the previous era. That this was so has tended to obscure the importance of the change in the relations of production. Moreover, "the functioning of these new relations of production necessitated the development of institutions and the new social stratum, a state bureaucracy responsible for controlling and supervising the reproduction of the new mode of production" (Godelier, 1977: 191). The elaboration of state institutions— instruments of coercion and administration and of ideological and political hegemony—provides the empirical circumstances attending the transformation to the state and the deeper social transformation to class society which necessitated it.

In both northern and southern zones, the formation of the state and its tributary system which had matured "in the womb of the old society" was influenced by the different "empirical circumstances," the historical conditions which generated it. In Kitara, the social transformation was synonymous with the emergence of Bunyoro, the name by which the kingdom came to be known to its neighbors by the late 18th century. What this terminological shift reflects is the differentiation of a new class of landowners and chiefs out of the upper echelon of the class of cultivators. This process of class formation so profoundly altered the content of the social relations of Kitara as to cause the entire social formation to be known by its new name, the land of the Banyoro or "freedmen." In Nkore, the crucial circumstance was the existence of pastoral clientage—*okutoizha*—which became a central mechanism for the extraction of surplus value when extended from herders to farmers. Clientage became a means of surplus appropriation from both agricultural and pastoral producers by a class of nonproducers at the apex of the pastoral stratum. Both these ruling classes were called into existence by the growth in the forces of production within the old societies—the growth of the laboring population and the stresses on the old modes of production caused by increased intensity of production and greater contact between the various elements of the evolving primary modes. Acting as a catalyst and midwife to the new tributary mode was the ecological stress of drought and famine and the social efforts to cope, survive, and control nature which these crises evoked. We begin by examining Kitara as it entered the time of troubles which marked the birth pangs of class society and the state.

Reports of drought and famine in the pastoral traditions of western Uganda are sparse and very casual (Steinhart, 1980). Even droughts that are known to have caused considerable dislocation in northern Uganda's mixed farming areas are often mentioned only as incidental background to the series of Nyoro invasions of neighboring territories. Such invasions are associated in oral accounts more with the warlike qualities of "hero-kings" than the ecological conditions which propelled herders to raid in order to replenish depleted herds (Webster, 1980a; Rennie, 1973; cf. Nyakatura, 1973: 72–73). The correlation between drought/ famine and pastoral expansion, agricultural dislocation, and state formation in Kitara and her southern marches is quite remarkable from the 16th to the 19th century.[9]

The number of wars fought by Kitara during the time of troubles compared to previous eras is eloquent testimony to the underlying transformation and internal dislocation and adaptation. Starting with the mid-17th century invasions of Chwa I (gen. 1626–1652) and the succession wars of Kyebambe I (gen. 1652–1679), the intensity and frequency of conflict, both dynastic and foreign, reached fever pitch in the reigns of Kyebembe II Bikaju (gen. 1706–1733) and his son, Olimi III Isansa (gen. 1733–1760).

A clue to the social significance of these wars comes from an examination of the Palwo traditions of the period collected by Adefuye (1973: 51–68; cf. Fisher, 1970: 128–144; Dunbar, 1965:

35ff; Uzoigwe, 1973: 49–71). From the Palwo perspective the period from c.1679 to c.1760 was one of dislocation and persecution. Prior to the reign of Winyi III (gen. 1679–1706), the Chope-Bugungu-Pajao areas of Palwo settlement had remained autonomous of the Kitaran court. The practice of the Queen Mother being drawn from Luo clans had remained in place from the time of the founding of the Bito dynasty. But the traditions report that the increasing Humaization of the court led in three stages to a reversal of this favored position. Under Winyi III, a prince of Huma parentage named Bikaju was sent by the court to directly administer the area for the first time. After an interregnum succession struggle, he emerged as *Mukama* Kyebambe II. When he transferred power to Isansa, his son by a Huma woman, the loss of Palwo influence was complete, and a Palwo exodus which had begun in c.1679 increased in pace and extent during the "Nyamdere" famine and the reputed "persecutions" of the "Bantu king."

In this version tradition assigns to "ethnic" and dynastic motives what I believe can be seen as the long-run consequences of pastoral expansion and penetration both of the Bito dynasty and of the agricultural lands around the pastoral core of Kitara. From another perspective, the expansion of Buganda into Kooki, Bwera, and the southeastern marches of Kitara in the reign of Duhaga I (gen. 1760–1783) marked not only a decline in Kitaran power but also the loss of valued grazing lands (Nyakatura, 1973: 84–88). The increasing autonomy of the pastoral societies of Nkore, Buhweju, and Buzimba on the southern fringe reflects the recession of Kitaran power and the shift of its economic locus as a result of the dislocations at the time of troubles (Steinhart, 1980). The final blow to Kitara's imperial status came in the waning years of the reign of Kyebambe II Nyamutukura (c.1786–1830) with the successful secession movement of Toro led by a Bito prince (Nyakatur, 1973: 92–95; Rukidi, 1969).

The chief consequences of the centuries-long transformation were the emergence of a class system and a new state structure erected on its base. The earlier literature has often referred to this new class system tangentially in terms of the "breakdown" of pastoral exclusivity in Kitara. Pastoralists moved in among the cultivators and settled in more permanent habitations in the arable areas. The pattern of community life was thus transformed along with the attitudes and values of the herdsmen:

> Village life thus sprang into existence, and communities, which before had been restricted to members of the same families, now increased in size and included members of various clans. Under the new circumstances of life herds were restricted to special places. . . . With the fusion of the two classes there came new rules for social life and a more settled form of government [Roscoe, 1924: 19; 23].

This "more settled form of government" in Kitara appears to reflect the emergence of a new stratum of political chiefs/lords and the reciprocal emergence of a class of subjects/tenants. There were three sources of recruits for the new chiefly elite. First, there were rich Bahuma who settled, abandoned seminomadic herding (or left it to herdsmen in need of cattle), and accepted territorial authority over people and land as the gift of the *mukama*. Second, the growth and dispersal of the Bito clan made royal princes and nonroyal but prestigious Bito clansmen available as appointees to territorial authority over similar official estates. And last, the elevation of leading members of agricultural society from village obscurity to positions as chiefs and royal councillors rounded out the new class. This last group was originally quite small and resulted from the emancipation of Bairu farmers and their ennoblement as freedmen called *Banyoro* "some generations ago," (Roscoe, 1923b: 10–12; 56). Capable of using their position in agricultural society to control clan or lineage labor and land holdings *(emigongo)*, these Banyoro became the backbone of the landlord chiefs. They intermarried with Huma and Bito, accumulated cattle (breaking the pastoral monopoly enjoyed by the Huma), and became the lords of official estates *(obwesengeze)*. There they acted as magistrates, law officers, and, most important, the collectors of tribute from the cultivators for passage to the *mukama* at the center and apex of the chiefly hierarchy. "In the Nyoro way of thinking . . . [political power came to be identified] with rights over land and over people who live on that land, and everyone who possesses such rights is *ipso facto* a chief" (Beattie, 1954b: 179; 1954a).

The emergence of a group of chiefs cum landlords who collected the tribute was the necessary concomitant of the emergence of a class of subjects cum tenants who were the direct producers of agricultural wealth. It was they who paid tribute as an obligation to the state *and* to retain access to land which they had ceased to "own" but merely occupied as tenants of the state.[10] This social and political transformation, I believe, took place some 5 to 7 generations before the opening of the colonial era (rather than 20 to 22 generations ago). It was a result of the increasing interaction of the two economies conditioned by changing ecological and demographic conditions. The growth to autonomy in the southern kingdoms from c.1750 to 1850 (Steinhart, 1980), the growth of the Nkore state (Steinhart, 1978a), and similar developments of territorial administration reported for Karagwe in northwestern Tanzania (Berger, 1968) and the growth of chieftaincies in Acholi (Atkinson, 1978) seem to support this relatively recent 18th century dating of Nyoro state formation based on the development of a subordinate tribute-paying peasantry.

A further word on the role of the Bito dynasty in the transformation from a Kitaran dyna-state to a Nyoro state is required. As an ethnically and linguistically alien group, the Babito were subjected to a process of naturalization which involved the acquisition of Bantu language and custom. This was accelerated through the immediate practice of intermarriage by the dynasty with women of important Huma families. This practice is symbolized in tradition by the marriage of Rukidi to Iremera, a wife of the last Cwezi dynast, Wamara, and a member of the (Huma) Balisa clan (Nyakatura, 1973: 66). The increasing pastoral orientation of the dynasty is a reflection of the maternal influence of several Balisa Queen mothers. An even more important result of the intermarriage was the procreation of nonroyal branches of the Babito clan, who over the three centuries from Rukidi to Bikaju had become the largest, most dispersed clan group in Kitara. The ability of Bito princes and ordinary Bito clansmen to marry well, often, and widely, with resulting growth in the next generation not only affected the size of the clan but also changed the status of the dynasty. As collateral branches married Huma aristocrats and later Banyoro commoners, the clan lost its alien status. Many Babito became commoners, without distinctions of wealth or power, but maintained a vague aura of prestige of distant kinship with the ruling family. Babito could be found at all economic levels, in the various social divisions[11] and in most geographical regions of the empire, creating the illusion that the Bito dynasty was a segment of a truly national institution, the Bito clan.

A second aspect of Bito naturalization concerns the association of other social strata and kinship groups in the institutions of dynastic and court life. The distribution of honors, titles, and privileges as varied and dubious as royal gatekeeper, keeper of the royal drum or spears, and royal dancers was made to members of varied clans on the basis of personal service and was later translated into hereditary office or privilege for the families or clans so honored (Nyakatura, 1973: 61–64; 1978: 95–101). This process of granting honorifics and courtly responsibilities increased the network of kinship and political associations focused at the Bito court, making of the office holders and their kin a hereditary class of honor, privilege, and duty attached to the dynasty. That this class of courtly, customary, and territorial office holders (*banyamirwa*) cut across the pastoral-agricultural division further served to naturalize and nationalize the dynasty and its elite of court officials called "crown wearers" (*bajwara kondo;* Beattie, 1971: 119ff). The multiethnic court surrounding the dynasty enhanced its image as a "national" leadership, above distinctions of caste, class, or clan and hence a neutral mediator of conflict between contending groups. Their ability to survive their initial identification with the pastoral interest and to parley this "national" image into political hegemony over both the Banyoro chiefly elite and the older Huma "aristocracy" is testimony to the adaptability of "Luo" leadership and the ideology of dominance (Cohen, Ogot, and Herring, 1979).

The collection of tribute in agricultural products, especially millet beer, by means of a hierarchy of chiefly landholders was the fundamental support of the Nyoro state. But the dynasty also exercised considerable control over the appropriation of surplus from the pastoral economy as well as the products of craft and the profits of commerce. Iron and salt-making and trade in those commodities and later in slaves, ivory, and guns—when these became important in the 19th century—were subjected to varying degrees of central control.[12] However, the kingdom and social structure were in no way the result of royal control of these strategic and valuable commodities (cf. Coquery-Vidrovitch, 1969). The revenue they produced for the rulers may have ameliorated the expropriation of the direct agricultural producers and lessened the burden of tribute. But it was tribute from the cultivators which defined the dominant mode of production and undergirded the state in the Nyoro social formation.

The transformation of Nkore, from a congeries of pastoral clans gathered around the mobile "court" of the Hinda *Mugabe* which was surrounded by other autonomous communities of herders and farmers, into a state of considerable power in the region was triggered in much the same way as the transformation of Kitara. That process, too, began with drought, famine, invasion, and a time of growing dislocation and violence. The memorable reign of Ntare IV Kitabanyoro (c.1699–1727±27) opened the doors to momentous changes, although it was only an initial step in the formation of a state to be known as the kingdom of Ankole. Drought and disease had led to a period of Nkore pastoral aggressiveness at the expense of Kitara in the Kyaka county of Toro District. A major invasion to counter these incursions was mounted by Olimi III Isansa and met with initial success, as is agreed in both Kitaran and Nkore traditions despite considerable confusion on the chronology (cf. Nyakatura, 1973: 80–84; K.W.,

1935, 1936; Karugire, 1971: 156–160). Nkore tradition (possibly eliding the 1730's invasion with an earlier one) states that after an occupation of some years, the Banyoro were defeated by the Rwanda (or by Ihangiro) and the remnants of the Nyoro army were scattered and victimized as they retreated and withdrew from Nkore. The death of many of the hapless Banyoro at the hands of Ntare IV's soldiers accounts for his most remembered praise name, Kitabanyoro, the Killer of the Banyoro (cf. Rennie, 1973: 15–20).

The consequences of this double crisis of famine and invasion are more firmly established (Karugire, 1971: 152–166). In the aftermath of the invasion, Ntare IV began a series of innovations in government and military affairs which foreshadowed later developments. The utter failure of the Nkore herdsmen to resist the initial invasion, to oppose effectively the occupation of the country, and their dependence on the power of southern neighbors for the defeat of the invading army shows that as a military power Nkore had made little progress since the days of Ntare I Nyabugaro. The absence of a trained, disciplined force left the kingdom's security in the hands of its pastoral warriors whose military virtues lay more in heroic recitations of their valor in raiding the cattle of others than in defending the pasture and water necessary to their own. To correct this situation, Ntare IV is credited with launching an experiment with a standing military force of organized regiments *(emitwe)* under the command of captains appointed for the purpose of the *mugabe*. Trained in archery as well as the use of the narrow-bladed Hima spear, these soldiers would not only give the Hima herds the protection supposed to be the obligation of all young Bahima but also would provide Ntare IV with an offensive weapon to carry out the policies of the Nkore state. The role of archery as well as the structure of the *emitwe* are indications that Nkore was coming under the influence of the expanding pastoral powers of Rwanda and Mpororo to the south and west (Kamuhangire, 1974).[13] The defeat of the first offensive action by Ntare's *emitwe* in a raid against "the seasoned warriors of Buhweju" (Karugire, 1971: 186; 162–164) led to the rapid abandonment of the military experiment but not of the southern influence it reflected.

The growing influence of the expanding regime in Rwanda was filtered through the briefly flourishing Bashambo empire of Mpororo (Baitwababo, 1969; Munyuzangabo, n.d.). Ntare IV pioneered diplomatic relations with Mpororo which raised the standing of both royal houses. He contracted two marriages to daughters of the Mpororo dynasty and in a very radical departure from tradition he refused to marry any wives besides these two, effectively eliminating any Hima clans from the future control of the powerful position of Queen Mother. This not only earned him the enmity of important Hima clans but it also made the Bahinda an exclusive dynasty, whose royal members would marry only other royalty, "separated from its subjects by blood as well as honors" (Steinhart, 1978a: 133). Finally, by assuring that the kingship would pass to a son of a Shambo woman, Ntare IV forged a link of mutual interest between the two dynasties which persisted long after Mpororo broke up later in the century (Karugire, 1971: 152–156; 190–194).

As if to compensate for the loss of status suffered by the Hima clans through the Mpororo connection, Ntare IV is credited with another innovation in the style of Ntare I Nyabugaro: the gift of titles and honors to members of various clans. These titled offices became inheritable clan possessions and served to extend the influence and patronage of the Hinda dynasty (Karugire, 1971: 160–162). One new office deserves special scrutiny: the keepers of the royal drum. Why was so central an institution of the Nkore state as the royal drum, *Bagyendanwa,* without its official overseer until the 18th century?[14] We are assured by Karugire (1971: 98–104; 138–139) that the drum was as old as the dynasty itself or even older, as it was reputed to have been made by the Mucwezi Wamara. Whether we accept its antiquity, "its central role as the embodiment of the state . . ." as Karugire (1971: 139) asserts, "could hardly be of recent origin," unless the state and the drum which symbolized it were equally recent developments?

It appears that it was from the reign of Ntare IV (about the first half of the 18th century) that the institutionalization of Bagyendanwa's establishment began, and that this was a gradual process from then onwards [Karugire, 1971: 100].

I believe that both the drum and the state began a gradual process of institutionalization from the early 18th century. This process was under the influence of Rwandan and Mpororo contact in part which is reflected in both the structure and symbolism of the Ankole state and society.

It was after the death of Ntare IV that the innovations of the early 18th century began to take hold. It is doubtful that the military and administrative systems tried by Ntare IV could have taken root in the loose soil of the pastoral community. For the full flowering of those systems, a developed, class-based social order comprising both herders and farmers, rulers and ruled, was needed. This social development was set in train by the events which occurred during the reigns of Macwa (c. 1727–1755±24) and his successors down to Mutambuka (1839–1867±14) and Ntare V (1867–1895). A new system of social relations and a state were erected in what became the Ankole kingdom.

Despite a remembered history of continued external and succession wars (Karugire, 1971: 167–199; Kiwanuka, 1971; Vansina, 1962), the 18th century was in many ways a period of geographical expansion and social progress for Nkore. The geographical expansion came at the expense of Mpororo and Bunyoro, both of whom suffered imperial decline and dismemberment (Nyakatura, 1973: 84–95; Kamuhangire, 1974: 55–67). The loss of power by Bunyoro had a direct influence on Nkore. Although most of the regions from which Kitara retreated managed to establish their autonomy, as in Buhweju, Buzimba (Morris, 1962), and Kitagwenda (Wheeler, 1972), the expansion of Nkore herding north of the Rwizi River into Nyabushozi, Kashari, and Ibanda was also made possible by Kitaran decline (Karugire, 1971: 164–165; 194–195).

More important for the development of the Ankole state was the collapse of Mpororo and Nkore's annexation of much of eastern Mpororo, especially Shema, Rwampara, and Igara, the last being the most densely populated county in Ankole District. Whatever the cause of the disintegration of Mpororo, two effects on Nkore are critical. First, the increasing and persistent migration of Bahororo (people of Mpororo) herders into Nkore itself meant the wholesale introduction of many of Mpororo's more stratified and authoritarian ideas and practices with associated terminology of class and status (Baitwababo, 1969: 50). Second, the eventual expansion of Nkore to the west made it, for the first time, the master of an extensive and prosperous agricultural region and its so-called Bairu population.

Perhaps we should recall that the process of expansion was itself a function of the troubles of the period. The periodic droughts meant the incursion of Hima on the wetter western hill country and the vulnerability of famine-stricken cultivators to those incursions. The persistent interregnum crises and civil wars may have exacerbated the problem as is indicated by the prohibition on cultivation that was ordered whenever a *mugabe* died until a successor was chosen (Katate and Kamugungunu, 1967: 164). The situation between c.1755 and c.1783 when no fewer than five successions took place, often involving a sustained power struggle, must have considerably vexed those cultivators who came under Hima sway. Furthermore, during the interregnum crises it was customary for Hima herdsmen to emigrate with their herds to beyond the borders of Nkore. There they awaited the righting of the drum which indicated an end to the civil wars between competing Hinda pretenders and their maternal kinfold and other supporters. The resulting migrations and interactions over a sustained period, I believe, gave rise to new social arrangements which came to characterize the Nkore social formation. Chief among these arrangements were the tributary and clientage systems which supported the Hinda monarchy and a new ruling class of wealthy, cattle-owning Hima lords.

By the late 19th and early 20th century, a system of territorial chieftaincy was described by the first European observers of Ankole. A rough hierarchy was headed by "the Bakungu chiefs who were always pastoral people and had under them as serfs many agricultural people who dwelt on their land, took charge of their goats, sheep and dogs, and supplied them with grain and beer" (Roscoe, 1923a: 15; 1915: 102–103; Gorju, 1920). Appointed by the *mugabe*, chiefs were often the most important and wealthiest Bahima in a given area, sometimes drawn from the princes of the blood *(banginya)* and recognized by the lesser Hima herdsmen as their local leaders. They were responsible for the collection and transmission of tribute *both* from the farmers and the herders of their district. The burden on the farmers of beer, millet, and labor services was often, in densely agricultural areas, further channelled through their own local headmen and chiefs (Roscoe, 1923a: 13, 20; 99; cf. Oberg, 1940: 136–150; Taylor, 1962: 107–110).

Cattle, nominally the property of the *mugabe*, were the major taxable resource and formed the units of wealth in a state-wide system of redistribution. A regular cattle tax of 2% appears to have operated through "tribute collectors" directly responsible to the *mugabe* (Roscoe, 1923a: 64). In addition, the *mugabe* had confiscatory powers over herds which he exercised as the most usual form of punishment. Both of these supplemented the control over tribute collection maintained by the Bakungu and regimental chiefs (Karugire, 1971: 53–55; 111–113; 203–205). It is important to remember that not all Bahima were wealthy in cattle or distinguished as chiefs and courtiers. Many poor herdsmen *(bashumba)* maintained themselves as Bahima by herding the cattle of wealthier men, who either lent cows to individual herdsmen or divided up their cattle and put each division under the supervision of a herdsman. "Chiefs and wealthy men seldom if ever wandered about the country with the cows. They built themselves permanent dwellings in kraals near the capital or in their districts" (Roscoe, 1923a: 64). And those wealthy men who "were known" and attended the *mugabe* might treat a poor, cattleless Muhima with the same disdain that was associated with the treatment of Bairu (Roscoe, 1923a: 17–20).

The burden of tribute probably fell most heavily on the Bahima who, if they owned cows, saw them appropriated by chiefs, princes, and the *mugabe*. If they did not, they would be liable to the most onerous labor services of herding the cattle and cleaning and maintaining the kraals of those who did (Karugire, 1971: 50–52; 1970). Yet even the humblest Muhima appeared to desire to maintain relations with Bairu that both preserved his superior status and secured access to agricultural produce. This desire explains the crucial role of clientage *(okutoizha)* in the production and reproduction of social relations of pastoral hegemony in the Ankole state.

Clientage arrangements probably existed among the pastoral Bahima from their first arrival in the region.[15] By this contract, cattle were given by wealthy patrons for the use of those with too few cows to sustain their families. In return, the client offered his loyalty and support in political affairs and services as herdsman and retainer at his patron's kraal. The contract established by the exchange of favors was terminable by either party and the return of a cow ended the obligation of the client. Any heifers born during the contract period belonged to the client as did the milk products or meat should the cow die during the contract's tenure. It was not unusual for contracts to pass from father to son establishing inheritable networks of patron-client relations from one generation to the next. At the apex of the network was the *mugabe*, "the giver of gifts," whose inexhaustible herds could be redistributed to both poor and wealthy Hima clients as a means of securing and symbolizing their political allegiance (cf. Mair, 1961; 1977: 136–141). At the bottom were those essentially cattleless herders who were maintained as Bahima by the loan of cattle *(empano)* and might hope to reestablish their own herds in better times. The operation of this social security insurance did not prevent a considerable amount of downward mobility as cattle-poor herders resorted to supplementary cultivation and intermarriage with Bairu (Denoon, n.d.: 1; Steinhart, 1967: 606–620; 1973).

Pastoral expansion appears responsible for the extension of clientage to the farming communities. But in going from one context to another the terms of the clientage contract were altered. The gift of a cow became the gift of a barren cow or bull, making the Mwiru client incapable of beginning his own herd. Still he had the use of the milk and meat if the animal died, which in time of famine was an important boon. This may explain the willingness with which poor and even wealthy farmers entered *okutoizha* relationships. Moreover, the limited demand of Hima herders for vegetable products and Iru labor must have mitigated the social inequality of the contract. As for political services, it is unlikely that many Hima would have valued the support of an Iru client. A few Bairu who left cultivation and settled at the kraal of a chief or the *mugabe*, becoming personal servants or courtiers *(bagaragwa)*, might receive cattle by special gift of the *mugabe*. Such dispensations, usually for extraordinary military service, led to a degree of upward mobility for a handful of Bairu, who accepted Hima values although they seldom lost the taint of low birth. Such mobility operated for such small numbers as to be socially illusory and ultimately to insure the maintenance of the system of class stratification (Karugire, 1970; 1971: 38–42).

By the end of the 18th century, the dual system of clientage ran from the *mugabe* down to the most impoverished of cultivators, across the major class and ethnic divisions of Ankole society. The class divisions only partially corresponded to the division between Hima and Iru. Wealth in the form of cattle was concentrated in the hands of a small group of Hima chiefs and lords, who did not personally attend their herds (i.e., work). Instead they employed poor herders to tend their cattle and poor farmers to provide beer, vegetables, and other menial services. A few prominent farmers, rich in land and family labor, might also number among the nonproducing class, although their position was masked by their continued role in the management of the village communities from which they arose.[16] At the other end, the producing class clearly consisted of *both* Iru farmers and Hima herders, upon whose labor rested the systems of tribute and of clientage and hence the structure of the Ankole state.

The state institutions of Ankole can be summarily described since they have been amply covered in the ethnographic literature (Oberg, 1940). At the center of political life was the *mugabe* and his court of several hundred retainers. No longer merely *primus inter pares* by the time of Mutambuka, the *mugabe* was an autocrat with powers of life and death over his Hima and Iru subjects. His court was the highest judicial body, his "decisions on any matter [being] final" (Roscoe, 1923a: 12), and the center of culture and "society" to which anyone with a claim to prominence came for extended visits. A courtly style, free from drudgery and given to poetic recitations (Morris, 1964) and the cultivation of fine manners, developed as the *mugabe's* residence became more fixed in the area near the modern site of Mbarara (Karugire, 1971: 200–201). There was no central bureaucracy; both the positions of prime minister and the governing council were colonial creations (Karugire, 1971: 110–111). The capital site never remained for longer than one reign and in times of disease was moved frequently. It never emerged as an urban or administrative center. The loose administrative structure of tribute collection by districts *(ekyanga)* controlled by Bakungu required no elaborate record-keeping or central offices (Steinhart, 1978a: 143–144).

The system of military administration based on *emitwe* attempted unsuccessfully by Ntare IV was developed by Rwebishengye (c.1783–1811±20) and Gasyonga I (c.1811–1839±17) and perfected by Mutambuka. When these regiments were garrisoned in border areas where they could be assigned herds for their support and where agricultural labor could be commanded, the *emitwe* system served both a military and an administrative and tax collection function (Karugire, 1971: 200–208). Military occupation along with pastoral migration provided the basis of contact and the structure of tribute collection, adjudication, and coercion among both farmers and herders. The kraal of the *omitwe* leader became a provincial capital, "the focus of social and cultural activities within the region," as well as local headquarters from which lesser chiefs were responsible for "tribute collection and . . . the organization of free labor for public works" (Karugire, 1971: 203–204). Although these regimental regimes lasted no longer than one reign, the change in command and regimental title did not so much disturb the administration of the region as reinvigorate it at each succession.

The military administration and tributary system in regions of agricultural settlement provided the revenue and labor control for making possible the transition to a rudimentary state. Tribute from herders and farmers made possible a life of leisure and distinction for the narrow ruling class around the *mugabe* and *bagyendanwa*. The elaboration of a monarchical ideology paralleled the elaboration of the cult of the drum and its physical establishment. Herds of cattle were collected and kraals and palaces built for the drum and its court which was second only to the *mugabe's*. The cult of *bagyendanwa* was the state religion, identified with the kingship and the possession of sovereignty and legitimacy (Oberg, 1940: 150–157). The drum's mystical functions provided religious support for the authority of the state. Nonetheless, the popular veneration of the Cwezi spirits and the growth of the antistatist Nyabingi cult among the subordinate classes reflect the lack of ideological hegemony of the drum cult and the state (Hopkins, 1970). Despite the absence of total ideological control, the evolution of the administrative, military, and ideological apparatuses of state power transformed the Nkore dyna-state inherited by Ntare IV in the 18th century into the considerable Ankole state which Ntare V bequeathed to the colonial powers in 1895.

We have seen how the emergence of class societies based upon a tributary mode of production laid the foundations for the simultaneous emergence of the state in the lacustrine region during the 18th and 19th centuries. By critically examining the royal traditions preserved by those who sought to glorify the state and its rulers, we have uncovered the class basis of exploitation and domination which undergirded the precolonial states of western

Uganda. Like everywhere, the monuments to the few were built upon the exertions of the many. The village cultivator and herdsmen built the palaces and tombs, made the tools and weapons, provided the food, clothing, and regalia of the kings, princes, and lords of the realms. Rudimentary as the systems of exploitation and accumulation were, they alone made possible the comparative luxury and attainments of the ruling class. But this is a fact of all early class social formations. What is different about the formation of Ankole and Bunyoro?

First, the ability of the ruling class to exploit both agricultural and pastoral workers made the burden on each less onerous. In order to expropriate the small surplus required by the state from farmers and herders, the ruling class did not have to destroy village, clan, or lineage organizations. The creation of an overarching state apparatus and the collection of tribute left the systems of agricultural and pastoral production essentially unaltered. The distribution of burdens between herders and farmers contributed to the melioration of class tensions between producers and nonproducers. Second, the persistence of the occupational and ethnic distinctions between Hima and Iru displaced class conflict onto a communal and cultural plane. The stability of the tributary mode and its lack of apparent revolutionary impetus can be seen to result from the melioration of exploitation of the peasantry by the availability of alternate sources of surplus value; the lack of disruption of peasant and lineage communities; and the displacement of class consciousness by ethnic and status consciousness.

Still, the tributary mode of production found in western Uganda was not static. A steady increase in population from the mid-18th century,[17] whether cause or result of the revolution in social relations, created pressure to increase the production of both agriculture and herding. It also provided the means to do so—labor being the factor of production in shortest supply. Periodic natural and political crises led to increasing state intervention in the organization and distribution of production and the involvement of more remote farmers, herders, and craftsmen in the production of surplus for the state-managed redistributive economy. The injection of western capitalism and the colonial state during the 20th century diverted this process while hastening the transformation of the African peasantry. By understanding the dynamics of precapitalist social formations in terms of their autonomous evolutionary direction and revolutionary potential, as in the growth of classes and states as described for Ankole and Bunyoro, it is hoped we can understand the direction and potential of these societies as they are encompassed within the world market and the capitalist mode of production, entering the dynamic of global revolutionary change manifest in the 20th century.

NOTES

1. The idea that the Bahuma may have internally differentiated from among local Bantu-speaking people (Posnansky, 1966: 6) has been effectively refuted by biological studies (Cook, 1969, and articles cited therein).

2. Scholarly, if occasionally subjective, estimates of the labor required for building Bigo range from 1000 men working for two to three months (Gray, 1935: 228) to 1000 men working one year (Posnansky, 1966: Note 11). Considering that the Hima population of Ankole alone was estimated at 25,000 with kraals of up to 150 people within which large-scale, collective action was organized (Oberg, 1943: 575–579), even the upper estimate does not seem outrageous for the voluntary efforts of pioneer settlers engaged in collective action.

3. Despite fanciful claims to genetic relationship to the Cwezi, Nyakatura (1973: 50–57) agrees that the Babito had to be trained in the customs of Kitaran cattle ritual and government practices. Contrast Atkinson (1978) on the spread of Nyoro political ideas to the Luo-speaking Acholi with Onyango-ku Adongo (1976), who credits the Luo with introducing the state among the Banyoro.

4. I am following Webster's use of regnal generations for Bunyoro chronology rather than Nyakatura's more conventional estimate by dynastic reigns.

5. Compare the description of a western Uganda famine in the early colonial era in Johnson (1908: 50).

6. Compare Atkinson (1978: 398–404) and Dyson-Hudson and Dyson-Hudson (1970) on cattle as a famine hedge among neighboring societies of northern Uganda.

7. The trade in salt was on a larger scale and involved some specialization among the Bairu (Good, 1972).

8. I have accepted the dating by reigns used by Karugire for Nkore as the most accessible.

9. See Webster (1979b: 13–14) for the dating of these droughts. I suspect another drought unmentioned in the traditions may have taken place between the 1740s and 1750s from evidence of a widespread sahelian drought of that period (Curtin, 1975: 54; Lovejoy and Baier, 1975: 570–572; cf. Herring, 1979: 60, on hydrological evidence for the same).

10. On the question of tributary versus feudal tenure, compare with Kea (1979) and contrast Crummey (in this volume).

11. "Today the Babito of Duhaga's sub-clan have ceased to be of great importance and many of them have become *bairu* only retaining the name of Babiito" (Nyakatura, 1973: 87–88).

12. On Nyoro trade, see Tosh (1970) and Uzoigwe (1972). On iron, see Sutton (1973: 15–16) and Hiernaux and Maquet (1948). On ivory and guns, see Beachey (1967, 1962).

13. Karugire (1971: 162) suggests that Buhweju was the inspiration for the introduction of archery. I believe that the Batwa archers of Rwanda are a more likely ultimate source.

14. Prior to Ntare IV, the Basita clan may have been the keepers of Wamara's drum rather than the Bayangwe clan, who were more closely associated with the Hinda dynasty (Karugire, 1971: 86–88; 96–97; 137–140). Moreover, the traditions that the drum was destroyed by the Nyoro, or that a Mururu from Mpororo painted the drum to look like Mororwa, the royal drum of Mpororo, raise unanswered questions about the authenticity, provenience and meaning of Ntare's drum (cf. Karugire, 1971: 100–101; 160).

15. For a comparison of clientage to European feudal contracts, see Steinhart (1967) and compare to the classic description of the feudal vassalage arrangements in Ganshof (1961) and Bloch (1964).

16. I am regretfully ignoring the exploitation by both farmers and herders of the labor of family members, especially women.

17. The evidence for population growth and its relationship to social change is inconclusive, but see Wrigley (1979).

REFERENCES

ADEFUYE, A. (1973) "Political history of the Palwo, 1400–1911." Ph.D. dissertation, University of Ibadan.

———— (1974) "Palwo Jogi." (unpublished)

———— (1976) "The Palwo: Emergence and crisis," pp. 232–250 in J. M. Onyango-ku-Odongo and J. B. Webster (eds.) The central Luo before the Aconya. Nairobi: East African Literature Bureau.

AMIN, S. (1976) Unequal development. New York: Monthly Review.

ATKINSON, R. (1978) "The history of the western Acholi." Ph.D. dissertation, Northwestern University.

AVINERI, S. (1969) Karl Marx on colonialism and modernization. New York: Doubleday.

BAITWABABO, S.R. (1969) "The origins and disintegration of Mpororo." (unpublished)

BEACHEY, R. W. (1962) "The arms trade in East Africa in the 19th century." Journal of African History 3: 451–467.

———— (1967) "The East African ivory trade in the 19th century." Journal of African History 7: 269–290.

BEATTIE, J. (1954a) "The Kibanja system of land tenure in Bunyoro, Uganda." Journal of African Administration 6: 18–28.

———— (1954b) "A further note on the Kibanja System." Journal of African Administration 6(4): 78–185.

———— (1971) The Nyoro State. Oxford, England: Oxford University Press.

BERGER, R. (1963) "Oral traditions in Karagwe." (unpublished)

BLOCH, M. (1964) Feudal society (2 vols). Chicago: University of Chicago Press.

BUCHANAN, C. (1969) "The Bacwezi cult." (unpublished)

———— (1974) "The Kitara complex: The historical traditions of western Uganda to the 16th century." Ph.D. dissertation, Indiana University.

———— (1979) "Courts, clans and chronology in the Kitara complex," in J. B. Webster (ed.) Chronology, migration and drought in interlacustrine Africa. London: Longman.

CLAESSEN, H. and SKALNIK, P. [eds.] (1978) The early state. The Hague: Mouton.

COHEN, D. W. (1968) "The Cwezi cult." Journal of African History 9: 651–657.

COHEN, D. W., OGOT, B. A. and HERRING, R. S. (1979) "The construction of dominance: The strategies of selected Luo groups in Uganda and Kenya." Presented at the Goethe Institute Conference, Nakuru, October.

COOK, G. D. (1969) "Lactase deficiency." Man 4: 265–267.

COQUERY-VIDROVITCH, C. (1969) "Recherches sur un mode du production Africain." Pensée 144: 1–78.

CURTIN, P. D. (1975) Economic change in pre-colonial Africa. Madison: University of Wisconsin Press.

DENOON, D. J. N. (n.d.) "A chronology for southwest Uganda." (unpublished)

DUNBAR, A. R. (1965) A history of Bunyoro-Kitara. Oxford, England: Oxford University Press.

DYSON-HUDSON, R. and DYSON-HUDSON, N. (1970) pp. 91–123 in P. F. M. McLaughlin (ed.) African food production systems. Baltimore: Johns Hopkins University Press.

EDEL, M. (1957) The Chiga of western Uganda. Oxford, England: Oxford University Press.

ELAM, Y. (1974) "The relationship between Hima and Iru in Ankole." African Studies 33: 159–172.

FISHER, R. B. (1970) Twilight tales of the black Baganda. London: Frank Cass.

GANSHOF, F. L. (1961) Feudalism. New York: Harper & Row.

GODELIER, M. (1977) Perspectives in Marxist anthropology. Cambridge, England: Cambridge University Press.

GOOD, C. (1972) "Salt, trade and disease." International Journal of African Historical Studies 5: 543–586.

GORJU, J. (1920) Entre le Victoria, l'Albert et l'Edouard. Rennes: Imprimeries Obarthur.

GRAY, SIR J. M. (1935) "The riddle of Bigo." Uganda Journal 2: 226–233.

HERRING, R. (1979) "Hydrology and chronology," in J. B. Webster (ed.) Chronology, migration and drought in interlacustrine Africa. London: Longman.

HIERNAUX, J. and MAQUET, E. (1948) L'age du fer à Kibero. Turvuren: Musée Royale de l'Afrique Centrale.

HINDESS, B. and HIRST, P. Q. (1975) Pre-capitalist modes of production. London: Routledge and Kegan Paul.

HOPKINS, E. (1970) "The Nyabingi cult in southwestern Uganda," pp. 258–336 in R. Rotberg and A. Mazrui (eds.) Protest and power in Black Africa. Oxford, England: Oxford University Press.

INGHAM, K. (1946) "The Amagasani of the Abakama of Bunyoro." Uganda Journal 27: 136–145.

JOHNSON, T. B. (1908) Tramps round the mountains of the moon. London: T. Fisher Unwin.

K. W. (1935 and 1936) "The kings of Bunyoro-Kitara." Uganda Journal 3: 155–160 and 4: 78–83.

KAMUHANGIRE, E. (1972) "Pre-colonial trade in southwestern Uganda." (unpublished)

———— (1974) "Bunyoro and Rwanda." Presented at the annual meeting of the Canadian Association of African Studies, Halifax, February.

KARUGIRE, S. R. (1970) "Relations between Bairu and Bahima in 19th century Nkore." Tarikh 3: 22–33.

———— (1971) A history of the kingdom of Nkore. Oxford, England: Clarendon.

———— (1972) "The foundation and development of the western kingdoms." (unpublished)

KATATE, A. G. and KAMUZUNGUNU, L. (1967) Abagabe B'Ankole (2 vols). Kampala: East African Literature Bureau.

KATOKE, I. (1971) "Karagwe: A pre-colonial state." Journal of World History 13: 524–529.

———— (1975) The Karagwe kingdom. Nairobi: East African Publishing House.

KEA, R. A. (1979) "Land, overlords, and cultivators in the 17th century Gold Coast." (unpublished)

KIWANUKA, M. S. M. (1971) A history of Buganda. London: Longman.

LANNING, E. C. (1960) "The earthworks of Kibengo, Mubende district." Uganda Journal 24(2): 33–196.

LOVEJOY, P. and BAIER, S. (1975) "The desert-side economy of the central Sudan." International Journal of African Historical Studies 8: 551–581.

LOWIE, R. (1927) The origin of the state. New York: Harcourt Brace Jovanovich.

MAIR, L. (1961) "Clientship in East Africa." Cahiers d'Etudes Africaines 2(2): 15–325.

———— (1977) Primitive government. Bloomington: Indiana University.

MARX, K. (1967) Capital (3 vols). New York: International Publishers.

MORRIS, H. F. (1962) A history of Ankole. Kampala: East African Literature Bureau.

―――― (1964) The heroic recitations of the Bahima of Ankole. Oxford, England: Clarendon.

MUNYUZANGABO, A. (n.d.) "The early history of Kajara and Rwampara." (unpublished)

MUSHANGA, T. M. (1972) Personal communication. Austin, January.

NYAKATURA, J. (1973) Anatomy of an African kingdom. New York: Doubleday.

―――― (1978) Bunyoro customs and traditions. Nairobi: East African Literature Bureau.

OBERG, K. (1938) "Kinship organization of the Banyankole." Africa 11: 129–159.

―――― (1940) "The kingdom of Ankole in Uganda," pp. 121–162 in M. Fortes and E. P. Evans-Pritchard (eds.) African political systems. Oxford, England: Oxford University Press.

―――― (1943) "A comparison of three systems of primitive economic organization." American Anthropologist, N.S. 45: 572–587.

OGOT, B. A. (1967) History of the southern Luo. Nairobi: East African Publishing House.

OLIVER, R. (1953) "A question about the Bacwezi." Uganda Journal 17(2): 135–137.

ONYANGO-KU-ODONGO, J. M. (1976) "The Luo-Bito Dynasty of Bunyoro-Kitara," pp. 118–130 in J. K. Onyango-ku-Odongo and J. B. Webster (eds.) The central Luo during the Aconya. Nairobi: East African Literature Bureau.

POLANYI, J. (1971) "The economy as instituted process," pp. 137–174 in G. Dalton (ed.) Primitive, archaic and modern economies: Essays of Karl Polanyi. Boston: Beacon.

POSNANSKY, M. (1966) "Kingship, archeology and historical myth." Uganda Journal 30(1): 1–12.

RENNIE, J. K. (1972) "The pre-colonial kingdom of Rwanda: A reinterpretation." Transafrican Journal of History 2: 11–44.

―――― (1973) "The Banyoro invasions and interlacustrine chronology." (unpublished)

ROSCOE, J. (1915) The northern Bantu. Cambridge, England: Cambridge University Press.

_____ (1923a) The Banyankole. Cambridge, England: Cambridge University Press.

_____ (1923b) The Bakitara or Banyoro. Cambridge, England: Cambridge University Press.

_____ (1924) Immigrants and their influence on the lakes region of central Africa. Cambridge, England: Cambridge University Press.

RUKIDI, SIR G. K. (1969) "The kings of Tooro." (unpublished)

STEINHART, E. I. (1967) "Vassal and fief in three lacustrine kingdoms." Cahiers d'Etudes Africaines 7: 606–620.

_____ (1973) "An outline of the political economy of Ankole." Presented at the annual meeting of the Western Association of Africanists, Laramie, April.

_____ (1977) Conflict and collaboration. Princeton, NJ: Princeton University Press.

_____ (1978a) "Ankole: Pastoral hegemony," pp. 131–150 in H. Claessen and P. Skalnik (eds.) The early state. The Hague: Mouton.

_____ (1978b) "From 'empire' to state." Presented at the Xth meeting of the International Congress of Anthropological and Ethnological Sciences, New Delhi, December.

_____ (1979) "The kingdoms of the march," pp. 189–213 in J. B. Webster (ed.) Chronology, migration and drought in inter-lacustrine Africa. London: Longman.

SUTTON, J. E. G. (1973) Early trade in eastern Africa. Nairobi: East African Publishing House.

TAYLOR, B. (1962) The western lacustrine Bantu. London: International African Institute.

TOSH, J. (1970) "The northern lacustrine region," pp. 103–118 in R. Gray and J. Birmingham (eds.) Pre-colonial African trade. Oxford, England: Oxford University Press.

UZOIGWE, G. N. (1972) "Pre-colonial markets in Bunyoro-Kitara." Comparative Studies in Society and History 14: 422–455.

_____ (1973) "Succession and civil war in Bunyoro-Kitara." International Journal of African Historical Studies 6: 49–71.

VANSINA, J. (1962) L'évolution du royaume Rwanda des origines à 1900. Bruxelles: Académie Royale des Sciences d'Outre mer.

WEBSTER, J. B. [ed.] (1979a) Chronology, migrations and drought in interlacustrine Africa. London: Longman.

_____ (1979b) "Noi-Noi, famines as an aid to interlacustrine chronology," in J. B. Webster (ed.) Chronology, migration and drought in interlacustrine Africa. London: Longman.

———— (1979c) "The reign of the gods." In J. B. Webster (ed.) Chronology, migration and drought in interlacustrine Africa. London: Longman.

———— (forthcoming) "The second Babito dynasty in Bunyoro," in D. J. N. Denoon (ed.) History of Uganda (Vol. 2). Nairobi: East African Publishing House.

———— (n.d.) "The deification of displaced dynasties." (unpublished)

WHEELER, A. (1972) "Kitagwenda: A Babito kingdom in southern Toro." (unpublished)

WILLIAMS, F. L. (1936) "Sowing and harvesting in Ankole." Uganda Journal 3: 203–210.

———— (1938) "Hima cattle." Uganda Journal 6: 17–42; 87–117.

WRIGLEY, C. C. (1959) "Some thoughts on the Bacwezi." Uganda Journal 22: 11–17.

———— (1979) "Population in African history." Journal of African History 20: 127–131.

6

THE SLAVE MODE OF PRODUCTION:
Precolonial Dahomey

ROBERTA WALKER KILKENNY
University of Guyana

Provocative questions relating to the nature and origin of slavery in Africa, posed by Rodney (1966) and Fage (1969), are only now being addressed in a meaningful and systematic fashion. In the past few years a number of case studies and collections have appeared which focus on the general topic of slavery (Grace, 1975; Meillassoux, 1975; Cooper, 1977; Miers and Kopytoff, 1977). But, these works tend to concentrate on the nature of slavery and to minimize the question of its origin and development over time. This is due in part to the greater availability of empirical evidence, on which many of the studies rely for the late precolonial and early colonial periods, than is available for earlier times. In at least one instance, however, it reflects the persuasion that the question itself

Author's Note: I would like to thank the participants in the 1977 symposium on the Cultivator and State in Precolonial Africa for their criticisms of an earlier version of this article, especially Joseph Mbwiliza, of the University of Tanzania, and Marcia Wright, of Columbia University. Thanks also go to Donald Crummey and Charles Stewart, both of the University of Illinois, for their constant encouragement.

157

is of little or no relevance (Miers and Kopytoff, 1977: 66–69). Miers and Kopytoff (1977) argue that to seek for a possible causation of slavery outside of Africa is to deny Africa an internal dynamism. Such a position minimizes the dialectical relationship existing between Africa's development (and underdevelopment) and the emerging capitalist, world economy from the 15th century onward and between the origin of slavery and its nature.

There is, in much of the work, a recognition that in order to understand the nature of slavery, we need to come to terms with the concept itself. Miers and Kopytoff (1977: 11) correctly warn against the unquestioned application of concepts which developed out of the study of the Western experience to the African experience. They, however, fall into this very trap themselves.

The reader is told to discard concepts of ownership, property, and the purchasing of people when considering African slavery as these concepts can also be applied to practices affecting free persons within lineage groups. They go on to state that "African lineages 'own' their members" and that "rights in wives, children, and kin-group members are usually acquired through transactions involving material transfers" (Miers and Kopytoff, 1977: 11–12). Viewing such lineage practices as being reflections of property relations is, in fact, imposing Western value judgments on an African reality. A closer examination of the payment of bridewealth, as one example of a "material transfer," reveals the fallacy of the Miers-Kopytoff argument.

Bridewealth is paid to the bride's lineage in order to secure certain rights to the labor and reproductive powers of the woman (Boserup, 1970: 50; Goody, 1976: 8; 43; Miers and Kopytoff, 1977: 8). That woman is not alienated from her lineage. She is still a member of her kin group and continues to have certain obligations to it, as the group does to her. Even the right to her labor power is not totally vested in the husband's lineage. The woman can acquire wealth independently of the husband and may pay back her bridewealth, thus freeing herself from her marital obligations (Boserup, 1970: 47). The payment of bridewealth cannot be said to reflect property rights in a woman as this concept can only apply to the total alienation of a woman, not only from her lineage but also from herself (i.e., from her labor power).

Although in no way peculiar to slavery, alienation from one's own lineage is generally accepted as a condition of slavery (Engels, 1970: 220; 1939: 199; Leacock, 1970: 52; Meillassoux, 1971: 63–64; Miers and Kopytoff, 1977: 14–15; Padgug, 1976: 4) even by social scientists with radically differing ideological positions. This alienation can come about through unredeemed pawnage, purchase, or capture. On the other hand, the question of property rights in an individual as being peculiar to slavery is the subject of some disagreement. The Miers-Kopytoff argument has already been stated. Unfortunately, they offer little by way of conceptual clarity. Opting for "slavery" instead of slavery, they suggest that where the word is employed, preference is given to the use of local terms for "slaves" and that descriptive information is supplied. The reader is then to determine, based on her/his own conceptualization of slavery, whether the case study reveals the existence of slavery, "slavery" (Miers and Kopytoff, 1977: 77), or perhaps some other form of subordination.

Greater conceptual clarity is offered by social scientists using a historical materialist approach, beginning with Marx. For Marx, production relations is the key determinant. "The purchase and sale of slaves is formally also a purchase and sale of commodities," but it is not one's vulnerability to sale which makes one a slave. A slave is distinguished from other laborers by the fact that the slave "works under alien conditions of production" (Marx, 1954–1959: Vol. 2: 32, Vol. 3: 776, 791), that is, possesses neither the means of production nor her/his own labor power. "The *effective possession* of slave property . . . depends on the capacity of the owner to set the means of production in motion" (Hindess and Hirst, 1975: 126; Engels, 1939: 178). The existence of such things as provision grounds[1] does not negate the veracity of the concept. "In slave labor, even that part of the working day in which the slave is only replacing the value of his own means of existence, in which, therefore, in fact, he works for himself alone, appears as labor for his master . . . the property relation conceals the labor of the slave for himself" (Marx, 1954–1959: Vol. 1: 505).

Production relations are but a part of a larger analytical framework, the mode of production (Hindess and Hirst, 1975). The slave mode of production has been conceptualized as one in which "slave labor forms the basis of production" (Hindess and Hirst, 1975: 126). It can also be said to exist when slaves produce an important proportion of the society's economic product (Padgug, 1976: 5). It should be noted that neither conceptualization in any way denies the possibility of slaves' existing in a society prior to the emergence of a slave mode of production. It is, however, implied that such persons would be relatively insignificant in effecting the overall material life of the society, despite the fact that from a subjective point of view the slaves' condition might be dismal (Leacock, 1970: 52).

A slave, then, can be defined as a laborer who is alienated from her/his own lineage, from the means of production, and from her/his own labor power. The slave mode of production comes into existence with the domination of the production process by slave labor and with the effective possession of slave labor by a separate class of slave owners. It is only after establishing the perimeters of the abstraction, slavery, that we can contribute meaningfully to the debate initiated by Rodney and Fage over its particular nature and origin in any given African society. For the purpose of this article, I have chosen to examine slavery in Dahomey from the 17th century through the 19th century.

Dahomey, a major participant in the transatlantic slave trade, was described as a slave-owning society by European visitors from the 1720s until the imposition of French colonial rule (Snelgrave, 1734; Dalzel, 1793; Norris, 1789; M'Leod, 1820; Freeman, 1844; Forbes, 1851; Newbury, 1960). The key questions are: (1) whether slaves, in fact, were present in Dahomey and, if so, from what period; (2) assuming the presence of slaves, what were the circumstances under which slavery developed and what were the conditions under which slaves labored; (3) whether a slave mode of production emerged; and (4) assuming the emergence of a slave mode of production, of what historical significance was it, that is, was the slave mode of production the determinant one in the Dahomean social formation (Poulantzas, 1973: 15–16) at any conjuncture in Dahomey's history. These questions can only be answered in light of the historical development of Dahomey.

The kingdom of Dahomey was located in an area of West Africa where the savannah extends to the coast. Its situation in an agriculturally poor area was further complicated by the presence of several swamps. The capital, Abomey, itself located on a plateau, suffered frequent droughts. Neither did Dahomey have access to the mineral resources (especially gold) that a number of other West African states commanded (Webster and Boahen, 1967: 102). These factors contributed to the development of a highly centralized state, in which agricultural production and trade were planned, controlled, and highly taxed (Webster and Boahen, 1967: 112), as well as to expansionist tendencies.

The conquest of Abomey in 1625, and the establishment of a royal dynasty by the Fon king, Dako (reigned c.1625–c.1650), marked the foundation of the Dahomean state. The indigenous population was assimilated through intermarriage and through the continuation of the "earth cults"[2] under the primacy of the new royal "cult" (Mercier, 1954: 213–214). The persistence of the "earth cults" was to have important consequences insofar as the "earth cult" priests occupied central positions and kept alive hopes of ending Fon domination (Herskovits and Herskovits, 1933: 180–181). A highly stratified state emerged, with the king at its head.

The highest stratum of society was occupied by the king's blood relations[3] and the clergy, neither of whom engaged in productive labor (Gough, 1972). It was in the king's interest that these persons be dependent on the state for their material sustenance as, given the ideological proppings of the state, they posed the greatest domestic threat to his regime.

While it was common for the king's eldest son to be named to succeed his father to the throne, it was not mandatory (Norris, 1789: 4–5). Any son who aspired to the throne could attempt to develop a following which would give physical support to his claim. While not impossible, this task was made difficult by the fact that the aspirant was not in a position to offer his followers either material reward or protection until his bid for the throne succeeded.

"Earth cult" priests were in a slightly better position than royal claimants to mobilize popular support. They maintained not only preconquest traditions but also rituals. Those rituals connected with fertility were perhaps of particular importance in this context. While not themselves engaged in productive labor, it was they who were believed to have the power to create conditions favorable or unfavorable to production and reproduction. They could call upon their followers to provide them with material sustenance in return for their services, thus giving them a degree of autonomy from the king. It was, therefore, of particular importance that the clergy be vulnerable to the power and sanctions of the crown.

The state bureaucracy was filled by "commoners" appointed by the king. Their lack of royal blood meant that they could not legitimately claim the throne; it was, therefore, considered safe to invest them with powerful political offices. Their loyalty and efficient service were guaranteed, ideally, by rewarding them with large landed estates, captives, and so on. They were also assigned members of the king's "harem" to watch over them.

The majority of the population was engaged in agricultural production, at something above subsistence level. The unit of production and consumption and of political organization and religion[4] was the patrilineal lineage which lived together in several houses, surrounded by an enclosure and associated with an agricultural plot (Polanyi, 1966: 70–73). This system resembles what has been termed the lineage mode of production (Coquery-Vidrovitch, 1976: 102–104; Dupre and Rey, 1973; Terray, 1975: 94). On the village level, also, a system of collective labor, the *dokpwe*, functioned. The *dokpwe's* functions were economic—

such as clearing fields and doing major construction work—and social—such as taking charge of elaborate funerals (Polanyi, 1966: 62–65). State intervention took the form of the exaction of tribute in the forms of produce and labor (Webster and Boahen, 1967: 112; Ronen, 1971: 10; Coquery-Vidrovitch, 1976: 107).

The state sought to establish tributary relations with other political entities as well, despite the fact that Dahomey was herself a tributary of Oyo until the early 19th century. The demand for foodstuffs was an important factor. As late as the 1850s when, as acknowledged slave raiders, the Dahomean army attacked Togo, the army's first demand was for foodstuffs—corn and yams—and cattle (Hurston, 1927: 655).

The capture of the coastal town of Whydah, during the reign of King Agadja (1708–c.1740), brought Dahomey into direct contact with European slave traders. The state developed a monopoly over the importation and distribution of guns, shot, powder, and cowries (Stoeber, 1969: 488; Polanyi, 1962: 40) with which it reinforced its paramountcy. The power and authority of the state, personified in the king, was further bolstered and reasserted by the "Annual Customs."[5]

It was at the "Annual Customs" that the infamous human sacrifices took place. Reports on the number of persons actually sacrificed vary greatly. Snelgrave (1734), Norris (1789), and Dalzel (1793) claimed that several hundred persons were killed at each "Customs." M'Leod (1820: 59–60) called such accounts exaggerated, the result of a desire on the part of Dahomean informants to magnify the king's grandeur and power. He reports that a Mr. James, officer of the Royal African Company, never counted more than 65 victims during any one of three visits. Frederick Forbes was aware of only 32 decapitations during his visit of 1849–1850 (Forbes, 1851: Vol. 2: 171). M'Leod's claim that the figures ranging in the hundreds are exaggerated is a plausible one. Snelgrave, Norris, and Dalzel were slave traders who sought to defend their own activities by portraying African society as being more inhumane than Western slave society.

It is, however, clear that the sacrifices were considered a vital part of the ritual. King Adadoza (reigned 1797–1818) would not be induced to lower the number of intended victims despite the high prices European traders were prepared to pay for captives (M'Leod, 1820: 65). Ryan (1975) suggests that the sacrifices may have been intended, in part, to increase the "production" of slaves. The ritual attracted adherents to the king by demonstrating his power and wealth. These adherents would then cooperate in procuring captives.

The "Annual Customs" was also the occasion when the king rendered judgments on matters beyond the jurisdiction of his officials and redistributed gifts and tribute he received during the course of the ritual, as well as trade goods and captives. Through favoring them with gifts, large quantities of cowries, and captives, the king was able to maintain the support of the various state officials.

Dahomean peasants also received captives, but, from their perspective, the receipt of cowries, the only legal tender in domestic markets (Polanyi, 1966: 40), may have been more important. Their effective use of captive labor was limited by the low level to which peasant production had developed at that time (Engels, 1939: 178; 199). Through the mechanism of redistribution, a situation was created in which the peasant, too, was dependent on the king.

Those captives not sacrificed or assigned to labor within Dahomey, the greatest number being sent to the royal estates (Le Hérissé, 1911: 52), would be sold to the European slave traders through the king's agent the *Yovogan*, at Whydah.

Dahomey apparently resisted involvement in the transatlantic slave trade, barring Allada slave raiders from penetrating the interior in 1670–1671 and again in 1687–1688 (Akinjogbin, 1967: 24). By the reign of King Tegbesu (c.1740–1774), however, the economy was deeply rooted in the trade (Akinjogbin, 1967: 208). The principal factor in this transformation was the reliance which the state had developed on European traders as a source of certain commodities, especially guns, which gave Dahomey a military technology far superior to her neighbors. For much of the precolonial history of Dahomean-European trade relations, the only commodity which the Europeans accepted was the slave.

With the decline in the demand for slaves, consequent to the Industrial and French Revolutions, and the growing effectiveness of the British blockade, Dahomey faced a crisis.[6] The pronounced dependence on European commodities reflected the underdevelopment of the Dahomean economy, in particular, and the social formation, in general. The only developed, exportable commodity was human. European industrialization, however, created a demand for a new commodity—palm oil—which Dahomey had the potential to supply.

King Ghezo (reigned 1818–1858), while continuing to participate in the transatlantic trade, actively encouraged the development of oil palm plantations. By the time of Frederick Forbes's visit, 1849–1850, King Ghezo had established his own plantation near Abomey (Forbes, 1851: Vol. 1: 31). A tax in kind was levied against other palm oil producers and attempts were made to institute a royal monopoly over the oil trade (Law, 1977: 574–575). A careful census was maintained of existing plantations to assure increased yields; and the Dahomean army was increasingly ordered away from slave raiding in favor of seizing territory in the rich Yoruba palm belt: Ado was attacked in 1844 and Abeokuta in 1851 and again in 1864 (Webster and Boahen, 1967: 112; 120). It is within this historical context that slave labor developed.

Pawnage, viewed by some writers as a form of slavery, could and did result in the event of heavy indebtedness. A child could be offered as a form of collateral until a debt was repaid. Should the debt not be repaid within the specified time, other arrangements were possible—the lender might marry a female pawn, a second pawn might be offered, the pawn might work off the debt, or the *dokpwe* might work off the debt (Polanyi, 1966: 68–69). The status of slave could only be acquired if the pawn went unredeemed and thus was alienated from his lineage and from the rights and obligations of lineage affiliation. As communal labor could be mobilized in the event of prolonged indebtedness, it would seem unlikely that a Dahomean pawn would suffer the misfortune of going unredeemed.

Dahomean citizens could be enslaved, but only under circumstances thought to be extraordinary—usually some real or imagined threat to the king. Given the central position which "earth cult" priests were thought to have in fomenting rebellion, it is not surprising that from the reign of King Wegbaja (c.1650–c.1685) onward, almost every Dahomean king ordered the enslavement of a number of "earth cult" priests, their families, and their disciples (Herskovits and Herskovits, 1933: 180–181). Followers of rival princes might also be enslaved, as was the case when Agotime, the mother of King Ghezo, and 63 of her supporters were enslaved prior to Ghezo's seizure of the throne (Herskovits and Herskovits, 1933: 181). Dahomeans could also be enslaved if found guilty of adultery (M'Leod, 1820: 49–50) and certain other crimes. Enslaved criminals, called *Oumesi,* were still considered Dahomean, although they had lost their rights to freedom and family (Le Hérissé, 1911: 56–57). Persons such as these, who were considered to pose a threat to the state, were not kept within Dahomey, but instead were sold to the Europeans. Who, then, were the persons Snelgrave identified as slaves as early as the 1720s and reported to be working the farm of King Agadja (Snelgrave, 1734: 106)?

By the time of Snelgrave's visit in 1727, captives were the dominant labor force on the royal estates. These estates were large expanses of land requiring a much greater input of labor than was possible using peasant production. The captives assigned there produced foodstuffs to sustain the large number of Dahomeans who were not engaged in productive labor, such as the royal relations, the clergy, the state bureaucrats, and the army, which was engaged in slave raiding and in expanding the area from which the state could exact tribute. The combined population of the palace and the standing army at one time was placed at more than 20,000 (Le Hérissé, 1911: 90). The army, especially, was a major consumer of foodstuffs. In the century from 1725 to 1820, the standing army doubled in size, from 3000 to 6000 persons; by 1845 it had again doubled (Webster and Boahen, 1967: 104). *Glesi*, descendents of the royal slaves, could keep a portion of what they produced, own property, and marry, but they could not leave the estate to which their parents had been assigned (Le Hérissé, 1911: 57). State officials also owned estates.

Unlike their counterparts on the estates, captives found with peasant families from perhaps as early as the 17th century (Aguessy, 1970: 76) did not constitute a distinct slave class (Meillassoux, 1971: 63; Terray, 1975: 112). Known by the Fon word *Kan-Noumon*, meaning a person without family (Auguessy, 1970: 76), their function in the production process was the same as that of other members of the lineages with which they were placed. Like junior blood relations, their produce was appropriated for redistribution within the lineage, which, in turn, paid tribute to the state. Social interaction, including intermarriage, was not significantly limited (Stoeber, 1969: 491–492). The children of slaves were considered *Danhomenou*, that is, born in Dahomey and, as such, could not be sold except under special circumstances as noted above. They, even more than their parents, took on the appearance of lineage members (Le Hérissé, 1911: 55–56). They worked a limited number of days, usually four, for their masters (Auguessy, 1970: 77). Descendents of female slaves and lineage members were still more rapidly assimilated (Aguessy, 1970: 78) into the patrilineal lineage structure.

If it was the captives deployed to the estates who constituted a distinct class of slave laborers, then it is to that sector that we must look to determine whether a historically significant slave mode of production developed.

With the shifting emphasis to palm oil in the mid-19th century, plantations developed quickly. In addition to those royal slaves deployed on the plantation near Abomey, large numbers were settled in the Whydah area (Le Hérissé, 1911: 90). Merchants as well as state bureaucrats owned estates devoted to the cultivation of oil palms and worked by slaves who may have been obtained from the king or, more likely, by purchase. Merchants may have been the principal owners of oil palm plantations. One Dahomean slave dealer was reported to own seven estates and 1000 slaves in 1850 (Forbes, 1851: Vol. 2: 175–176). Brazilian traders, based on the coast, had oil palm plantations as well. Domingo Martinez was said to own several (Ross, 1965: 81; 83).

Producing for the vital export market meant that the slaves' labor took on greater economic and political importance. Integration into the world capitalist market meant a dramatic increase in the degree of exploitation (Marx, 1954–1959: Vol. 1: 226) and a qualitative change in the nature of social control. Plantation slaves lived in villages (Forbes, 1851: Vol. 1: 115), socially isolated from Dahomean citizens. Their isolation and high numbers made opportunities for personal advancement or the advancement of their children through a process of gradual assimilation virtually impossible to achieve. Plantation slaves controlled neither their own person nor that of their descendants. The slave could be disposed of in a wager, through trade, by sale, or as punishment; the king could order imprisonment or death (Le Hérissé, 1911: 54). As *Danhomenou,* their children could not be sold, but they continued to live in the slave villages (Le Hérissé, 1911: 52) laboring for their parents' owner (Miers, 1975: 129). Except in the course of resistance, they did not own their own labor power; the fruit of their labor was appropriated without recompense. Assuming that all of the slaves' labor was not demanded by the king, a portion of the slaves' produce could be retained (Le Hérissé, 1911: 53). On the king's estates, slaves worked under the supervision of a royal official (Forbes, 1851: Vol. 1: 31), the *Sogon.* Merchants also retained persons to manage their estates. While there is not much evidence of class consciousness, the fear of a rebellion by Yoruba captives in 1855 (Law, 1977: 573) would suggest that class consciousness was at least nascent.

The European attitude toward slavery in Dahomey was ambiguous. Frederick Forbes, a British naval officer, visited Dahomey in hopes of convincing King Ghezo to cease participation in the transatlantic slave trade. Instead, he argued, captives should be retained and made to cultivate the soil (Forbes, 1851: Vol. 2: 185–193). This ambiguity continued into the early colonial period. Clearly, the French colonial powers did not want to risk disrupting production (Newbury, 1960: 54). In fact, they themselves made use of forced labor in order to increase production. The French established a number of *villages de liberté* beginning in 1887, obstensibly for the resettlement of homeless ex-slaves. These villages were used as labor camps by the local colonial administration. It was not until the 1905 shooting of a French official by a suspected slave trader that strong action was taken (Hopkins, 1973: 226–227). A decree was issued abolishing slavery, but even this did not affect persons already enslaved. New job opportunities and new avenues for social mobility arising out of the colonial economy probably were the major factors in effectively ending slavery (Crowder, 1968: 183–184).

There are at least two other studies (Stoeber, 1969: Augessy, 1970) which address the question of the place of slavery within the Dahomean social formation. Stoeber (1969) argues that, though slavery existed, a slave mode of production did not develop. He sees the rights which slaves had to private property and to a portion of their produce, as well as their gradual assimilation, as indications of feudal rather than slave relations. Aguessy (1970), on the other hand, maintains that a slave mode of production did exist. This mode, *l'esclavage semiservage,* coexisted and competed with other slave modes—*l'esclavage domestique* and *l'esclavage de traite,* as well as with peasant production—and never gained predominance. The society, then, cannot be conceptualized as a slave society. In my view, the Aguessy analysis seems to be the more accurate.

Coquery-Vidrovitch (1971; 1972: 51) argues that the transition from the slave trade to the palm oil trade did not pose a crisis for Dahomey because the state survived the transition. But what of the social formation as a whole? Coquery-Vidrovitch's claim that both trades involved the same privileged persons is contradicted by Ross (1965) and Aguessy (1970: 87–89), both of whom offer evidence of a drastic decline in the economic power of the Brazilian merchants despite their attempts to adjust to the new demands. Even her claim that the state survived needs to be reexamined in light of the fact that the transition precedes the French colonial occupation by only a few decades, and may in fact have been a contributing factor to French overrule.

The transition to oil palm production meant a realignment of Dahomean economic activity. Whereas the old export-destined commodity, slaves, had been procured from outside of the kingdom, the new commodity, palm oil, was produced within. Property relations vis-à-vis the land were also changing as land increasingly came to be claimed as private property. Plantation owners, interested in reaping the greatest possible profit, redeployed captives away from the transatlantic trade to the plantations in ever-increasing numbers. There, slaves were the sole labor force. Isolated from the free population and highly exploited, unlike slaves assigned to the lineages, plantation slaves remained unassimilated. While the tributary mode of production continued to dominate both lineage production and the slave mode of production, the slave mode of production became a major factor in the structuring of the Dahomean social formation, growing to absorb over one-third of the population by the beginning of the 20th century (Newbury, 1960: 57).[7]

NOTES

1. The provision ground was an area of land set aside by the plantation owner and used by the slave to grow foodstuffs. In some cases the slave was allowed to market the produce.

2. "Cults" were associated with the natural environment (water, land, etc.) and observed by the original inhabitants of the area.

3. Royal blood was traced through both the male and female lines.

4. I refer in this instance to the ancestor "cult."

5. Despite its name, the "Annual Customs" appears to have taken place only after the Dahomean army returned victorious from its wars of conquest and/or slave raids and following the coronation of a new king.

6. The nature and extent of the crisis is subject to debate and will be returned to later in the essay.

7. See Kea (1979) and Mason (in this volume) for their discussion of the impact of slavery and the slave/servile mode of production on the Gold Coast and the Bida State, respectively.

REFERENCES

AGUESSY, H. (1970) "Le Dan-Home du XIXe siècle était-il une société esclavagiste?" Revue Française d'études Politiques Africaines 50: 71–91.

AKINJOGBIN, I. (1967) Dahomey and its neighbors. Cambridge, England: Cambridge University Press.

BOSERUP, E. (1970) Woman's role in economic development. New York: St. Martin's Press.

COOPER, F. (1977) Plantation slavery on the east coast of Africa. New Haven, CT: Yale University Press.

COQUERY-VIDROVITCH, C. (1971) "De la traite des esclaves à l'exportation de l'huile de palme et de palmistes au Dahomey: XIXe siècle," pp. 107–123 in C. Meillassoux (ed.) The development of indigenous trade and markets in West Africa. Oxford, England: Oxford University Press.

———— (1972) "Research on an African mode of production," pp. 33–51 in M. Klein and G. Johnson (eds.) Perspectives on the African past. Boston: Little, Brown.

———— (1976) "The political economy of the African peasantry and modes of production," pp. 90–111 in P. Gutkind and I. Wallerstein (eds.) The political economy of contemporary Africa. Beverly Hills, CA: Sage.

CROWDER, M. (1968) West Africa under colonial rule. London: Hutchinson.

DALZEL, A. (1793) The history of Dahomey. London: G. & W. Nicol.

DUPRE, G. and REY, P.-P. (1973) "Reflections on the pertinence of a theory of exchange." Economy and Society 11(2): 131–163.

ENGELS, F. (1939) Anti-Duhring. New York: International Publishers.

———— (1970) The origins of the family, private property and the state. New York: International Publishers.

FAGE, J. (1969) "Slavery and the slave trade in the context of West African history." Journal of African History 10: 393–404.

FORBES, F. (1851) Dahomey and the Dahomans (2 vols.). London: Longman.

FREEMAN, T. (1844) Journal of various visits to the kingdoms of Ashanti, Aku and Dahomi in Western Africa. London: John Mason.

GOODY, J. (1976) Production and reproduction. Cambridge, England: Cambridge University Press.

GOUGH, I. (1972) "Marx's theory of productive and unproductive labour." New Left Review 76: 47–71.

MARX, K. (1954–1959) Capital (3 vols.). Moscow: Progress Publishers.

MEILLASSOUX, C. [ed.] (1971) The development of indigenous trade and markets in West Africa. Oxford, England: Oxford University Press.

———— [ed.] (1975) L'esclavage en Afrique précoloniale. Paris: Maspero.

MERCIER, P. (1954) "The Fon of Dahomey," pp. 210–234 in D. Forde (ed.) African worlds. Oxford, England: Oxford University Press.

MIERS, S. (1975) Britain and the ending of the slave trade. New York: Africana Publishing Company.

———— and KOPYTOFF, I. [eds.] (1977) Slavery in Africa. Madison: University of Wisconsin Press.

NEWBURY, C. (1960) "An early enquiry into slavery and captivity in Dahomey." Zaire 14: 53–67.

NORRIS, R. (1789) Memoirs of the reign of Bossa Ahádee. London: W. Lowndes.

PADGUG, R. (1976) "Problems in the theory of slavery and slave society." Science and Society 40: 3–27.

GRACE, J. (1975) Domestic slavery in West Africa. New York: Harper & Row.

HERSKOVITS, M. and HERSKOVITS, F. (1933) "A footnote to the history of Negro slavery." Opportunity 11(6): 178–181.

HINDESS, B. and HIRST, P. (1975) Pre-capitalist modes of production. London: Routledge and Kegan Paul.

HOPKINS, A. (1973) An economic history of West Africa. New York: Columbia University Press.

HURSTON, Z. (1927) "Cudjo's own story of the last African slaver." Journal of Negro History 12: 648–663.

KEA, R. A. (1979) "Land, overlords, and cultivators in the seventeenth century Gold Coast. (unpublished)

LAW, R. (1977) "Royal monopoly and private enterprise in the Atlantic trade: The case of Dahomey." Journal of African History 18: 555–577.

LE HERISSE, A. (1911) L'ancien royaume du Dahomey. Paris: Larose.

LEACOCK, E. [ed.] (1970) The origin of the family, private property and the state. New York: International Publishers.

M'LEOD, J. (1820) A voyage to Africa. London: John Murray.

POLANYI, K. (1966) Dahomey and the slave trade. Seattle: University of Washington Press.

POULANTZAS, N. (1975) Political power and social classes. London: New Left Books.

RODNEY, W. (1966) "African slavery and other forms of social oppression on the Upper Guinea Coast in the context of the Atlantic slave trade." Journal of African History 7: 431–443.

RONEN, D. (1971) "On the African role in the trans-Atlantic slave trade in Dahomey." Cahiers d'études Africaines 41: 5–13.

ROSS, D. (1965) "The career of Domingo Martinez in the Bight of Benin, 1833–64." Journal of African History 6: 79–90.

RYAN, T. (1975) "The economics of human sacrifice." African Economic History Review 2(20): 1–9.

SNELGRAVE, W. (1734). A new account of some parts of Guinea and the slave trade. London: James, John and Paul Knapton.

STOEBER, H. (1969) "Der europaïsche sklavenhandel und die feudale produktionsweise an der westafrikanishen sklavenküeste." Ethnographisch—Archaolöegische Zeitschrift (Berlin) 10: 487–500.

TERRAY, E. (1975) "Classes and class consciousness in the African kingdom of Gyaman," pp. 85–135 in M. Bloch (ed.) Marxist analyses and social anthropology. London: Malaby.

WEBSTER, J. and BOAHEN, A. (1967) History of West Africa. New York: Praeger.

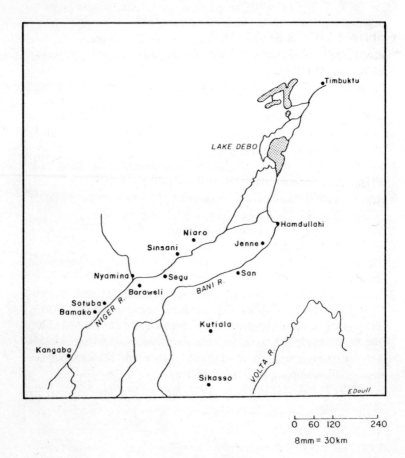

Middle Niger Valley

7

FISHING FOR THE STATE: THE POLITICAL ECONOMY OF THE MIDDLE NIGER VALLEY

RICHARD ROBERTS
Stanford University

Despite their diverse origins, the fishermen of the Middle part of the Niger River, from Bamako to Ansongo, were all more or less subordinated to the dominant states in the region during the 18th and 19th centuries. The exact relationships of dependence are unclear, in part as a consequence of Shehu Ahmadu of Masina's attempts to rewrite the history of this relationship (Levtzion, 1971). But Shehu Ahmadu's early 19th-century revisions of the *Tarikh el-Fettach,* which attempt to highlight the servile nature of Niger fishermen, only underline the important role fishermen played in the structure and history of the states in this region.

This article explores the relationship of one such group of fishermen, the Somono, to the dominant states in the Middle Niger

Author's Note: I wish to thank both the Canada Council for a Graduate Fellowship which made research in Mali, Senegal, and France possible and the Izaak Walton Killam Trust for a postdoctoral fellowship which gave me the opportunity to develop some of my ideas. Dalhousie University's Research Development Fund provided a small grant to defray the costs of interlibrary loans.

valley over a period of 200 years. The earliest relationship between the Somono and the Segu Bambara state (c.1712–1861) resembled a "social contract" involving a high degree of volition. This volition declined as the Somono came to play an increasingly important role in the structure of the Segu state. The Somono were eventually inserted into the actual process of reproducing the form and economic expression of the state. The state in turn recognized the Somono's importance and fostered them through special recruitment and privilege. Once established, the relationship between the Somono and the state underwent considerable change during the course of the 19th century as the pagan Bambara state was conquered by the Futanké under al-Hajj Umar in 1861 and once again when Segu was conquered by the French in 1890.

Because of Shehu Ahmadu's revisions of the *Tarikh el-Fettach*, the single best source for the social and economic history of the medieval empires is suspect. Parts of the *Tarikh el-Fettach* (Kati, 1964) remain intact and the two other chronicles of the era, the *Tarikh es-Soudan* (Es Sa'di, 1900) and the *Tedzkiret en-Nisiran* (Anon., 1966), provide some data for a socioeconomic reconstruction of the period. Monteil, (1927), Cissoko (1968, 1975), de Sardan (1975), Tymowski (1967, 1970), Niané (1975), and others have made considerable use of these sources, but problems of reconstructing the nature of the social relationships remain. Oral traditions, especially with the appearance of Delafosse's (1912) work, often suffer from the problem of literary feedback (interview, Mamby Sidibé). Moreover, fishing and boating resemble the occupational specialization of the strictly endogamous castes widespread throughout the larger Malinké cultural zone (N'Diaye, 1970; Vaughan, 1970). This may have caused confusion about the degree of subordination and servility involved in the relationship between fishermen and the state.[1] Thus, it may be impossible to establish a historically valid account of this relationship, especially for the medieval period.

Such may not be the case for a history of the Somono, however. Both oral tradition and written descriptions exist. And the Somono have not been the object of a serious historical enquiry, which means surviving oral traditions do not seem to suffer from literary distortions.

The Somono and the Bozo form the major fishing groups of the Middle Niger region. The largest concentration of Bozo is in the interior delta and lacustrine region of the Niger (Daget, 1949, 1956; Malzy, 1946; Gallais, 1958, 1967). Most Somono are located in the heartland of the Middle Niger valley, up- and downstream from Segu. Small colonies of other fishers, such as the Sorko, are to be found working Lake Debo and along the Bani (Gallais, 1967). However, the Sorko are primarily associated with the Niger bend (Ligers, 1966), where they formed an important component of the Songhay state.

The term *Somono* means fisherman or, more exactly, boatman.[2] As such it is an expression of an occupation, whereas Bozo refers to an ethnic group. The Bozo claim to have been the earliest inhabitants of the river and they have maintained their own language, cosmology, and religious practices. In contrast, the Somono form a professional group composed of many ethnically different elements including Soninké, Malinke, Bambara, Bobo, Minianka, and Bozo. All Somono speak Bambara and they were progressively Islamicized during the course of the 18th and 19th centuries.

There is no question that the Bozo were among the boatmen of ancient Mali. They provided a tax in fish and transport services to the local governors at Ja, Kokri, and Kilenze (Daget, 1956: 51; Perron, 1930). However, the small Bozo population was dispersed over large distances and their occasional resistance to authority (Ligers, 1966: IV, xii; Daget, 1949: 31; Daget, 1956: 74) may have prevented their full integration into the structure of the state. Because the river facilitated internal communication, provided a relatively inexpensive means of commercial transport, and provided an abundant source of nutrition, the successive states of the Middle Niger region may have encouraged the development of an additional group of fishermen to augment the scale and frequency of these services (interview, B. & M. Koné; Tymowski, 1970). This was especially pressing for the Segu Bambara state located at the southern extremity of Bozo dispersion. It is quite possible that in fostering the expansion of a group of fishermen, the Segu state was drawing upon an existing tradition of fishermen-state relationships which certainly predated the 19th-century revisions of the *Tarikh el-Fettach*.

The traditions of the Somono, especially those recorded by successive Europeans during the course of the middle- and late-19th and early-20th centuries (Mage, 1868; Soleillet, 1887; Delafosse, 1912; Monteil, 1924), stress the circumstances surrounding the insertion of the Somono into the productive activities of the state by means of a "social contract." The term *social contract* may be misleading because is implies a judicial relationship made between equals. The relationship between the Somono and the state was much more than this. While the Somono were clearly subordinated to the state, they retained a high degree of independence in the forms of their production and in their social identity. More important, however, the Somono and the state (represented in the person of the *faama* [Bambara: ruler, king] and his critical position in the state's military organization) participated in the reproduction of each other's social forms.[3] I shall explore the interstices of social reproduction in the course of the following discussions on the Somono and the political economy of the Middle Niger valley.

The Somono and the Bambara, c.1712–1861

Traditions concerning the rise of the Segu Bambara state are fairly consistent, although the accounts differ on chronology (Monteil, 1924; Delafosse, 1912; Tauxier, 1942; Bîme, 1952; Ward, 1976). Until the late 17th century, the Middle Niger valley experienced some form of imperial rule, first under ancient Ghana and then Mali. Effective Songhay rule never permeated the region and the Arma do not appear to have established political authority there. Rather, expanding demand for slaves both in Africa and across the Atlantic encouraged a transformation in the political and economic forms of state organization in the region (Curtin, 1969, 1975; Roberts, 1980a).

At the beginning of the 18th century, Mamari Kulubali led his bachelor's age set (Bambara: *ton,* association) through a social revolution against traditional Bambara society. Traditional Bambara society was based on an annual grain agricultural cycle which provided the material basis for gerontocratic rule (Meillassoux, 1960; Lewis, 1979). The society reproduced itself generation after generation as the cadets became elders with their own cadets to exploit. Mamari's social revolution consisted in removing the bachelor's association from the generational structure of Bambara society and establishing it as an independent social and political unit. This new unit was able to reproduce its form through the recruitment of new members (*tonjonw,* Bambara: slaves of the association), primarily through warfare and enslavement, many of whom were already young men. Through these actions Mamari Kulubali established the nucleus of a new state whose very structure and cohesion depended upon continued predation (Bazin, 1975; Roberts, 1980a).

Predation became both the primary expression of the state and the means through which the state dominated the social formation[4] of the Middle Niger valley. The Bambara distinguished three kinds of military operations based on the degree of state involvement. *Kélé* was the official military campaign staged during the dry season and was the most productive form of enslavement because the full weight of the state and its support services were brought to bear. A second form of warfare was *soboli,* conducted by a mounted cavalry troop of around 40 warriors. Cavalry raids could be mounted in any season and it usually had the approval of the king. Finally, *jado* was simple brigandage. Brigandage was usually undertaken by a band of 10 to 20 warriors, although individuals could do so as well. Moreover, brigandage was strictly clandestine because it promoted disorder within the state (Meillassoux, 1964; Bazin, 1975; Curtin, 1975; interview, I. Fané).

The division of the booty and the incidence of these forms of warfare are central to an understanding of the Segu Bambara political economy. Depending on the organization of production, the various techniques of warfare produced different kinds of slaves.[5] Two kinds of slaves were produced: "big slaves," who were not marketable, and "black slaves," who were marketable. In the annual campaign and the cavalry raid, one-half to two-thirds of the booty belonged to the king. The remainder was distributed among the warriors. The king also redistributed some of his slaves to the warriors and praise singers. Since brigandage was juridically outside the law, all slaves thus captured were inherently marketable and retained by the warriors. Unless they wanted to risk being caught with the evidence of their illegal enslavement, warriors were obliged to sell their slaves quickly and for whatever price they received.

Whatever the king retained, after the division of the booty and redistribution, was divided into "big" and "black" slave categories (Bazin, 1975). "Big" slaves were reinserted into the apparatus of the state, which at once permitted the state to conduct wars and also to conduct them on an enlarged scale. A portion of the "big" slaves was designated as recruits to the elite guard; these were usually boys who were too small to remember their previous lives and who would owe their complete allegiance to the king. Another portion was used to replace the ranks of the warriors; a third portion was sent to work on the state fields (*forabajonw*, Bambara: slaves of the big field). Produce from these fields and from the state herds tended by the *forabafula* (Bambara: Fulbe slaves of the state) supplied the capital and the active army with food. Captured ironworkers were attached to the state in order to repair firearms and make lead balls. A final portion was given to the Somono, the Segu fishermen.

Within the militarized Segu state, the relationship between the Somono and the state was based upon the reproduction of productive relations. In 1864 Mage recorded the basis of this "social contract":

The Somono are of Soninké origin. They maintain they fell as slaves into the hands of the king of Segou, who proposed to them to make canoes and fish for him. They succeeded very well and the king gave them slaves to teach their trade. Thus, after each expedition, he gave them a portion of his share of slaves. The Somono expanded along the littoral, forming in each village a type of corporation, which lives apart, works and transports [goods and people] by canoes, of which they have a monopoly, and which provides them with many cowries, especially on market days [Mage, 1868: 373–374].

In return for a steady stream of new recruits and the exclusive right to navigate and fish the river, the Somono paid a special tax in cowries and fish; provided ferry service and canoe service for the movement of information, material, and troops; manufactured and carried gunpowder into the battle; and repaired and built the walls of the king's palace and other fortifications in the state. Because of the importance of these services, the Somono had the special protection of the king and were never enslaved (Mage, 1868: 374; Delafosse, 1912: II, 285; Soleillet, 1887: 308; Bîme, 1952: 21; interviews, C. Kulubali, B. Kamité, K. Koné, II; M. &. B. Koné). Thus, the state sponsored the expansion of a group of fishermen who in turn provided goods and services crucial to the continued ability of the state to make war.

Through the operation of the "social contract," the state inserted itself in the reproduction of the Somono mode of production. This occurred in two ways: (1) through renewal of the social relations of production and (2) through the extraction of a portion of the social product. By providing a steady stream of new recruits, the state encouraged both an expansion of production and a change in the technical capacity to fish. Somono fishing was based on a mixed use of small and large nets. Individuals fished with small nets from shore or from a canoe. Large nets, some stretching as far as 300 meters or more, were cooperative ventures. While the "social contract" with the Segu state gave the Somono the exclusive right to fish the river (as opposed to the Bozo, who only fish the small tributaries, backwaters, and marshes), their capacity to do so depended upon the manpower under their control. The large nets which spanned the greater part of the river were potentially more productive than either fishing with small nets or fishing the streams and ponds; its use was dependent upon an organizational ability and adequate labor power. The Somono had this capacity only because the state involved itself directly in the production process.

But the Segu state's control over the river was a gradual process. Somono expanded up and down the river from Segu, founding settlements or distinct quarters in already established villages (Soleillet, 1887: 308; Jaime, 1894: 44–45). Somono settlements on the right bank of the river appeared with a curious regularity: they were often 15 kilometers apart (Gallais, 1967: I, 108; interview, B. &. M. Koné). The frequency of settlement reveals a discipline imposed from above. But it also points to one of the important roles the Somono played within the Segu state: communication. The Somono thus formed a series of relay stations which facilitated the movement of information and passengers. In 1863 Mage and his European companion, Dr. Quinton, were taken by canoe to Segu from Nyamina, an important port on the main western trade route:

> Each of our canoes received a skipper and two crew at Yamina; besides, at each village one gets a crew which thus relays from station to station. This operation takes a certain loss of time, especially at night, when one must wake the boatmen. This service, however poor it may be, had been, I was told, organized by El Hadj [Umar] for his needs. This was the beginning of order which I could not but applaud. But I later learnt that this, as all else, the conquerors took from the vanquished, and that this service had existed since the creation of the Somonos [Mage, 1868: 202–203].

Despite fundamental changes in the region's political economy, as I shall explain below, the Somono relay network was in operation 15 years later (Soleillet, 1887: 310–312).

The relay system described by the midcentury travelers was not instituted fully formed. At the beginning of the 19th century the relay system did not operate as smoothly nor were the Somono so well ensconced all along the river. During Park's second visit in

1805, a canoe owner near Segu refused to comply with a requisition of his canoe:

> Bookari [Monzon's agent] sent four of the Somonies over to the
> town on the opposite side of the river to . . . requisition a canoe for
> carrying a part of our baggage. The people refused to give the
> canoe and sent the Somonies back without it. Bookari went imme-
> diately with all the Somonies; and having cut the owner of the
> canoe across the forehead with his sword and broke his brother's
> head with a canoe paddle, he seized one of his sons and brought him
> away as a slave with the canoe [Park, 1815: 264].

Park's remarks indicate that at the beginning of the century, the
Somono had not yet achieved hegemony over the river. They also
indicate the incomplete submission of the population to the Segu
Bambara state.[6]

As a group the Somono did not form a homogeneous unit. Many
were recruited as part of the king's share of captured slaves.
Others, such as the Bozo of Banankoro, were part of a deported
community resettled close to the Segu heartland during the reign of
Da Monzon (reigned, 1808–1827; Gallais, 1967: II, 430; interview, C. Dembélé). Others became Somono by individually
choosing to become fishermen and thereby accepting submission
to Somono chiefs and the state (Monteil, 1924: 32; Ortoli, 1936:
169). Somono social boundaries were therefore permeable. Their
identity revolved around an occupation, a political relationship
and, gradually throughout the 18th and 19th centuries, the development of an Islamic and pacific tradition. This stood in contrast to
the aristocratic and pagan warrior tradition of the Bambara and the
militant Islam of the Umar's *talibés* (Arabic: *talib;* students, followers).

Oral traditions maintain that the Somono were Muslims, which
set them apart from both the slave warriors and from the Bozo. But
the original Muslim segment of the Somono was the Djiré family
of Segu. The Djiré were probably of Maraka (Soninké) origin and
were the imams of Segu and the marabouts of the Segu kings.
Although they were considered Somono, they did not fish (inter-

views: K. Kané I; B. Kamité, B. & M. Koné; Perignon, ASAOF 1G248, 1900). In the early 19th century the Somono still consumed beer (Park, 1815: 264). Yet by the 1860s the Somono would eat no meat which had not been ritually slaughtered (Mage, 1868: 206). This change lends support to the contention that the Somono were forcefully converted to Islam by the Umarians after their conquest of Segu in 1861 (Ortoli, 1936: 169).

Somono control over the river may have occurred only during the reign of the Ngolossi. The "social contract" with the Somono was first established during the Kulubali era. Under the Kulubalis (reigned c. 1712–1757) the peculiar character of the state was established; this period also witnessed the Segu state's first expansionist phase. Yet Mamari Kulubali's death precipitated a long struggle for succession and power between Mamari's descendants and the warrior aristocracy (Monteil, 1924; Tauxier, 1942). During this time the state's control over outlying areas was severely weakened. Under Ngolo Jara (reigned, 1766–1790) the Segu state was once again expansionary. Both Ngolo and his successor Monzon introduced reforms which gave greater stability to the administrative structure. Ngolo Jara also established a special relationship with the Somono, with the Thiero clan in particular, whom he made chiefs of the Somono (interview: I. Fané; Monteil, 1924: 49). In so doing, Ngolo replaced the Dembélé who apparently formed the original Somono core and who were the Somono chiefs under Mamari Kulubali.[7]

The Somono chieftaincy had both judicial and material prerogatives. First, the Somono chief adjudicated cases between Somono defendants; the king reserved the right to decide cases between clans. Second, the Somono chief was instrumental in the division of new recruits given by the king, the distribution of whom could influence the numerical and political viability of the various Somono clans. Third, the Somono chief opened the *bassama*, the large collective fishing during the low water period. He collected a handsome share of the social product or the entire catch of the first day (interviews, K. Kané I; B. & M. Koné, Deherme, 1908: 289). And fourth, the Somono chief assembled the king's share of the revenue derived from ferrying, which was considerable. In 1796 Park described this operation:

> [The king of Segu] employs a great many slaves in carrying people over the river, and the money thus received (although the fare is only 10 shells for each individual) furnishes a considerable revenue for the king in the course of a year [Park, 1807: 293].

A century later the costs of passage across the river had risen and these costs were assessed on the value of the goods involved:

simple passage	80K (K=cowrie)
passenger with a bar of salt	200K
passenger with a basket of kola	400K
donkey without a load	160K
donkey with a load	600K
horse without a load	1200K
pack oxen without a load	800K
pack oxen with a load	100[0]K
up to 100 head of sheep	80K
over 100 head of sheep	one third off
cattle	160–200K
over 10 donkeys of horses, loaded or unloaded	one third off

(Source: Correnson, ASAOF 1G 336, 1910).

There are a number of variations for the division of the ferrying revenues. A standard practice divided these into three equal shares: one for the king, or the village chief; one for the Somono chief; and one for the ferrymen (Binger, 1892: I, 12–13). Another variant divided the revenue into two equal shares: one for the king or chief and the second divided equally between the Somono chief and the ferrymen (Robin, AM 1D 186, 1909). Yet another variant gave the entire proceeds of market day ferrying to the sailors (Anon., AM 1E 20, n.d.).

Although the establishment of Somono hegemony over the river was gradual, exclusive control over the riverine economy had important implications for the social formation established at

Segu. First, it indicates the effects political economy had on the development of an integrated regional market and the development of a social division of labor. Second, it indicates the role of the state in providing cohesion to the social formation at the same time as it structured overlapping modes of production in domination.

Predation was the economic expression of the state and booty was the social product. The division of booty into shares for warriors and the king and between marketable and nonmarketable categories influenced the commercial environment of Segu. A steady stream of marketable slaves encouraged the expansion of Maraka long-distance trade and the development of an important plantation sector in and around Maraka cities. The slaves who were retained in Maraka society came to outnumber freemen by two or three to one (Roberts and Klein, 1980). These slaves produced surplus grain and cotton cloth which were sold to the Moors of the Sahara, shipped down the Niger to Timbuktu, or carried southward to the kola-producing regions (Roberts, 1980b; Lovejoy, forthcoming).

Nonmarketable slaves formed important agricultural communities around Segu which produced food for the royal court and for the army. Captured Fulbé became herders for the state's occasionally large herds, much of which were derived from capture. They also provided a steady stream of meat. Other "big" slaves were inserted into the ranks of the Somono who provided fish for the state and provided transport and communication services. Bambara agriculturalists who had voluntarily subordinated themselves to the state provided tribute in the form of an annual tax payable in cowries and grain. Captured villages were often deported to other regions where they provided the annual tax as well as special supplementary supplies of food to neighboring garrisons. Thus, the social formation established by the Segu state contained social groups articulating different modes of production.[8]

The cohesion of the social formation was determined on two levels: first, by the state which involved itself in either the productive process itself (*tonjonw, forabajonw, forabafula,* Somono,

Maraka) or in the distribution of the social product (Bambara farmers) and, second, through the growth of specialized producers servicing the same market and integrated at the level of exchange. The state encouraged specialized production and market development by providing internal security, which permitted safe movement of goods and the opportunity to expand production, adjudicated conflicts between merchants and local chiefs (often in favor of the former), and supplied a market police to control irregularities and especially to watch over malpractices in the gold trade (Carrère and Holle, 1855: 186–187). Commerce suffered during droughts and periods of internecine conflict (Cissoko, 1968). When conditions were propitious, however, Bambara farmers brought grain as well as condiments and handicrafts to the market; Somono brought fresh and dried fish, tobacco, and rope products which they exchanged for the grain and cotton they did not produce; the Fulbé, both free and *forabafula,* exchanged livestock and milk for grain and fish; and the Maraka exchanged locally produced cloth as well as an assortment of goods they imported, including desert salt, kola, and luxury goods from the Maghreb and Europe. The circulation of goods from these specialized producers on both sides of the Niger was facilitated through the regularized ferry services provided by the Somono. Moreover, the Segu state was in the cowrie zone. Cowries, gold, and slaves formed standard currency units (Johnson, 1970; Lovejoy, 1974).

THE SOMONO AND THE UMARIANS, 1861–1890

To what extent was the relationship between the Segu state and the Somono, based as it was on the organization and capacity to produce, reproduced within the Umarian state? Evidence from Mage, who was held under house arrest in Segu during the first few years following the conquest of Segu, suggests that the basis of the relationship was altered. The Futanké required the Somono to provide the same services, but changed the nature of their involvement in the production process of the Somono:

> The Somono have the same obligations but not the same resources.
> They no longer receive slaves after the expeditions, in which they
> carry the powder and the replacement firearms on their heads. But,
> in contrast, when a Futanké prince has the need to "eat" a slave, in
> order to get the retail value, to pay debts to an ironworker or
> leatherworker, he goes to a wealthy Somono, and takes a slave
> whom he wants, and if the master complains or does not want to
> give the slave, he is beaten [Mage, 1868: 374].

Changes in the nature of the Somono-state relationship under the
Umarians reflected the general decline in the capacity of the new
state to reconstitute the social formation established under the
Bambara.

The Umarians conquered Segu in 1861 following their victorious sweep through Kaarta, Beledugu, and the western shore of the
Niger. But their conquest was incomplete; they never pacified the
region and this had important implications for the form of the state
and the economy (Roberts, 1980a). Their inability to reestablish
internal security undermined economic specialization and
threatened the very nature of the social formation itself. In place of
the established zones of commercial activity in the Middle Niger
valley, with linkages to the local economy, the Umarians encouraged a westward (and "homeward") orientation. From Futa
Toro and Futanké bases in western Kaarta came new recruits,
firearms, munitions, and horses. These funneled through Nioro
and onto the western corridor to Nyamina and Segu (Kanya-
Forstner, 1969: 77–79; Oloruntimehin, 1972: 232). Moreover, the
Umarians used the river as a political and military instrument:
They prohibited the movement of goods downstream from Mopti
and upstream from Nyamina, in part to control the circulation of
weapons and goods to their enemies and in part to starve Timbuktu
into submission (Soleillet, 1887: 273, 277, 310; Jaime, 1899:
159). These restrictions on the circulation of goods and on the
transportation industry had severe repercussions for the Somono
and for the cohesion of the social formation.

Between 1863 and 1865 the Maraka of the important commercial towns of Sinsani and Nyamina revolted against the Umarians.

The Maraka had complained of excessively heavy taxation and of arbitrary appropriation of trade goods and surpluses (Bellat, ASAOF 1 G184, 1893; Mage, 1868: 275). The Maraka were also feeling the consequences of the dislocation of the regional economy. Endemic insecurity interfered with the desertside trade and interrupted the free movement of goods to the kola regions of the south. The revolt of the Maraka was successful, but resulted in the collapse of the flourishing commercial cities of the region. The revolt also deprived the Umarian state of the substantial taxes the Maraka had traditionally paid the Bambara.

Bambara farmers seem to have responded to the new political economy by reducing the acreage planted and by storing their cereal surpluses far out into the bush. Gallieni noted in 1881 that the Bambara feared Futanké raids in which everything of value including small livestock and grain stores was confiscated (Gallieni, 1885). The Futanké were also suffering the consequences of their incomplete conquest and the dislocation of the regional economy. Food soared to five times the normal price in Segu (Mage, ASAOF, 1G 32, 1865). Nor were the decisive military successes of the earlier years repeated. Large campaigns were singularly unsuccessful; the *talibés* began embarking on uncontrolled raids. They took whatever they could find and hid a part of their booty in order to avoid sharing it with Ahmadu Sheku. Ahmadu's reduced capacity to redistribute wealth further alienated the *talibés,* especially as economic conditions declined.

The Umarians, considering themselves conquerors, but dismayed at the lack of material benefits, began to coerce the local population. The Somono were a natural prey: Because of their control over the riverine economy with its access to fish, transport, and ferrying revenue, they had good nutrition and a fairly good income. Mage noted that the Somono were "in general very rich . . . . The Somono lived better than the *talibés,* meat and fish were ordinary parts of their diets" (Mage, 1868: 373–374; 377). In addition to the weekly household tax of 20 cowries payable each Friday, the Somono were victims of individual *talibé* predations (interview: B. & M. Koné):

When a *talibé* arrived at a village, he deposited his horse in one household [to be fed and cared for], his saddle in another, and his bridle in yet another. One could not wear elegant or richly embroidered clothes; if one did, a *talibé* would simply take it and it became his [interviews: B. & M. Koné; K. Kané, I].

In October 1864, during the Maraka revolts, Ahmadu began to fear a rebellion of the Somono. "He deprived them of their canoes and their firearms; thereby depriving them of their means to escape and also their principal means of existence; thereafter they could only fish from dry land" (Mage, 1868: 373). It is not clear how successful Ahmadu's prohibitions were, because the Somono were again ferrying troops and supplies in mid-1865 (Mage, 1868: 513). Ahmadu may have had to rescind this order precisely because the Somono were so crucial to the state. However, the speed with which the Somono were so crucial to the state. However, the speed with which the Somono abandoned the Futanké for the French in 1890 may indicate how deep their resentments were. At Mopti, Tijani organized a militarized flotilla, which may well have reflected his continued need to have command over the river, as well as the possible reluctance of the Somono to provide this function (Jaime, 1894: 156; 159).

The experience of the Somono during the Umarian period only exemplified how changes in political economy influenced social relations between groups and the very cohesion of the social formation. The new state continued to require the services of the Somono, but deprived them of the productive capacity to fulfill these functions. Moreover, the new state changed the nature of the environment in which these functions were performed. The inability of the Umarians to reconstitute the basis of the social formation in turn influenced the stability and expansion of the state itself.

THE SOMONO AND THE FRENCH, 1883–1905

French conquest of the Middle Niger valley was gradual and the earliest form of the colonial state differed little from its Bambara and Futanké predecessors. The Somono initially benefited from the trader-based economy encouraged by the French (Suret-Canale, 1971) through their control over the riverine economy and especially over transport. By 1905, however, the colonial state and the peculiar political economy it expressed had fundamentally transformed the established patterns of domination.

The French arrived in Bamako in 1883 only to discover the precarious nature of their expansion. Between 1879 and 1883 the French advanced rapidly from the upper Senegal to the Niger establishing a series of forts along the way. Supply of food, material, and communication was thinly spread and even the intrepid Colonel Desbordes acknowledged the need to consolidate their position before further expansion (Kanya-Forstner, 1969: 96). Nevertheless, the French in Bamako were concerned to justify their presence on the Niger through diplomatic and commercial advances (Ward, 1976). They proceeded on two fronts: first, they formed alliances with anti-Futanké Bambara of the left bank and, second, they wanted to show their allies and economic benefits of French rule by encouraging economic activity in Bamako and by freeing the river from political control and restrictions. In 1885 the French launched the first of several gunboat missions down the Niger. The Delanneau mission went as far as Nyamina; Caron went as far as Timbuktu in 1887; and Jaime again reached Timbuktu in 1889. These missions succeeded both in winning several friendship treaties and in demonstrating the French technological superiority. The steam-powered gunboats were a source of amazement and interest, although their constant need for fuel made them dependent upon local villages.

However, commercial activity in Bamako was to remain sluggish until the Umarian state was conquered. Bamako had been important in the regional economy for a brief period in the first half of the 19th century (Roberts, 1978). The demand for grain to supply the French colonial army with food encouraged an expansion of production which had important implications for the structure and performance of the city's economy (Roberts, 1980c). By 1893 Bamako was the entrepôt for the administration's grain trade and Bamako's share of the total trade of the region had greatly expanded.

Between 1884 and 1889 the French were concerned with consolidating their hold in Kayor, in Upper Senegal, and along the *route de ravitaillement* from Kayes to Bamako. By 1889 the French were ready to advance against the Tokolor empire (Kanya-Forstner, 1969; Oloruntimehin, 1972). In early 1890 the French left Bamako and advanced against Segu. As the French colonial army marched along the left bank, a large flotilla of Somono canoes moved parallel with it. At Nyamina, the local Somono chief placed all his canoes at Archinard's disposal and promised that the Segu Somono would do the same. Indeed, the Somono were crucial to the success of the campaign by transporting troops and material to the Segu side of the river and by bringing news that the Futanké had fled (Archinard, ASAOF 1 G105, 1889–1890).

The French recognized the important role the Somono played in the conquest and the importance of insuring that this relationship continued. In his discussions with Mari Jara, whom Archinard crowned king of Segu, he noted that:

> The Bozos and Somonos are by reason of their usual occupations placed under the exclusive authority of the French. If the *faama* has something to request of the Bozo or Somono, he can only do so through the intermediary of the French [resident] who may accept or reject the request [Archinard, ASAOF 15G 172, April 11, 1890].

The special place of the Somono in the new colonial state was reiterated in the treaty with the chief of Saro (Archinard et Ousman Taroaré, AM 1 E5 Sept. 20, 1890) and was probably reproduced in every major town along the river.

French policy indicates the importance they attached to controlling the river. Indeed, placing the Somono under the exclusive control of the French resident at Segu only thinly disguised the "puppet" nature of Mari Jara's reign. Moreover, direct control over the Somono brought with it some of the same benefits as the previous rulers exercised:

> In addition to the revenues due to the French government in exchange for the protection it accords the Bozo, they are charged, as

it is their practice, to provide for the palace of the [French] resident. The Somonos will [also] provide the small garrison under the title of taxes with fish and other foodstuffs. Rice, millet, fish, salt, milk, eggs, meat on the hoof, and karité are required by the resident in the form of taxes [Archinard, ASAOF, 15 G172, April 16, 1890].

In reformulating the "social contract" with the Somono, the French were reproducing the form if not the content of the relationship well-established by previous African regimes. This relationship entailed special privileges for the Somono. While the French commitment to free movement along the river could not tolerate an exclusive preserve for the Somono, the Somono were not treated on the same footing as other African people. William Ponty made this point explicit in a 1900 report, which explained the Somono "hostility" to certain French requisitions described by the Segu commandant:

The commandant would have been less surprised by this attitude if he had better understood the character and history of the confederation of fishermen. At all times, even under the rule of the blacks, these people have always shown a certain independence which the chiefs have permitted them. Never did the kings of the land draw upon their ranks to recruit slaves; they have always been free, and on their side have always provided precious services to the inhabitants in ferrying; in our time they have preserved certain privileges in exchange for certain duties; they are freed from paying the [head] tax, and in return they put at our disposition their flotilla when circumstances demand. . . . It is thus in our interests for justice to not treat them as other blacks [Ponty, ASAOF 2 G1-12, June 1900].

Since the Somono were under the exclusive authority of the French, they owed neither services nor taxes to local chiefs. This certainly aided Somono control over capital, which they invested in commercial and transport activities.

Once the river was liberated from the political restriction of Umarian rule, the Somono's control over the transport industry placed them in an excellent position to reap benefits from a revived commerce. The Bamako grain market put more cash into the hands of grain producers, which encouraged a larger movement of both imported European and local African goods in the region. Moreover, since grain has a low weight-to-volume ratio, inexpensive transport was crucial to the commercial viability of the grain market. It was six times more expensive to move one ton of grain overland than by water (Commandant, AM 1E 18, 1892). The Somono became entrepreneurs of transport, hiring themselves out, hiring their own crew, and often buying grain for speculation (interview: B. Kulubali; Commandant, AM 1R69, 1st quarter 1900).

Between 1893 and 1905 the Bamako grain market dominated the regional economy of the Middle Niger valley. It created both opportunities and strains (Roberts, 1980c; Roberts, forthcoming). In 1905 these opportunities and strains came to a head, when the slaves of Banamba began a massive exodus from their masters (Roberts & Klein, 1980). These freedmen provided abundant wage labor, which had never been in sufficient supply for the burgeoning colonial economy. Other freedmen cultivated grain and groundnuts, some collected wild rubber, and still others settled in the important market towns of the region and became weavers, artisans, boatmen, and fishermen. Somono privilege was gradually eroded by the demand for sailors to move increasing quantities of grain. Both the administration and private metropolitan commercial houses participated in the Bamako grain market and built barges to carry the grain to Bamako (Meniaud: 1912, I, 89). It is quite possible that increased demand for labor to man the barges and to move the grain broke the Somono monopoly over riverine transport. Without the corporate character of the Somono to control the supply of labor, wages, and canoes, established commercial practices may have weakened. In 1913, for example, the Somono of Nyamina complained that the Société Commercial de l'Ouest Africain recruited sailors but did not pay them (Commandant, AM 1 E 20, March 1913).

The French conquest revitalized the economy of the Middle Niger valley. The Somono initially benefited from the expanding economy because of their control over the riverine sector. But their exclusive privilege of navigation and fishing was not maintained. Nor did the French directly reproduce the Somono's capacity to produce, as had been their lot under the Segu Bambara. Although the French did establish a special judicial relationship with the Somono, this did not translate into changes in the scale of production. Indeed, because the French were committed, at least in principle, to encourage the free circulation of goods, the Somono monopoly over the river was eventually eroded. Moreover, the end of slavery in the region resulted in free labor which further eroded the Somono's exclusive control over fishing and navigation. Many Somono retained an important share of the riverine economy, but their success depended more on commercial acumen than on special economic privilege.

The relationship between the Somono and the state is indicative of a number of variables involved in the political economy of the Middle Niger valley. First, it expressed the nature of the social relations between groups (occupational groups and/or classes). The *faama* of the Segu Bambara state and the Somono related to each other on the level of production relations. The Umarian *talibés* extracted surplus from the Somono without encouraging the reproduction of relations of production. And the French fostered a special relationship with the Somono based on judicial privilege.

Second, the relationship between the Somono and the state expressed the character of the social formation. Under the Segu kings, the cohesiveness of the social formation was determined on two levels: (1) through the state's involvement in the various social and occupational groups' capacities to produce and (2) through the encouragement of a commercial environment favorable to the emergence of a social division of labor. Under the Futanké, the inability of the new state to establish internal security fundamentally altered the economy and society of the Middle Niger valley as it had existed. Moreover, the Futanké were more or less under constant seige, which severely constrained the spatial dimension and cohesiveness of the social formation. Under the French, the structure of the social formation underwent considerable change over the course of two and a half decades. At first the French were unable to stimulate commercial activities and thereby promote a social division of labor. Only with the expansion of the Bamako grain market did a certain cohesiveness to the social formation again appear, based on an interaction at the level of exchange.

And finally, the history of the Somono indicates a possible interpretation of the origin of specialized occupational groups and ethnic identities in West Africa. Barth (1967) suggested that social boundaries and ethnic identities were based, as least partially, on control over economic niches. The history of the Somono supports this assumption. But it also refines the historical causality involved: Occupational specialization was encouraged by the rise of states and by the specific influence states had on the nature of the social formation. More research on the relationship between the state, political economy, and social formation is needed before we can fully understand the levels and varieties of interaction between them. But it is certain from this study and from others in this anthology that further research along these lines promises fruitful results.

NOTES

1. The widespread fuzziness about the degree of subordination and servility of fishermen in the social structure of the Middle Niger region may reflect the occupational snobbery of farmers. Many agriculturalists, who may engage in occasional dry season fishing, view the occupation of fishing as degrading. Réné Caillé, writing in the late 1820s, reflected this general bias: "All the negro boatmen who navigate the river are slaves . . . . Noble men believe that they will degrade themselves in engaging in this activity" (Caillé, 1830: II, 245). Caillé's perceptions and those of other Europeans may have been insensitive to the subtleties of the relationship between fishermen and the state. While the Bozo rendered services to the state, and were therefore *aservis* (Malzy, 1946:

102), they conserved their original activities and their independence (Gallais, 1958: 122). The suspect *Tarikh el-Fettach* maintains a similar confusion: "The word Fanfa, which is fanafi in plural, designates a chief of slaves, but is also used to designate the skipper of a boat" (Kati, 1964: 179). Whatever confusion may have surrounded the Bozo, the relationship of the Somono to the state was much clearer, at least during the Segu Bambara period.

2. The derivation of the term *Somono* is not clear. It may be derived from the term *komo* (Bambara: to fish the marigot), which the Sorko use to mean *captifs de pêche* (Ligers, 1966: II, 121). Gallais (1967: I, 84) claims that the *komo* were the boatmen of ancient Mali, although I have not seen supporting evidence for this assumption.

The possible constituent elements of Somono are *so*, house; *mono* (syn. mana), flame; *somo*, one who is far from his family; *no*, place. There are two reasonable combinations. One is suggested by I. Fané, *soumaniké*, to push (a canoe), which becomes *soumanikéla*, one who pushes, a paddler. The other combination reflects a Muslim interpretation, suggested by K. Kané, I, *son*, to accept, and *mana* (syn. *mono*), the flame, and by extension, God; thus one who accepts God.

3. By social reproduction I understand the renewal on a continual basis of the means and forces of production in the same social forms. The concept is derived from Marx, *Capital*:

> Whatever the form of the process of production in a society, it must be a continuous process, must continue to go periodically through the same phases. A society can no more cease to produce than it can cease to consume. When viewed, therefore, as a connected whole, and as flowing on with incessant renewal, every social process of production is, at the same time, a process of reproduction [I, 531].

The term *social reproduction* has gained currency in anthropological and historical studies and offers one of the most sensitive analytical tools for a reconstruction of the dynamic of precapitalist societies. It does so by underlining a necessary historical dynamic in all societies: continuity. But at the same time it hints at the dialectic of continuity: the tensions of those who want stability and those who want change. Social reproduction may or may not be a conscious social process, but it is embedded in the very nexus of social relations of production and in the division of the social product (Meillassoux, 1960, 1972, 1977; Lewis, 1979; Roberts, 1980a).

4. Marx and Engels used the terms *social formation, society,* and *state* with relative carelessness (Legros et al., 1979). By social formation I understand the oftentimes complex temporal, spatial, and social entity associated with a state or a region which forms a more or less integrated unity. The nature of this unity will depend upon the ways in which it is structured by domination (Balibar, 1972). Hence, each social formation has a historical specificity although social formations may share common characteristics (determination, determinant mode of production, means of appropriation, class relationships, forms of social reproduction, etc.).

5. I use the expression "to produce slaves" in a qualified and explicit sense. Elsewhere (Roberts, 1980a) I have argued that the process of enslavement was crucial in transforming an individual's judicial status and thereby infusing him with a double identity: as a human being but also as a commodity. Without wanting to draw a metaphysical analogy, enslavement is similar to a hunter transforming game into meat and a lumberjack transforming trees into lumber. All these cases involve labor whose object is to transform a resource into utilizable use and exchange values. The items thus produced draw part of their value from the fact that labor is embodied in them as a consequence of work.

6. Following the death of Ngolo Jara in 1790, a succession dispute between half-brothers polarized the Segu state and resulted in a bloody civil war (Bambara: *fadé kélé,* war between brothers). During this period the effective limits of the Segu state declined dramatically.

Much of my reconstruction of the Somono during the early Segu Bambara period relies upon a single European source, Mungo Park. Although Mungo Park was an indomitable traveler and an often acute observer, what he witnessed during his fairly short sojourns along the Niger may indicate peculiar events and not patterns. I would like to thank David Robinson for this cautionary note.

7. There is some disagreement about this sequence in the traditions. See especially the interview with C. Kulubali and the genealogy of Thiero, cited in Perignon (ASAOF 1G 248, 1900).

8. This very schematic overview of the overlapping modes of production should only be used to illustrate the complexity of the social formation. These correlated modes of production only suggest the articulated dominance in each group:

tonjonw: petty commodity production (Marx, n.d.: I, 713)
Bambara farmers: lineage mode of production

Somono: lineage mode of production
Maraka: slave mode of production
forabajonw: slave mode of production
forabufula: slave mode of production.

This schematic illustration is unsatisfactory because it is static, it does not reveal the processes of social reproduction, and because it reifies modes-of-production analysis.

REFERENCES

Printed Material

ANON. (1966) Tedzkiret en-Nisian (O. Houdas, trans.) Paris: Maspero.
BALIBAR, E., (1970) "Basic concepts of historical materialism," pp. 199–308 in L. Althusser and E. Balibar (eds.) Reading Capital (Ben Brewster, trans.). London: New Left Books.
BARTH, F. (1969) Ethnic groups and social boundaries. Boston: Little, Brown.
BAZIN, J. (1975) "Guerre et servitude à Segou," pp. 135–181 in C. Meillassoux (ed.) Esclavage en Afrique précoloniale. Paris: Maspero.
BIME, A. (1952) Ségou, veille capitale. Angoulôme: H. Corignan and J. Landraud.
BINGER, L. (1892) Du Niger au Golf de Guinée par le pay du Kong et de Mossi, 1887–1889. Paris: Hachette.
CAILLE, R. (1830) Journal d'une voyage à Tombouctou et à Jenne. Paris: Imprimerie Royale.
CARRERE, F., and HOLLE, P. (1855) De la Sénégamie Française. Paris: Firmin Didot frères.
CISSOKO, M., (1968) "Famines et épidémies à Timbouctou et dans la boucle du Niger, XVI au XVIIIième siècle." Bulletin de l'Institut d'Afrique Fondamentale B, 20: 806–821.
_____ (1975) Tombouctou et l'empire Songhay. Dakar: Nouvelle Editions Africaines.
CURTIN, P. (1969) The Atlantic slave trade: A census. Madison: University of Wisconsin Press.
_____ (1975) Economic change in precolonial Africa: Senegambia in the era of the slave trade. Madison: University of Wisconsin Press.

DAGET, J. (1949) "La pêche dans le delta central du Niger." Journal de la Société des Africainists 29: 2–79.

_____ (1956) "La pêche à Diafarabé: étude monographique." Bulletin de l'Institut d'Afrique Française B, 28: 1–97.

DEHERME, G. (1980) L'Afrique Occidentale Française. Paris: Bloud.

DELAFOSSE, M. (1912, reprinted 1972) Haut Sénégal Niger. Paris: Maisonneuve et Larose.

ES SA'ADI, A. (1900) Tarikh es-Soudan (O. Houdas, trans.). Paris: Publications de l'Ecole des Langues Orientales Vivantes.

GALLAIS, J. (1958) "La vie saisonnière au sud du Lac Debo." Cahiers d'Outre Mer: Revue de Géographie de Bordeaux et de l'Atlantique 2: 117–141.

_____ (1967) Le Delta intérieur du Niger. Dakar: Institut Fondemental d'Afrique Noire.

GALLIENI, J. (1885) Mission d'exploration du Haut Niger: Voyage au Soudan Français: Haut Niger et pays de Ségou. Paris: Hachette.

JAIME, Lt. (1894) De Koulikoro à Tombouctou sur la canonnière, "Le Mage." Paris: Les Librairies Associes.

JOHNSON, M. (1970) "The cowrie currencies of West Africa: Parts I and II." Journal of African History 11: 17–49; 331–353.

KANYA-FORSTNER, A. (1969) The conquest of the Western Sudan: A study of French military imperialism. Cambridge, England: Cambridge University Press.

KATI, M. (1964) Tarikh el-Fettach (O. Houdas and M. Delafosse, trans.). Paris: Adrien Maisonneuve.

LEGROS, D., HUNDERFUND, D., and SHAPIRO, J. (1979) "Economic base, mode of production and social formation: A discussion of Marx's terminology." Dialectal Anthropology 4(3): 243–249.

LEVTZION, N. (1971) "A seventeenth century chronicle by Ibn Muktar: A critical study of the Tarikh el-Fettach." Bulletin of the School of Oriental and African Studies 34(3): 571–593.

LEWIS, J. (1979) "Descendants and crops: Two poles of production in a Malian peasant village." Ph.D. dissertation, Yale University.

LIGERS, Z. (1966) Les Sorko: Maitres du Niger. Paris: Librairies des Cinq Continents.

LOVEJOY, P. (1974) "Inter-regional monetary flows in the precolonial trade of Nigeria." Journal of African History 15(4): 563–585.

_____ (forthcoming) "A history of Kola in West Africa." Cahiers d'Etudes Africaines.

MAGE, M. (1868) Voyage dans le Soudan Occidental. Paris: Hachette.

MALZY, P. (1946) "Les Bozos du Niger et leurs modes de pêche." Bulletin de l'Institut Française d'Afrique Noire 8: 100–132.

MARX, K. (n.d.) Capital. Moscow: Progress Publishers.

MEILLASSOUX, C. (1960) "Essai d'interpretation du phénomène économique dans les sociétés d'autosubsistence." Cahiers d'Etudes Africaines 4: 38–67.

——— (1964) "Historie et institutions du *kafo* de Bamako d'après la tradition des Niaré." Cahiers d'Etudes Africaines 14: 186–227.

——— (1972) "From production to reproduction." Economy and Society 1(1): 93–105.

——— (1977) Femmes, greniers, et capitaux. Paris: Maspero.

MENIAUD, J. (1912) Haut-Sénégal-Niger. Paris: Larose.

MONTEIL, C. (1924) Les Bambaras du Ségou et du Kaarta: Etude historique, ethnologique, et litteraire d'une peuple du Soudan Français. Paris: Larose.

——— (1927) "Les empires du Mali: Etude d'histoire et de sociologie soudanaise." Bulletin du Comité de l'Afrique Occidentale Française 12.

N'DIAYE, B. (1970) Les castes au Mali. Bamako: Editions populaires.

NIANE, D. (1975) Le Soudan Occidental du temps des grands empires. Paris: Presence Africaine.

OLORUNTIMEHIN, R. (1972) The Segu Tukulor Empire. New York: Humanities Press.

ORTOLI, J. (1936) "Une race de pêcheurs: Les Bozo." Bulletin de Recherches Soudanaines 4: 152–178.

PARK, M. (1807) Travels in the interior districts of African. London: W. Bulmer.

——— (1815) Journal of a mission to the interior of Africa in 1805. London: John Murray.

PERRON, M. (1930) "Traditions claniques des groupements Bozos et Somonos du Moyen Niger: Recueillés dans la région du Macina." Bulletin d'Agriculture Générale Coloniale 23: 439–453.

ROBERTS, R. (1978) "The Maraka and the economy of the Middle Niger Valley, 1790–1905." Ph.D. dissertation, University of Toronto.

——— (1980a) "Production and reproduction of warrior states: Segu Bambara and Segu Tokolor." International Journal of African Historical Studies 13(3): 389–419.

_____ (1980b) "Long distance trade and production: Sinsani in the nineteenth century." Journal of African History 21(2): 169–188.

_____ (1980c) "The emergence of a grain market in Bamako, 1883–1905." Canadian Journal of African Studies 14(1): 55–81.

_____ (forthcoming) "Ideology, slavery, and social formation: The evolution of Maraka slavery in the Middle Niger Valley," in P. Lovejoy (ed.) Ideology of slavery in Africa. Beverly Hills, CA: Sage.

ROBERTS, R., and KLEIN, M. (1980) "The Banamba slave exodus of 1905 and the decline of slavery in the western Sudan." Journal of African History 21(3): 375–394.

SOLEILLET, P. (1887) Voyage â Ségou, 1878–79, redigé par les journaux par Gabriel Gravier. Paris: Challamel Aîné.

SURET-CANALE, J. (1971) French colonialism in Tropical Africa, 1900–1945 (T. Gottheiner, trans.). London: Hurst.

TAUXIER, L. (1942) Histoire des Bambaras. Paris: Librairie Oriental Paul Geuthner.

TYMOWSKI, M. (1967) "Le Niger, voie de communication des grands états du Soudan occidental jusqu'à la fin du XViè siécle". Africana Bulletin 6: 37–95.

_____ (1970) "La pêche à l'époque du moyen age dans la Boucle du Niger." Africana Bulletin 12: 7–26.

_____ (1973) "L'économie et la société dans le bassin du moyen Niger, Fin du XVI-XVIIIe siécles." Africana Bulletin 18: 9–64.

VAUGHAN, J. (1970) "Caste systems in the western Sudan," pp. 59–92 in A. Tuden and L. Plotnicov (eds.) Social stratification in Africa. New York: Free Press.

WARD, J. (1976) "The Bambara French relationship, 1880–1915." Ph.D. dissertation, University of California, Los Angeles.

Archival Sources

National Archives, Republic of Senegal, Section Afrique Occidental Française (ASAOF).

ASAOF 1G 32. Mage. Correspondence, 1865.

ASAOF 1G 105 Archinard. Rapport militaire du compaigne, 1889–1890.

ASAOF 1G 185. Bellat Renseignements historiques sur le pays de Sansanding et du Macina, 1893.

ASAOF 1G 248. Perignon. Généralites sur Haut-Sénégal et Moyen-Niger, 1900.

ASAOF 1G 336. Corrensen. De l'organisation de la justice chez les populations de la région de Ségou, 1910.

ASAOF 2G 1-12. Ponty. Rapport politique sur la situation des territories de Haut Sénégal Niger pendant le mois de juin 1900.

ASAOF 15G 172. Archinard. Palabre avec Mari Diarra, 11 April 1890.

_____ Archinard. Instructions particulières pour le resident de Segou, April 16, 1890.

National Archieves, Republic of Mali (AM).

AM 1D 186. Robin. Réponse au questionnaire sur les coutumes indigènes, cercle de Bamako, 1909.

AM 1E 5. Archinard. Treaty with Ousman Taroaré, chief of Saro, September 20, 1890.

AM 1E 18. Commandant. Letter, September 3, 1892, Bamako.

AM 1E 20. Anon. Passage du Niger, no date (probably 1915).

AM 1E 20. Commandant. Rapport politique, Bamako, March 1913.

AM 1R 69. Commandant. Rapport commercial et agricole, Ségu, 1st quarter 1900.

Oral Informants

All interviews were taped and have been deposited with the Archives of Traditional Music, Indiana University, and with the Institut des Sciences Humaines, Bamako, Mali.

DEMBELE, C. Banankoro, December 12, 1977. Notable.

FANE, I. Tesserela, March 15, 1977. Cleric.

KAMITE, B. Markaduguba, December 20, 1976. Cleric.

KANE, K. (Session I). Segu. December 11, 1976. Somono notable.

_____ (Session II). Segu, January 6, 1977. Somono notable.

KONE, M. and B. Segu, December 11, 1976. Somono notables.

KULUBALI, B. Segu, February 27, 1976. Grain merchant.

KULUBALI, C. Segu, February 26, 1977. Notable.

SIDIBE, M. Bamako, November 25, 1976. Historian.

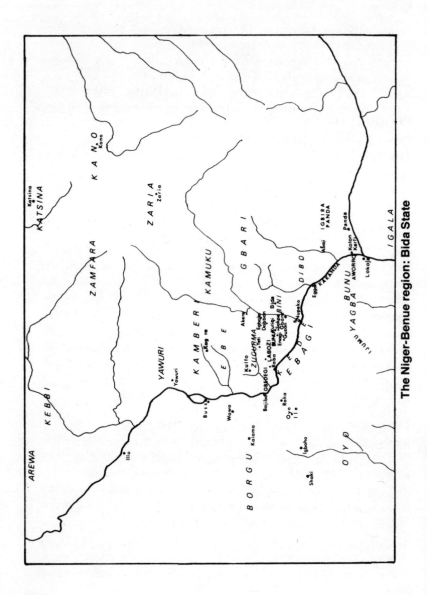

The Niger-Benue region: Bida State

8

PRODUCTION, PENETRATION, AND POLITICAL FORMATION:
The Bida State, 1857–1901

MICHAEL MASON
Concordia University

After faltering for several decades, merchant capital finally anchored itself in the waters of the Middle Niger River in the 1860s. This was to be an event of the greatest moment in the history of the peoples of this area, and indeed in the whole of the Central Sudan. Certainly they had already seen some evidence of the encroaching world market—trade goods of European origin had filtered down from the north and had trickled up from the south. In some cases villages in the area had been raided and plundered and their inhabitants sold as slaves in distant markets. But social relations remained unaltered as precapitalist, lineage-based production was largely unaffected by these slight stirrings of change.

Now a new epoch was beginning. It was to be distinguished from the previous epoch by the accelerated expansion of capitalist

Author's Note: An earlier form of this article was given at the Conference on the Economic History of the Central Sudan, Kano, January 1976. I would like to offer my thanks to the organizers and other participants of that conference whose comments have encouraged me in my revisions.

relations of exchange and the concomitant transformation of indigenous relations of production. It shall be my main concern here to try to explain this, that is, to use the notion of a changing mode of production in order to illustrate the fundamental shifts which were taking place in Nupe at all "levels." That these changes brought to a close the precapitalist epoch and linked Nupe indissolubly with the advanced capitalist world beyond seem to me to justify the periodization of history not in terms of precolonial and colonial but in terms of precapitalist and capitalist. The distinctive quality of the capitalist period is the process, apparent since the 1860s, which links production within Nupe to the needs of capitalist reproduction elsewhere. This process is one of domination and subordination at several levels: that of the mode of production, whereby the mode within Nupe is dominated from without; that of social relations, whereby the villagers are dominated by the Bida ruling class and their appointees; and that of political formations, whereby the existence of the Bida state is determined by its external dependency. This process was manifest in and facilitated by a dominant local class which, conscious of their interests and the interests of merchant capitalism to which they were allied, reordered social relations. They did this by means of a state the existence of which was the expression and the defense of the emergent relations of production.[1]

NUPE: c.1725–1857

We should begin with the affirmation that in the period under discussion, the term *Nupe* is taken to refer simultaneously to an area and the people living in that area, a land and people in the parlance of geographers. Nupe in this period included a wide range of social formations; Nadel, writing in the 1930s, referred to these as "subtribes." The number and history of these prior to the late-19th century is unknown. It is my assumption that they shared a mode of production based on the lineage although the forms of the division of labor within the lineage mode may have differed. By "forms of labor" I mean specific circumstances under which men labored and were relieved of their surplus product: slavery, which existed on a limited basis from the early 19th century at least, was one such form. It should be emphasized that these forms of the division of labor are not the same as modes of production.[2] Within the lineage mode of production, there may also have been differences in means of production, that is, in the relationship between "nature" (the geographical and ecological conditions in which men existed), tools, techniques, ideas, and human labor power.

It is only from 1827 when the first European report on Nupe was composed that we begin to get a detailed view of the changes taking place in Nupe, although these are mainly at the political level.[3] In the western part of the country, competition for domination over the local social formations had developed with an intensity which can only be completely understood with reference to the revolutions which had taken place to the north, in Hausaland and Borno, and to the south, in Yorubaland. In Nupe the leading revolutionary agents were several, three being indigenous and one foreign. Each had a force of armed men and each force was maintained materially by plunder and kidnapping. Those kidnapped were exchanged for war materials, most notably horses and firearms. By c.1830, the force led by the foreigner, the Fulani preacher called Mallam Muhammedu Dendo, had become dominant. Its success in large part derived from its identification with Islamic reform and its acceptance of the material price implied by this connection. In concrete terms the alliance with the reformed states to the northwest yielded military aid in return for tribute. This aid was to prove decisive in the next decades.

Dendo's lineage and those associated with it sought to superimpose themselves upon the villages of Nupe by force sustained by ideological manipulation. These villages, never previously incorporated within the boundaries of a large state (unlike those in the more well-developed northern savanna), may not have initially been capable of surplus production sufficient to maintain the forces which were seeking to impose new economic and political relationships on the area. The numbers of these forces were quite enormous—one British visitor estimated that there were 25,000 warriors raiding in the country (Laird and Oldfield, 1832: vol. 2: 77; 86). Slave raiding and looting were the ready methods of securing the means to sustain these bodies of men. Here is a description of this primitive form of accumulation:

> They [the slave raiders] travel very quickly taking the unsuspecting inhabitants by surprise. They seldom fail in capturing hundreds of prisoners as well as cattle, horses &c. The slaves are disposed of to the Arabs; some are sold at towns on the banks of the Niger, and eventually reach the seaside [Laird and Oldfield, 1832: vol. 2: 90].

The arbitrary terror of these bands afflicted the whole of the rural population. Rev. Crowther described their povery and insecurity as he saw it in 1857, at the end of a long period of war:

> The farmers are the most numerous class of people in Nupe. They are mostly Pagans, and the most oppressed of the inhabitants; from the nature of their work in the fields they are the greatest sufferers during the time of war, or political disturbance. Their produce, the results of a whole year's labour, on these occasions falls into the hands of soldiers, who eat up every thing, as the locusts devour the grass of the fields. At such times, not only their produce is exposed to plunder, but the implements of husbandry are liable to be snatched away from them by the soldiers, and sold for a few cowries, and their persons are also in danger; if saleable they are caught and sold into slavery. . . . The only way to save themselves is to abandon themselves to the mercy of the soldiers and keep out of the way. From these and other causes this people . . . always remain poor. Besides these disadvantages, they are subject to heavy taxes, which are annually exacted from them . . . on the death of any of the . . . inhabitants (of the villages) if he or she be a person of property half of it is claimed by the chief to whom he is tributary [Crowther and Taylor, 1959].

Up to this point there is little evidence of shared interest among the leaders of the war bands: that is, we cannot speak yet of "class." In fact, just the opposite was the case. The sons of Mallam Muhammedu Dendo continued to attack one another, each with his own band, each in an attempt to establish a new political regime and new social and economic relations. Such was the instability that no single town emerged as a secure center until Bida was founded in 1857. On the other hand, the basis of a more systematic exploitation resting not on plunder but on the consistent removal of surpluses from the villages was beginning to emerge. The "heavy taxes" which Crowther refers to in the above passage are in evidence by the early 1840s and probably before. We know, for instance, that the Kakanda town of Kinani paid 20,000 cowries a year in 1841, a sum equivalent to the cost of a child in the slave market (Schon and Crowther, 1843: 537; Allen and Thompson, 1846: 99).

But what was the relative importance of taxation or tribute in the years prior to 1857? Certainly we can agree that it was of primary importance in a number of West African formations, such as in the system of states in the Central Savanna. Compared to slave raiding up to c.1860, I would suggest that taxation remained a secondary source of revenue for those who exploited the producers. Part of our problem is, of course, sources; we simply know too little about this period. But it is my impression that the years prior to 1857 were too full of strife between rival lineages for anything approaching a tributary *system* to have emerged, that is, for there to have emerged new social relations defined as being simultaneously economic, political, and social.

We must now raise the question of the significance of commerce for the rulers of the state. So far as we can tell from either literary or cartographical sources, there were neither major interregional markets nor significant trade routes within Nupe prior to the period of the warring lineages, that is, c.1830. The major highways which carried the long-distance trade between the Gulf of Guinea and the savanna were, in the 18th and early 19th centuries, both further to the east and to the west of Nupe. This may suggest that the surplus produced within the lineage mode was little in excess of the immediate needs of social reproduction.

Let us consider these routes, first the eastern one. This connected, via the entrepôt of Panda, the lower Niger valley with southern Hausaland as well as the towns of the Benue valley. Access to the goods which flowed along this route (which is a different matter from the monopolizing of trade or the effective taxing of traders) was one of the most earnest aims of the new parties which rose to power in the 1820s. To the end of having greater access to goods from the north and the south, the new parties in Nupe destroyed the commercial circuits which passed over the peripheries of Nupe. One of these was that which joined Zaria in the North to the Niger and which passed through Panda. This route was suppressed through the destruction of Panda in the period of 1830–1860. The victims of its destruction were the riverain Igalas as well as the trading interests of Idah, the Kakanda canoe owners, and the Igbirra merchants of Koton Karfi and Panda itself. These remained the implacable enemies of the rulers of Nupe throughout the larger part of the 19th century.

Now let us look at the road which skirted the western edge of Nupe. The major market town on the southwestern frontier of Nupe was Raka. The commercial significance of this town declined into obscurity in the 1820s in a wave of raids directed against market centers in this area as a whole. These centers included Bussa and Kiama. In the place of Raka rose the new center of Raba, both a river port and a market town, in the same style as Eggan further downriver had come to supplant Panda. In these new centers there is no suggestion that either tax or tolls were levied on trade. Nor, so far as I know, is there any indication that the would-be rulers of Nupe had attempted to establish for themselves an exclusive monopoly over external trade. The exception may be in the area of kolas, although the nature of the royal monopoly here is not clear to me. Overall, then, the situation appears to be similar to that in the Akan states where Daaku remarks:

> As for the organization of trade, the evidence suggests that no Akan state monopolised this to the exclusion of its subjects. On the contrary all subjects were encouraged to participate in it [Daaku, 1971: 17].

In Kulfo market where Clapperton stopped in 1826, visiting merchants gave presents to their hosts, the *masugida,* but not to the Nupe rulers (Clapperton, 1829: 136–139). And it was in the houses of these hosts that their goods were either sold or given to commission agents, but not to royal representatives. Raba, which in 1830 when the Lander brothers visited it was both a "ferry" and a capital, was one of the two main centers in Nupe for the sale of slaves. All of the "principle inhabitants," to use Richard Lander's term, were involved in the trade (Lander & Lander, 1832: vol. 2: 298). At Eggan, the principal river port in the same period, there seems to have existed neither monopoly nor exclusive rights of any other kind.[4] So it seems that there were not markets in Nupe which in themselves could yield profits from exchange sufficient to maintain ruling groups of anything but the most petty proportions. In short, we see no evidence of rulers in Nupe sustaining themselves principally from the profits of trade.

NUPE c.1857–1901

According to Nadel, "tax" *(edu)* had been collected throughout the Bini area from at least the early 19th century by the rulers of eastern Nupe prior to the advent of the emigrant insurrectionaries. We have already indicated that from 1841 *edu* had been paid to the emigrant regime. By 1857, Crowther tells us, the people of Nupe were "subject to heavy taxes which are annually extracted from them." Nadel indicates that from the reign of *Etsu* Masaba (1859–1873) to the reign of *Etsu* Maliki (1882–1895), taxes rose increasingly until *"u de iyaka à,"* there was no limit. He also suggests the mechanisms by which taxes were collected and distributed:

> [The] Nupe kingdom was divided up into smaller and larger "countries" comprising each a town with its dependent villages and *tunga* which were administered as fiefs through feudal lords or *egba*. The *egba*—a member of the royal house or of the office holding nobility, or a court slave—received the fief from the king together with his rank with which the fief remained permanently linked. Mokwa

was known as the town of the *Shaba*, Egga as the town of the *Ndeji*, Kutigi and Enagi belonged to the *Ndatwaki*, and so on. Promotion to a higher rank brought with it appointment to another, more lucrative, fief. The feudal lord lived in the capital and rarely visited his possessions. The local affairs, the collection of tax, were in charge of his representative, one of his slaves or serfs who was resident on his land as *egbagi*, Small Delegate. Of the tax collected in these fiefs, again a money tax, a quarter went to the king and three quarters were retained by the *egba*, who returned a small share to his *egbagi*, salary and commission in one. Sometimes the towns or districts also paid an additional tribute in kind both to *Etsu* and *egba* [Nadel, 1942: 116–117].

Nadel adds that the appointment of village chiefs was subject to royal confirmation.

The Nupe cultivators not only parted with a part of their surplus product in the form of tribute but they also exchanged another part of it for imported goods. The substitution of textiles made in Europe for those made locally seems to have diminished local production. This exchange was mediated by the expansion of a money economy, although the extent to which this prevailed is not evident. Overall, however, a trend is apparent. I would argue that we are witnessing, over the period 1857–1901, a qualitative change in the mode of production within that part of Nupe which was governed by Bida. To summarize, we have indicated (1) increased taxation, (2) payment of tax partially in money, (3) political domination from outside the village, and (4) the growth of a market for both imported goods and agricultural commodities. These changes in economic and political relations which are apparent are accompanied by mutations in social relations which are less visible. The ensemble of these transformations may allow us to propose that there has emerged from within the body of the precapitalist lineage mode of production a successor mode determined essentially by the needs of the Bida regime for tribute. If we call this a "tributary mode," then we can capture in a somewhat abstract, heuristic way what has taken place in the Nupe villages.

But if the villagers, or peasants as we may now reasonably regard them, were increasingly governed by the demands of the rulers of Bida, these rulers were themselves bound up with a world which they hardly recognized. The agents of this world were the European and, to a lesser extent, African, merchants. The vulnerability of the hold of the rulers of Bida over the peasants who paid them tribute was partly a function of the close ties which had emerged between these rulers and the merchants on the Niger. When the Europeans adjusted the price of commodities downward, as we shall see they did in the late 1870s and the 1880s, the fractions of the Bida ruling group which benefited most from the relationship with the capitalist world had to contend with a widespread peasant revolt supported by dissident members of their own class.

Now let us consider slave labor and its place in the Nupe political economy. We should recall here that the exploitation of war captives was a normal feature in a number of societies in 19th-century West Africa. In Nupe there is no convincing evidence that the use of captives on farms or plantations existed on a widespread basis prior to the late 1850s. From this point onward, however, from the end of the struggles between the members of Mallam Dendo's lineage and the attempt to found a political and commercial capital at Bida, captives were settled in villages on a regular basis. The number of such villages founded under the five *etsuzi* (kings) who ruled central Nupe between 1857–1901 is indicated below:

Regnal period	1857–1859	1859–1873	1873–1882	1882–1895	1895–1901
No. of new villages	55	694	484	311	57

The captives in question were taken either during the wars between the members of Dendo's lineage or during subsequent campaigns of expansion. They were therefore people who would earlier in the century have been sold to the slave buyers from the north and the south. That this was not to be their fate from c.1860 onward was due in part to the international diminution in demand. But of greater significance was the conviction of *Etsu* Masaba (1859–1873) that the value of the labor of captives was mainly in production to sustain a town-based ruling class (which was no longer occupied so fully in raiding) as well as to yield commodities for the European market, and this value was greater than their market value as slaves. This view was not universally accepted, however. Another faction in the capital upheld the old export trade in slaves. This was headed by the *etsu*'s sister, Habiba, who is known to have done business with Madame Tinubu, the queen of the Lagos slave dealers (F.O., 2/32). Habiba's opposition to Masaba went so far as to lead her to revolt against him in 1867. But in the end it was she who was on the losing side in a struggle to adapt to the local needs of merchant capitalism.

Slaves on the Nupe plantations which thus began to proliferate from the reign of *Etsu* Masaba onward did not become naturalized through adoption by the lineages of their owners. This was so for several reasons. First, these slaves did not work together with their owners' lineages as they did, for example, in Zaria to the north. Second, in the area where most plantations developed, there were probably more slaves than there were free peasants, so integration into local society was impaired by the sheer weight of the slaves' numbers. Finally, naturalization had a very short space of time to work as the era of the plantations lasted only from 1857 to 1901 at the very longest. We must assume, therefore, that the social relations of the captives' villages differed from those of peasants' villages insofar as they were determined by the captives' relations to their captors.

The question arises: was there a distinctive "slave mode of production?" I would say no. Slavery was a form of labor not a relationship of production. There was no distinctive, fundamental relationship between slaves and slave owners: In Zaria, slave labor was a form of labor within the tributary mode of production. In Nupe, although slaves did not live together with the lineages of their owners, we do not see that the social relations between slaves and their masters were fundamentally different from the relations between the lords or *egbazi* (sing. *egba*). and the peasants who paid them tribute. Slaves and peasants both paid tribute. Otherwise, the slaves kept their own products. Here is W. B. Backie who visited Nupe in the early years of *Etsu* Maliki's reign:

> Three-quarters of the labouring population, whether free or slave, are at liberty to have their own farms, and to sell the bulk of their own crops. Thus though a small farmer may himself be a slave, the larger his crops the larger his profits, and in working hard he is not labouring . . . for the benefit of his master, but for his own immediate behoof; and thus, though a large part of the population of . . . Nupe are slaves, the labour on the small farms is not strictly "slave labour" [Cotton Supply Association Reporter, 1858].

If we assume that fundamental social relations cannot be simply defined as an economic relation (i.e., by the slave's payment of surplus to his master) but that it should be seen as a relation of class power sustained and reproduced by different and indistinguishable means (economic, political, and ideological) and that this relation of class power pervades every aspect of society, then we should see that there is but one relation in Nupe and that is the one which we have called "tributary". This mode colored all relations between masters and slaves and between lords and peasants. The power of the individual members of the Bida ruling class over their slaves was hardly different than their power over the peasants who paid them tribute. We see no brutalized exploitation peculiar to the institution of slavery in the New World. For in Nupe, as distinct from Jamaica or Georgia, if the masters sought to exploit their slaves that bit extra, they might find themselves with no labor at all, for flight was always an alternative. Of course this alternative was constrained by the perils of the road and by the possibility of recapture.

We should, at this point, indicate the existence of a people living within Nupe (although not exclusively within) whose productive existence was based on the lineage but whose environment was entirely different and whose political history was, up to mid-century, quite distinct. I refer to the Kedes, the Nupes whose domains were the rivers of Nupeland and beyond. Kede history, in common with that of the landward Nupes, becomes increasingly intertwined with that of merchant capital on the river Niger. The transformation of Kede life had already begun by the middle of the 19th century. Lineage-based production (in which the forces of production were different from those on land in that they include canoes, lines, nets, and harpoons in place of hoes, scythes, bows, and arrows) was being partially modified by the concentration of productive wealth in the hands of the few. It was Reverend Crowther who perceived this change. Canoes, he noted, were not owned by those who worked them. Some "belong to the kings . . . [while] others [belong] to some persons of rank . . . others again are owned by persons of some property" (Crowther and Taylor, 1959: 200–201). This process was tied to the expansion of commerce which placed the opportunities for trade in salt in the hands of those who had command over the means of transporting this salt along the Niger and Benue.

Back on the land, slaves and peasants both produced surpluses which were rendered in cowries and kind. The bulk of the latter was horticultural and was consumed in the capital to which it was taken by the villagers themselves or by their patrons or owners' representatives. But of more importance for trade was control over the production of the sivicultural and artisanal goods of rural Nupe for it was these which attracted what appears to be an expanding stratum of Nupe merchants. Of sivicultural products, three were of major importance: kolas, shea nuts, and palm products. The trade in kolas had by the 19th century become the only royal monopoly we are aware of and in the previous century may have been one of the main attractions for the northern merchants who came to Nupe. Labozi, the center of the kola-growing district, was said by Baikie to have been one of the oldest towns existing in the country (Baikie 1867: 105). Kolas from the forest here had the advantage of comparative nearness to the markets of Hausaland and were said to have been prized above the nuts from Gonja for their own sake. We know nothing of the quantity of Labozi kolas produced in the 19th century. Nadel suggests that slaves were sent to the kola plantations by the king (Nadel, 1942: 90) and it may be that by controlling the main factor of production here, the *etsu* assured himself of a greater share of the harvest.

Shea butter trees grew throughout Nupe and their fruits were too accessible to be monopolized. The "butter" produced by the processing of the shea fruits became the main export of Nupe from the time of the efflorescence of European trade on the Niger in the 1860s. Between 1864 and 1879 shea butter exports rose from 6 or 7 tons to 1500 tons per year. As this expansion coincides almost exactly with the expansion of slave plantations, it may be that slave labor was a major factor in production for this trade. Thus, although shea nuts could be picked freely and shea butter produced, transported, and sold by anyone, those members of the Bida ruling class who had control of the largest numbers of tribute paying and slave villages profited most from this trade. The labor required in the production of palm oil might also have been dominated by the most powerful men in the kingdom although we are less sure of this.

Of this artisanal exports of Nupe, textiles were primary in importance. It was Barth who commented: "The Nupe have excelled in industry from very remote times and rival the inhabitants of Kano in the arts of weaving and dyeing (Barth, 1857: vol. 3: 121). In the early part of the 19th century, slaves taken from Nupe to Hausaland were highly valued for their skills as weavers (Denham and Clapperton, 1826: 113). By the second part of the century, the situation had reversed itself and foreign slaves were being brought to Nupe. It is thus evident that it was accepted practice to employ slaves as craftsmen as well as laborers both within Nupe and beyond. Besides acquiring labor, a "small master" in Nupe might also invest in textiles produced by free weavers. Such were numerous, especially in the large commercial towns like Eggan where in

1841 Crowther saw 200 looms in use (Schon and Crowther, 1843: 172–174). Looms were easily and inexpensively produced while weaving itself was a skill which was neither highly specialized nor in any way esoteric.[5] As soon as a piece of woven cloth was finished, assuming it was to be marketed and not otherwise exchanged, it was probably handed to a merchant who might seek to enhance its value by having it dyed or tailored. Then it might be sold again, perhaps for export. Thereafter it might pass through several hands and increase in price several times until it reached its final destination in Lagos or Kano or beyond.

Given the market value of textiles throughout most of the 19th century, the Bida rulers sought slaves who could serve them as weavers as well as farm workers. If such were the case, then a substantial proportion of the tens of thousands of cloths which were exported from Bida annually in the middle of the century (Cotton Supply Association Reporter, 1858) would have been produced by slave labor. As far as the Nupe evidence is concerned, therefore, this gives us further reason to disagree with Catherine Coquery's contention that the economic base of the state rested upon control over long-distance exchange (Coquery-Vidrovitch, 1969). Rather, it was, as Terray maintains, control over labor, and particularly over peasant and slave labor, which was the goal of the Bida rulers (Terray, 1973: 315–345).

Of the Bida ruling class, the *etsu* was the most powerful member. Besides controlling the largest number of commodity producers, he benefited from a most singular commercial advantage. By virtue of his political position, he had precedence as an importer of firearms and munitions from the foreign merchants. Trade with the European ships which ascended the Niger did not begin until his representatives got guns and powder. As firearms were essential to the reproduction of servile labor, the *etsu*'s privileged access to the major source of their importation gave him an advantage not only over his local rivals but also over rival kingdoms. This privilege was acceptable to the rival lineages within the capital for as long as their share in the wealth of the kingdom was assured. But when they became less willing to accept royal domi-

nance, competition for their trade came to an end with the formation of a buyers' monopoly, as we shall see below, and the prices
for the goods which their captives and clients produced plummeted
on account of the contract between the monopolists and the *etsu*.
The solidarity of the Bida ruling class was thus sundered. It is to
this and the consequent decline of the state as the vehicle of class
solidarity and dominance that we now turn.

It is apparent that the 1860s and 1870s were something of a
golden age, if not for the producers of Nupe, then at least for their
exploiters. The gilding of these times was a consequence of the
linking of the producers to the capitalist world market. The gilded
class which served as intermediaries between the capitalist mode
and the domestic modes depended for their existence on their
mediating function. They were highly vulnerable to changes over
which they had no control. Thus when prices rose, all was well for
them; their sumptuary standards rose and their function in the
extended reproduction of the social system remained beyond
doubt. But this changed when commodity prices on the West African coast began to decline. The effects of this reached the Nupe
Niger in the 1870s, and the first reaction to this came from the
merchant capitalists who began to amalgamate in order to effect a
monopoly.[6] By 1879 their mergers had resulted in the formation of
a single trading company on the Niger, the United African Company. In 1879 this company prevailed on the *etsu* to grant a monopoly of trade which would exclude all of their rivals, the most
notable being the coastal Africans and the French, the latter having
arrived in earnest in 1878. The *etsu*'s reasons for granting a monopoly, assuming that he had an inkling of what such entailed, may
have been the company's willingness to supply him with a large
consignment of arms and power at a particularly desperate political moment. He had become involved in a campaign in Akoko to
the south which, if he lost, could have threatened his supply of
labor and tribute from the whole of northeastern Yoruba and Afen-
mai, and perhaps his political status as well. The *etsu* may have
understood that by granting a monopoly, some of his rivals would
become distressed, but he could not have predicted the scale of the

consequences of his action. To see this let us look at the effect of the monopoly on one of the groups trading in Nupe, the ivory traders. Down to 1879 the heads of the ivory caravans which came to Nupe from the east had grown accustomed to having gifts pressed upon them at the opening of trade with the Europeans. With the United African Company in a monopolistic position, this practice was ended abruptly. Instead, according to one observer, "the caravanners had to solicit sale from the Company and accept one-fifth of the price they used to receive a few months before (Flegel, 1890: 52–53). The results of this collapse in what had become the accepted levels of profit for the African merchants was the great rebellion of 1881–1882 which shook the state to its foundations. There can be no doubt that the uprising was a direct consequence of the new monopoly. As the German traveller Flegel commented:

> The treaty (conferring the monopoly) could not be maintained by King Umoru for it was not only to the disadvantage of all his subjects . . . but also to the king himself and the nobles who earlier had lived in luxury on the fat of the trade [Flegel, 1890: 53].

The rebellion was supported not only by the Kede nobles whose salt profits had been threatened but also by members of the Bida nobility and by the small-scale Sierra Leone merchants. It was repressed successfully only with the assistance of the ships and guns of the Europeans. Thereafter followed a brief flutter of free trade until the main competitors of the United African Company, the French, agreed to sell out in 1884. This left the British, in the words of George Goldie, the head of the newly emergent National African Company, "alone on the Niger."

The Niger had become a British river in spite of the *etsu*'s complaints about the effects of monopoly. His grudging acquiescence was admitted when Goldie agreed to increase the subvention paid to him from £400 to £2000 per annum. If we assume that competition had braked the downward slide of commodity prices in the 1870s and early 1880s, then we might suggest that the monopoly which prevailed from 1884 onward released this brake. This monopoly precipitated renewed political crisis of a type which afflicted the ruling elements in states over the whole of Africa. The crisis stemmed from the fact that merchant capitalism in its monopoly phase could lower commodity prices to such a level as to rule out the existence of the large intermediary class whose symbol was the Bida state. This class could only exist in a skeletal form under the conditions imposed by British monopoly. Its members could not, however, contemplate their own demise, and they sought other means by which they might perpetuate themselves. This brought them, as we shall see, into greater conflict with the British.

As trade became less rewarding for the rulers of Nupe in general, old political wounds began to open. These had been plastered over in the earlier period of prosperity but appeared again with the increased competition for a diminishing supply of goods. The *etsu* himself was shielded from the harsher effects of the cold economic wind which now blew up the Niger by the increased subsidy which had been paid to him. Some of his privileges, at least, could still be maintained but only at the cost of the growing rift between himself and the members of the other lineages within the ruling class. So as divisions widened, he was drawn closer to the Europeans on whom he depended increasingly for the means to secure his authority. This was especially the case with arms. The British realized this when they threatened that if the *etsu* did not honor the treaty which gave them a monopoly:

> the Company would be compelled to blockade Nupe and to divert the trade of all the Christians to Borgu, Zaria, Bautshi, Adamawa and other states which did observe their treaties [CMS CS A3/1882].

What emerged in the late 1880s was that the ruling class turned on itself:

> The Nupes are going from one extreme to another. The princes are at loggerheads among themselves, and all of them with the king [CMS C3 A3/1892].

As the maintenance of previous levels of consumption now required more exports, and thus mastery over more men, no longer was the king able to persuade his rebellious princes that peace offered more material advantages than arbitrary plunder.

As the British merchants had effected destabilization within the Bida state, so they found it necessary to restore order. The first instance of this was in 1888 when they drove the *Benu,* the prince in whose domain the British factories at Lokoja stood, out of that town. Thereafter, they declared, Lokoja was to come under the authority of the Royal Niger Company, not Bida. As Lokoja was in an area regularly exploited for plunder, captives, and tribute, the town became a haven for fugitives. By offering sanctuary to the victims of oppression, the agents of British capitalism, both merchants and missionaries, were able to garb themselves in the mantle of humanitarianism. Within just a few years, William Wallace, the Royal Niger Company's chief agent, had extended his authority over the hinterland of Lokoja as well. The consequences of this was the loss to the Nupe princes of an even larger province of revenue. The effect of this was commented on by one of the missionaries at Lokoja:

> The Mohammedans' slave hunts are being progressively checked by the Royal Niger Company. These things have created general discontent in the minds of the Nupe rulers who against their desire have been submitting to the power of the Company [CO 446/14].

The general discontent prevailing in Bida could only have been aggravated by the threat of attack by Sir George Goldie if Nupe bands crossed the Benue into Bassa country or the Niger into Igala seeking new resources. The only choice left to the Bida warlords was to more effectively exploit those territories within reach. So in the period 1893–1895, the villages of Yagba, Bunu, Aworro, and Ijumu were plundered as they never had been in the past. But this desperate strategy led only to more difficulty, for it brought the Nupe war bands into conflict with ever-widening military patrols of the British company.

The last chapter of Bida's independent political history was written during the reign of *Etsu* Abubakar (1895–1901). Suspicion of British political designs had continued to mount from the early 1890s. Confrontations between the soldiers of the company and the followers of the war lords increased in frequency. Renewed French interest in the Niger served to advance the schedule of conflict. In order to assert their unqualified claim over the Niger, the British launched, in December 1896, the "Niger Soudan Campaign." Bida fell after a battle which one excited missionary likened to Plassey (Church Missionary Intellegencer). Thereafter, all Bida activity south of the Niger and to the east of the Chanchaga was ended when the British installed puppet rulers over the formerly Bida-controlled towns of Pategi and Koton Karfi. The political dependence of these towns was guaranteed by patrolling detachments of the West African Frontier Force.

More destructive to the economy of Bida than the decline in trade prices and the loss of territory was the loss of the control over men. Not only were the sources for captive labor cut off but also new sanctuaries for runaways were created. The Kedes, who since their defeat of 1881 had ceased to share any interests with the rulers of Bida, were probably not unwilling to transport escapees across the Niger. The cry of the slave owners supports this assumption: "All our slaves are running away to the south of the river" complained one of the leading princes (CO 147/124). Trade with the company declined even further as the sinews of the economy weakened. For the British it was merely a matter of waiting for the next stage in the relationship with the Bida ruling class to begin. This came with the occupation of Bida in early 1901. This was no Plassey. As the Mounted Infantry of the colonial army charged in one gate of the town, the rulers of the kingdom galloped out of the other. There was as little resistance as might have been expected in a capital in which the rulers had become internally divided as well as increasingly separated from their depressed supporters. The eviscerated but accommodating administration which emerged from the ruins of the collapsed emirate presided over an economy which was different from that which had immediately preceded it.

Economically it could no longer hope to expand on the basis of slave production and politically it was to become only the local intermediary of colonial rule. Whereas previously the characteristic forms of exploitation took the form of the relationship between the lord on one hand and the peasants or slaves who paid him tribute on the other, in the colonial period, class power was mediated by the state.

CONCLUSION

The question of the nature of the precolonial African state has diverted historians since African history first emerged on the academic syllabus as a distinct area of study in the early 1960s. In this essay I have sought to examine the question again but in a somewhat different light. I have not sought autocentric forces capable of generating political elites nor have I looked for evidence of the transhumance of political ideologies. Instead, I have sought the foundations of the state in relation to the effects of the expansion of capitalism on indigenous social structures. Thus I have assumed that there is no autonomous sphere of politics and that the origins of political processes must be rooted in shifts in the mode of production. In the case of Nupe, these shifts were the concomitant of the penetration of merchant capitalism into the Middle Niger basin. Their form was that of the intensification of servile relations. This did not lead, in any developmental way, to a gradual transition to capitalist relations but rather fostered the preservation and extension of precapitalist relations of production. The tributary mode of production was expanded, having inserted within it a form of production based on slave labor. This tributary mode was sustained by a specific kind of class power which was manifest in a form of servile relationships, between rulers and ruled. This was a personal relationship but its stability was dependent on the existence of a state which could guarantee its security. The survival of both class and state was determined not by an autocentric process but by a historical development external to them, namely, the transformation of capitalism elsewhere. Thus the pattern of subordinate development in Nupe, as elsewhere on the periphery of capitalism, which in the 20th century must be seen as being self-perpetuating, is seen to have its origins in the 19th century.

NOTES

1. An elaboration of this story can be found in Mason (1980).

2. This suggestion is made by Godelier (1978: 87).

3. These events are chronicled in unsurpassed length in Mason (1980).

4. See Crowther and Taylor (1859) or Schon and Crowther (1843) for a description of this town.

5. I owe my enlightenment on this point to Phil Shea of Maiduguri.

6. An account of this is given in Flint (1960).

REFERENCES

African Times (1884) September 1.

ALLEN, W. and THOMPSON, T. R. H. (1846) Narrative of an expedition in 1841. London: n.p.

BAIKIE, W. B. (1867) "Notes on a journey from Bida in Nupe to Kano in Hausa". Journal of the Royal Geographical Society 37.

BARTH, H. (1857) Travels and discoveries in Central Africa. New York: n.p.

Church Missionary Intelligencer (1897) Vol. 48.

CLAPPERTON, H. (1829) Journal of a second expedition. London: n.p.

COQUERY-VIDROVITCH, C. (1969) "Recherches sur un mode de production africain". Pensée 144.

Cotton Supply Association Reporter (1858) no. 1, August.

CROWTHER, S. A. and TAYLOR J. (1959) The gospel on the banks of the Niger. London: n.p.

DAAKU, K. (1971) In C. Meillassoux (ed.) The development of indigenous trade and markets in West Africa. London: n.p.

DENHAM, D. and CLAPPERTON, H. (1826) Narrative of travels and discoveries. London: n.p.

FLEGEL, E. R. (1890) Vom Niger Benue: Briefs aus Afrika. Leipzig: n.p.

FLINT, J. (1960) Sir George Goldie. Oxford, England: Oxford University Press.

GODELIER, M. (1978) "Infrastructures, societies and history". New Left Review 112.

LAIRD, M. and OLDFIELD, R. A. K. (1832) Narrative of an expedition. London: n.p.

LANDER, R. L. and LANDER, J. (1832) Journal of an expedition. London: n.p.

MASON, M. (1980) The foundations of the Bida Kingdom. (unpublished)

NADEL, S. F. (1942) A Black Byzantium. Oxford, England: Oxford University Press.

SCHON, J. F. and CROWTHER, S. (1843) Journals . . . of the expedition up the Niger in 1841, London: n.p.

TERRAY, E. (1973) "Long-distance exchange and the formation of the state." Economy and Society 3.

Archival sources

CO 147/124 (1899). "Report by Sir George Goldie" enclosed in Morley to Salisbury, April 29.

CO 446/14 (1901). Lugard to C.O.

CMS C3 A3/1882/24 Johnson to Crowther, January 6.

CMS C3 A3/1882/47 Johnson to Crowther, January 13.

CMS C3 A3/1892 J. J. Williams, "Annual Report." November 12, 1891.

F.C. 2/32 (1857). Baikie to Russell. September 2.

9

STATE AND SOCIETY:
19th-CENTURY ETHIOPIA

DONALD CRUMMEY
University of Illinois

Ethiopia is perhaps the first, and certainly the largest, African state to experience internally generated social revolution. Beginning in 1974, popular demonstrations and military mutiny led to peasant insurrection, the deposition of Haile Selassie, and the end of imperial government. Subsequent developments saw the extension of state ownership to include the principal financial institutions, factories, and large plantations. Of still greater and continuing importance, popular pressures led first to the nationalization of all rural, agricultural lands and then of all urban lands and housing. A weak revolutionary government, unable to exercise direct control itself, vested control of rural lands in peasant associations and of urban lands in neighborhood associations (Ottaway and Ottaway, 1978). In one sweeping move, the Ethiopian people gained control of their main productive asset and embarked on an irreversible step forward. The revolution which began in 1974 marks a turning point in Ethiopian history.

As yet students of Ethiopia have failed to produce an adequate conceptualization of the revolution against its local background.

Already by 1976 both Ethiopia's rulers and their principal opponents had adopted Marxist-Leninist concepts as their main mode
of expression (Ethiopia, Provisional Military Administrative
Council, 1975, 1976; Ottaway and Ottaway 1978: Chap. 7).[1] No
one has yet explained how this came about. Nor has anyone yet
adequately related those concepts to the deeper background of the
revolution.[2] The bulk of Marxian thought concerning Ethiopia has
contented itself either with crude notions of Ethiopian feudalism or
with exaggerated notions of the extent of capitalist penetration into
the country. Such explanations have thus mechanistically adduced
capitalist imperialism as the principal force against which the revolution was launched (Addis Hiwet, 1975; Cliffe, 1974).[3] The ultimate truth of the latter argument has obscured its immediate inap-
propriateness.

Implicit in what follows is the view that the Ethiopian revolution
may be related to Ethiopian history. The necessary concepts for
doing so are the concepts espoused by the revolution's leaders, the
Marxist concepts of historical materialism. These concepts have
not yet been deployed against the wealth of recent historical research concerning Ethiopia. Although little of that research has
been informed by questions appropriate to historical materialism,
nonetheless, many of the findings of that research are capable of
materialist reinterpretation. Such a reinterpretation would have the
further value of suggesting priorities for subsequent research.

This essay will try to demonstrate the applicability of certain of
the concepts of historical materialism to an understanding of
Ethiopian history in the 19th century. Limitations of space and the
essay's thematic focus preclude an adequate conceptualization of
the revolution, but the essay should provide for an understanding
of the broad context of the revolution. The following pages will
argue that the premodern Ethiopian polity, the Solomonic state,
rested upon a moderately developed class structure, one in which a
ruling nobility extracted surplus from a subject peasantry primarily by means of tribute and not strictly by means of rent. The
argument continues that this state has often been confused with the

monarchy, a confusion which substitutes an excrescence of the state for its essence. In reality, any adequate definition of the state must take proper account of the nobility. The argument has greatest force with respect to the period known as the *Zamana Masāfent* (1769–1855), when, without alteration of either ideology or basic social relations, the monarchy was drastically reduced in power. It was this state which was revived in the latter 19th century in a dialectic with European imperialism, a dialectic which greatly affected the boundaries of the reconstituted Ethiopia, but which saw remarkably little foreign influence introduced into the empire's social relations. Social relations in Ethiopia in the last quarter of the 19th century evolved along autonomous lines, the rulers of northern Ethiopia using imported military technology to increase the pace at which they subjugated the kingdoms and peoples of the south, southwest, and southeast. These developments had no immediate effect in northern Ethiopia. However, in the conquered territories, with a few notable exceptions, they led to large-scale alienation of land from the hands of local people into the hands of the conquerors and/or to the introduction of servile status for the conquered. The result in southern Ethiopia was a social order and structure of class relations with a striking resemblance to a feudal mode of production (Marx, 1965; Hindess and Hirst, 1975). The reconstruction and expansion of the empire in the later 19th century considerably enhanced the office of the emperor, not least by expanding the material base of imperial power through giving the crown rights to reallocate conquered lands. Nonetheless, until the Italian invasion of 1935, the monarchy remained primarily a tool of noble class rule. Not until the restoration period of the 1940s did Haile Selassie succeed in establishing an autocratic rule which separated the monarchy from the nobility. Only then, in an intimate dialectic with the monarchy, did the forces of capitalism effect a significant impact on the country; and in a set of developments which lie beyond our proper frame of reference, only then did Ethiopia begin to develop internal contradictions of revolutionary potential. Nonetheless, as late as 1974, the great bulk of Ethiopian cultivators remained firmly within a feudal nexus, a fact which gives the present comments pertinence to the current revolution.

The principal insight of historical materialism to be employed here is the necessary relationship between the state and its underlying mode or modes of production, and the further notion that the means of surplus extraction are the critical link between the two (see above, Chapter 1). Marx (1908, III: 919) argues: "The specific economic form in which unpaid surplus labor is pumped out of the direct producers, determines the relations of rulers and ruled." He goes on to argue that the conditions of social production form the "hidden foundation" of the state, the state being "the political form of the relations between sovereignty and dependence." In some real sense these relations "between sovereignty and dependence" are *class* relations, relations of inequality which tend to perpetuate themselves from one generation to another, although as Hobsbawm (1971) has remarked, "Class," in the context of precapitalist societies, may be "an analytical construct which makes sense of a complex of facts otherwise inexplicable." And the state is here seen as the locus of an ongoing coercive power acting in support of authority.

The Solomonic state in Ethiopia rested on a mode of production which vested the principal means of production—land, seed, and oxen—in the hands of the direct producers, the peasants. The state thus lacked material, economic means of dominating the peasants and consequently sustained itself primarily by political and ideological factors and by force.[4] The Solomonic state emerged in the late 13th century and rapidly came to base itself on the Amharic- and Tegreññā-speaking peoples. These peoples, who may conveniently be referred to jointly as Abyssinian, had a developed cereal agriculture which used the plow (Crummey, 1979). We lack direct evidence about social relations in the Solomonic polity until the 16th and early 17th centuries, and when we do get it, the evidence is ambiguous and hard to interpret (Pankhurst, 1966).

Not until the 19th and 20th centuries does a fairly clear picture come into focus. That picture reveals the Abyssinian peasantry largely in control of the land. Peasants exercised their control of the land in several broad ways. The more prevalent system was one known as *rist,* the transmission of land by inheritance, in roughly equal portions through children of both sexes. Notional descent corporations, also controlled by the peasantry, mediated the process of inheritance and allocated fields on the basis of such claims. Under the *rist* system, the tenure of actual fields was subject to constant revision and reallocation (Hoben, 1973). The principal alternative system of peasant land control was a system based on residence, not descent. This system ostensibly granted agricultural land on an equal basis to all residents of a particular territorial unit, such as a parish or village (Bruce, 1976). It involved regular periodic redistribution through agencies controlled by the peasants, and it was found exclusively in the Tegreññā-speaking provinces where it involved only a minority of the cultivators. Peasant control of the land, whether by inheritance or by periodic village redistribution, characterized the Abyssinian territories until the revolution of 1974. Peasants also owned their own oxen and seeds, so that they fully controlled the immediate process of agricultural production. Although autonomous in the immediate sphere of agricultural production, these same peasants formed the basis of one of Africa's more enduring polities.

The Abyssinian peasants sustained a sizable nobility by a variety of devices. Firstly and fundamentally they recognized the right of the state to extract surpluses as tribute. Although rich with economic and material content, this right was primarily a political one and its justification was ideological. Associated with the claim to tribute was a claim that the king "owned" all the land in the kingdom (Pankhurst, 1966). However, this claim was explicitly countered by the peasant claim to inalienable rights to their land, rights conditioned only by the requirement that they pay tribute. Clearly the peasant sort of ownership was a good deal more solid than the royal kind. The level of surplus extracted through tribute was never less than a tenth of total production, and often ran rather higher. It was composed of a mix of corvée and of either a levy by percentage of the peasants' production or of a fixed amount of some major local commodity such as honey or cattle (Crummey, 1979; Gebre-Wold, 1962; Cohen and Weintraub, 1975). Additionally the peasants recognized a variety of superordinate land rights whereby gentry and nobility enjoyed more or less public or private rights, generically known as *gult,* to receive these tributes. The incidence and form of these noble rights to land varied both according to area and through time, and their determination at any given point is often a major historical problem. In addition to regular tribute, the state recurrently subjected the peasantry to the direct support of troops by billeting (Littmann, 1902; Gebre-Wold, 1962; Caulk, 1978). Generally it is my impression that the cumulative levels of surplus extraction from the Abyssinian peasants during the 18th and 19th centuries ran to at least around 30%. However, we may be mistaken in seeking too systematic an understanding of surplus extraction. Perhaps its most significant aspect, more significant even than its cumulative weight, was its arbitrary and irregular nature (Bruce, 1976). In this view class struggle would take the form of unending attempts by the nobility to devise fresh, or to revive ancient, modes of bilking the peasants, while the peasants with equal determination and imagination resisted. Finally, throughout much of the 19th and 20th centuries, warfare was endemic to the Abyssinian polity. Plunder was a major device for supporting this particular form of noble sport, and in this case the peasants paid by the most direct means of all. Tribute was sustained by ideology. There were many components to Abyssinian ideology, most of them religious. The Solomonic legend legitimated the state by legitimating its kings through genealogical connection with the kings of Israel, and beyond them to divine election. The Orthodox Church further preached a message of submission to rulers ordained by God.[5] And force sustained ideology. The penalty for refusal to pay tribute was permanent alienation of land.

In addition to tribute and force, the nobility enjoyed other devices for its support. In particular, rent arising from noble titles to direct access to the land was by no means uncommon, although far less common than in feudal Europe. In some areas the nobility enjoyed very considerable rights to control land and held the position of private landlords (Weissleder, 1965; Kea, 1979). These areas seem to have been few, although their extent has never seriously been determined. More commonly the nobility supported itself by means of political offices, access to which was determined by an uneasy mix of hereditary right and external appointment. For example, very few offices were widely recognized as being strictly hereditary. Equally, very few offices were viewed as being independent of the claims of particular lineages. Power of appointment lay with the court, with respect to the highest offices or provincial governorships, and with the higher nobility with respect to inferior offices. The system was thus one of subinfeudation. Appointers paid very careful attention to the utility of the appointees, largely measured in terms of their potential local influence and therefore their social standing. Appointers were generally content to play off the local rivalries of their subordinates in making appointments. Offices frequently had lands attached to them ex officio, and in this respect they approached fiefs and were interpreted as such by contemporary European travelers (Lefebvre, 1845; Beke, n.d.). Further access to land depended on the nobility competing directly with the peasantry to claim land by inheritance. It was an unequal competition. One of the principal points of articulation between the peasantry and the state came through the courts. In pre-20th century Ethiopia, there were no secular courts independent of the nobility who presided over them. Although the right of appeal to the king was a fundamental feature of Abyssinian concepts of justice, this right could not be exercised through any systematic hierarchy of courts. Land played a large part in litigation. Peasant landholding, particularly under the system of inheritance, was inherently unstable. Abyssinian peasants inherited only *rights* to land, not particular pieces of land, and the recognition of rights in tangible form was an imperfect business. Moreover, each peasant always had rights more extensive than he was able to effect, while no one's right ever went unqualified by the conflicting right of another. The price of peasant control of the land was thus a system which greatly encouraged peasant conflict and tended to undermine peasant solidarity. Peasant institutions, such as the notional descent corporations, were inadequate to contain the many conflicts which arose. Ultimate resolution of land conflicts consequently lay with the nobility, and the nobility did not hesitate to use its position to enhance its own holdings (Hoben, 1973; Bruce, 1976). Unequal shares were allocated, the rich and powerful openly receiving much more than others. Again a system ostensibly based on inheritance and descent proved quite adept at incorporating powerful strangers, through the invention of convenient ancestors for them if necessary. In its resolution of land conflicts, the nobility played a crucial role in the reproduction of the social order and of the system of social production by determining the limits of peasant land control and by gaining land for itself.

Previous commentators have identified the Abyssinian state with the Solomonic court (Markakis, 1968; Ricci, 1968; Taddesse Tamrat, 1972; Doresse, n.d.). Recent scholarship has tended to emphasize the absolutist practice and aspirations of that court (Doresse, n.d.; Taddesse Tamrat, 1972). This tendency has obscured the class context of the state and has thereby construed it too narrowly. If the Abyssinian state is to be identified with the Solomonic court, then it is essential to see that court as the controlling apex of a structure of appointed officials which ultimately allowed the extraction of crucial surpluses from the peasantry.[6] Until the 20th century, such was not the case. Rather, the court balanced and manipulated, and sometimes overrode, the claims of the nobility to particular offices. The court was confined by a social and class structure which it never challenged. Ideology held that the king was for all and that all had equal right to the king's justice, but the absence of any separate *system* of royal courts, outside of those run by the nobility themselves, made this claim an empty one to most subjects (Perham, 1948; Rubenson, 1966). Moreover, although we know that Abyssinian rulers devoted a reasonable amount of time to judicial activities, we have little information on the reach of the ideological claims made on behalf of this judging. The practice of the royal court was to sanction and regulate the affairs of the nobility. In this respect it had a crucial role to play. Abyssinian rules of inheritance and descent are ambilineal, stressing the rights of claimants derived through either of their parents (Hoben, 1973). Particularly with respect to offices these rules have a pronouncedly male bias, but there is no obligation to respect seniority let alone primogeniture. Consequently, claimants for offices abounded and the extremely fluid nature of the Abyssinian family, associated as it is with ease of divorce and frequent remarriage, lent an unstable character to the affairs of the nobility. This gave the royal court an extremely important role as ultimate arbiter of conflicts among the upper nobility, placing it in a comparably crucial role with respect to the reproduction of the nobility as a class as the nobility enjoyed with respect to the social formation as a whole. Thus the primary function of the court was the maintenance and reinforcement of the class rule of the nobility, and only as a very secondary function did it regulate relations between the nobility and the peasantry.

It is important neither to reify this notion of the "nobility" nor to construe the nobility's existence as a class with too rigid a character. Class, as we ought to expect in this precapitalist context, was fluid and ill-defined. Class rule in the Solomonic state was not buttressed by notions either of "estate," as in Europe, or of "caste," as in India. Indeed, there were no sharp lines of demarcation as one moved up the social structure, clearly marking one layer from another, however great the distance traversed from top to bottom, unless it was the line of prestige at the top marking royal from nonroyal. At the top of society and distinct from royalty, but more powerful than all but the reigning monarch, there were the *makwānnent,* the great lords or princes (sing. *makonnen;* Crummey, 1979), and at the bottom there were the *bālāgar* or *gabārē,* the peasants, country people, or farmers. However, the *makwānnent* were simply members of a much larger class, the members of which, particularly in its lower reaches, were known as *bālābbāt* (sing.). The term literally means "one who has a father" (Markakis, 1974), that is to say someone of recognized social standing, and it covers the range of both "gentry" and "nobility" in the language of European feudalism, tilting perhaps somewhat toward the former. At the bottom a *bālābbāt* would be simply a rich peasant whose descendants could rapidly sink to anonymity. Nonetheless, it was from among the *bālābbāts* that appointments were made, and the *shums*, or appointees, formed the administrative basis of the Abyssinian state. The *shums* as officials, and the *bālābbāts* as a social group, formed the principal point of contact between the Abyssinian state and the Abyssinian peasants.

From the 1770s to the 1850s, the Abyssinian polity lacked an effective central authority. Struggles of the nobility during the 1770s succeeded in subordinating the king and the royal court to the control of a succession of nobles (Bruce, 1790; Guidi, 1912; Weld Blundell, 1922; Abir, 1968). The decades following the 1770s saw the emergence of regionally based lineages and nobles who competed with each other on the battlefield, seeking the enlargement of their tributary rights. None succeeded in establishing an enduring supremacy. Yet the period saw neither significant changes in basic social relations nor in the broad framework of ideology. The class structure of Abyssinian society was largely untouched by this period, known as the *Zamana Masāfent* (the Era of the Princes). Rather, class relations continued to work themselves out on much the same basis as they had previously, inasmuch as we can discern patterns from earlier periods. For example, neither major new forms of tribute or rent may be dated to the *Zamana Masāfent*[7] nor does the period show major movements among the peasantry which the imposition of such new exactions ought to have provoked. Thus the nobility did not view the subjugation of the monarchy as an opportunity to transform class relations between itself and the peasantry. Rather, the various noble lineages, and individual nobles, saw this subjugation as an opportunity for aggrandizement *vis-à-vis* other lineages and individuals.

The result was almost a century of bloody strife, which, unlike the bloodshed of the medieval period (13th through 16th centuries) or of the later 19th century, bore very directly on the Abyssinian cultivators, over whose fields, in a quite literal sense, the nobles fought.

The nobility justified its rule along the same lines as the monarchy had. It did not abolish the monarchy, and throughout the period the monarchy remained available to sanction appointments to the highest ranks of the nobility or to sanction grants of land to major churches.[8] The alternative to using the monarchy as a tool was ignoring it, and for many purposes nobles now acted autonomously (Huntingford, 1965). They justified their rule along lines analogous to those of the court. Strict dynastic Solomonic legitimacy was claimed by no one, since this would have been synonymous with assumption of the throne, and this did not take place until 1855. Just as many regional rulers attempted to ignore the *fainéant* kings, so too they ignored strict Solomonic ideology. On the other hand, the rulers of Gojjām and Dāmot made much of their descent from the dominant imperial figure of the mid-18th century, a woman (Fantahun Birhane). The main ideological thrust of the noble rulers of the *Zamana Masāfent* was Christian Orthodoxy. The 17th century had seen the rise of divisive schools of Christian doctrine within the Ethiopian Orthodox Church. By the later 18th century three distinct sects opposed one another, and different rulers sought to legitimate their rule by claims to doctrinal rectitude, generally carefully tailored to the inclinations of locally based monastic parties (Crummey, 1972). In addition, wherever possible the nobles postured as champions of Christianity against Islam, and they further exploited ethnicity (Abir, 1968; Crummey, 1975). Thus, the *Zamana Masāfent* saw adaptations in ideology, but it saw no transformations.

In essence, the Abyssinian state perpetuated itself through the *Zamana Masāfent* by means of a few striking adaptations. The royal court virtually disappeared as such, but its style and structure reappeared thinly disguised in the courts of the regional nobles. Physically the noble courts showed the same pattern as that of the kings (Taddesse Tamrat, 1972; Griaule, 1934). Customs and institutions such as itineration and the imprisonment of contenders continued. Offices and court hierarchies were reproduced holus-bolus (Fantahun Birhane, 1973; d'Abbadie, 1868). Only the tip of the state was altered, its framework and its foundation endured. The nobility constituted that framework and foundation. And the nobility supported itself by exactions from the peasantry.

The years following the 1850s saw the reconstruction of Ethiopia's imperial institutions and the expansion of the Ethiopian state to include vast new territories. These developments took place in an era of growing European imperialist activities in northeast Africa. External forces fed imperial rule in Ethiopia and stimulated and fed Ethiopia's territorial expansion. These same external forces had no impact on social relations within the old Abyssinian territories and little direct impact on social relations within the new territories. Ethiopia's rulers, especially Menilek of Shawa, attempted with some success to control commerce, but they showed little interest in, and had virtually no impact on, systems of production (Caulk, 1966, n.d.). The Abyssinian state retained a tributary posture with respect to trade.

Ethiopia's imperial institutions were restored by a succession of three men: Tēwodros II (r. 1855–1868), Yohannes II (r. 1872–1889), and Menilek II (r. 1889–1913). They did so largely by subordinating their noble rivals by force and by exacting tribute from them. In this way the last quarter of the 19th century saw a great enhancement in the power of the Ethiopian emperors. External developments also played their part. A succession of victories in foreign wars, particularly the victories of Gundat and Gur'a in 1875 and 1876 and of Adwā in 1896, greatly enhanced the emperors' prestige (Rubenson, 1976). Nonetheless, the emperors never moved beyond their class context, but rather their office continued as a potent instrument preserving the class rule of the nobility.

The reign of Tēwodros was turbulent and there has been a recurrent tendency among younger Ethiopians to interpret that turbulence in terms of attempts by the emperor to liberate the peasantry from feudal exactions. Contemporary records give scant support for this view, stressing rather tussles between the court and the church over tribute, tussles which grew more acute as the emperor failed to subdue his rivals, but which issued in victory for the church (Crummey, 1978). There is nothing in Tēwodros's career to suggest anything other than a particularly intelligent, at times enlightened, and charismatic nobleman (Crummey, 1969). Neither Yohannes nor Menilek carries the least aura of social radicalism (Marcus, 1975; Zewde Gebre-Sellassie, 1975). So far as their landed policies are concerned, Yohannes is associated with lavish grants of land to the churches of Tegrē province (Gebre Medhin Kidane, 1972; Rosen, 1974; Bruce, 1976), while Menilek can claim a number of changes, none of which measurably improved the conditions of the country's cultivators. On the one hand, Menilek systematized the appropriation and redistribution of conquered lands in such a manner as to ensure the perpetuation of a local indigenous ruling class alongside, but generally subordinate to, the immigrant colonists (Gabra Sellāsē, 1930: Chaps. 30, 34; Garretson, 1974; Gebre-Wold, 1962). He also made universal the payment of the tithe in the lands immediately subject to him, a move which was designed to regularize the support of imperial troops at a time of distress for the peasantry (Garretson, 1974; Gebre-Wold, 1962). This move has frequently been presented as a reform benefiting the peasants, a group to whose burdens it, in fact, probably added. Restored imperial rule perpetuated the rule of a landed nobility in the Abyssinian territories and extended that rule to the south in more direct forms.

More generally, Menilek has enjoyed the reputation of a modernizer (Pankhurst, 1964). This reputation is shallowly based. Prior to the emperor's death in 1913, the most progressive change to affect the peoples of the empire as a whole was the imposition of a *pax Amharica*. It was only a relative peace as the nobility continued to prove itself fractious. Otherwise, change affected the country and its government only superficially. A national bank was founded and coins issued for the first time in a millenium. Posts and telegraphs were introduced; a cabinet form of government was nominally created; modern machinery appeared in Addis Ababa, which was eventually connected to the coast by railroad; a cadastral survey was begun; and modern education and medicine were introduced. The government attempted to keep pace with military technology. The bulk of these developments affected only the capital, Addis Ababa, although the telegraph did serve modestly to enhance the capital's control of the provinces. Moreover, the enhanced power of the emperor ebbed with the health of Menilek (Marcus, 1975; Rosenfeld, 1978). For virtually two decades, from 1909 onward, the nobility regained the upper hand, and power in the Abyssinian polity was again diffused. Menilek was effectively *non compos mentis* from 1909 onward. His appointed successor, *Lej* Iyāsu, proved inept and unsuccessful in his dealings with the magnates of his grandfather's court. The result was his deposition and a compromise in 1916 vesting power simultaneously in Menilek's daughter Zawditu as empress and in Tafari Makonnen (later Haile Selassie) as regent (Caulk, forthcoming). Their relations were at best cool. Not until the late 1920s did the regent succeed in gaining a really substantial position of leadership. And although he succeeded to the throne in 1930 and began a program of ostensibly progressive change, this had little effect before the Italians invaded in 1935. Thus, the crucial developments in the country in the late 19th and early 20th centuries concerned the expansion of the Abyssinian state and the extension of the rule of the Abyssinian nobility into the southern regions.

Decades before the 1870s when the Egyptians burst into the Ethiopian highlands as forerunners of European imperialism, the Abyssinian polity had begun to expand. Growth points existed in Tegrē, Gojjām, and Shawā, all of whose rulers conducted regular forays into neighboring territories inhabited by non-Christian peoples. These forays were primarily designed for plunder, the bulk of which was controlled by the rulers who used it to support their armies and retainers, and who dispensed it further to such useful allies as the clergy (Simone). Since the 18th century, Shawā had grown steadily. Tegrē and Gojjām exhibited the same potential. The advent of Egyptian and European imperialism added an extra incentive, the desire to preclude hostile occupation of valuable territories, and modern firearms provided the means for much faster expansion. Modern firearms also played a major role in determining the internal struggle for control (Caulk, 1972). Thus, the primary thrust to Abyssinian expansionism arose from the dynamic of Abyssinian society and politics. European imperialism played a secondary role. As a result, the new forms of social relations imposed in the conquered territories had a markedly feudal character, but bore no signs of capitalist influence.

Abyssinian rule in the newly conquered territories was sustained by two main devices. First, in a number of cases local rulers adjusted themselves to the armies of conquest, submitted to the Abyssinians, and were thus coopted into the national ruling class. Such was the case with the ruler of Jimma or the Oromo princes of what is now Wallagā province. In these cases comparatively little land alienation took place and the cultivators suffered little immediate change in their social status. However, in most cases military conquest preceded an area's incorporation. Generally a higher degree of subjugation followed conquest than followed submission, although circumstances varied. For example, although similar in many respects, including the commitment of their rulers to resist conquest, the kingdoms of Wallāyta and Kafā suffered rather different fates. In the former case rather more of the preconquest ruling class was absorbed into the structure of Abyssinian control than in the latter case (Tsehai Berhaneselassie, 1969; Orent, 1968). The most intensive effects of conquest were felt by the peoples of the Rift Valley and the eastern highlands. These peoples—whose scale of social organization tended to be small, and many of whom lived in stateless societies—saw quite radical changes in their conditions of life as they lost large amounts of their land and suffered a sharp reduction in social status (McLellan, 1976; Addis Hiwet, 1975: 34–36). In these cases, and to a lesser extent also in the cases of those who submitted more voluntarily, Abyssinian rule based itself on immigrant garrisons, known as *katamā*. The *katamā* were supported by lands, by tributes, and by the services of local cultivators who were attached to the members of the garrisons in servile relationships. The term for this relationship was *gabbār,* the meaning of which approximates "serf" (Gebre-Wold, 1962; Gilkes, 1975: 13–14; 121–122).

The class structure which evolved in southern Ethiopia in the early 20th centure contained open antagonisms. The rulers were largely, although by no means wholly, immigrants. Their culture was visibly foreign. They practised Orthodox Christianity, which was true of only a small minority of the southern peoples, and that in a vestigial form; they spoke a foreign language, Amharic; they dressed differently; they ate differently; they served an alien lord. Thus, in southern Ethiopia, class tended to assume the character of ethnicity. Objectively, the situation was much more complex. While the bulk of the immigrants were Abyssinians, either Amhara or Tegrē, a sizable minority of them were recently and/or partially assimilated Oromo. And Abyssinian rule in the south was everywhere, although in varying degrees, associated with preconquest classes and elites. Nonetheless, ethnic and cultural differences reinforced class differences and made social relations in southern Ethiopia far tenser and prone to open conflict. Thus, in 1935–1936, at the time of the Italian invasion, and again in 1974 rather widespread rebellion marked the area (Getachew Kelemu, 1970; Ottaway & Ottaway, 1978).

With some justification, observers have viewed the social situations in southern Ethiopia as rather more fully feudal than the situation in the Abyssinian provinces. For example, the Abyssinian conquerors alienated large tracts of southern lands and reduced many of the local cultivators to tenancy relationships. In Illubābor, the most badly affected province, tenancy relations may have affected 75% of the cultivators, and 73% of the cultivators were wholly dependent on tenancy. More typical would be Kaffā where the comparable figures would be 62% of all cultivators involved in tenancy relationships, and 59% wholly dependent on tenancy; or Wallagā 59% and 54%. Arussi was comparatively lightly affected by these standards, with possibly 52% of its cultivators affected by tenancy relationships and 45% of its cultivators wholly dependent on tenancy.[10] A situation in which at least half the cultivators, and sometimes two-thirds or three-quarters, were affected by tenancy contrasts very markedly with the Abyssinian north where the comparable figures are about 20% of all cultivators involved in tenancy and around 12% or less wholly dependent on it (Crummey, 1979). In addition to asserting a much more direct control over the land in the south, the Abyssinian conquerors also imposed a more distinctly servile status on the southern cultivators, whose position rather more closely resembled that of serfs than did the position of the northern cultivators. Finally, also in the feudal vein, Abyssinian rule in the south was even more militaristic in character and flavor than it was in the northern heartlands. However, in political terms Abyssinian rule was rather less characteristically feudal since Addis Ababa kept a much closer control over the top offices in the south than it did on those in the north and prevented the emergence of a locally based nobility in the south. Abyssinian colonists in the south needed the support of Addis Ababa. On the other hand Abyssinian control of the south served the north in several ways. The process of conquest provided rich opportunities for bravado, plunder, and more long-term enrichment through control of new lands. Northerners, particularly gentry, clergy, and nobility, all benefited from the conquest, although it is very difficult to see what the northern cultivators got from it except respite from the attention of their rulers. After the conquest was complete, the distribution of lands continued to prove a highly valuable asset to the royal court, one which had still not exhausted itself prior to the revolution of 1974 (Cohen, 1973). And finally the rule of southern lands proved a fine expansion of opportunity for the higher reaches of the Abyssinian nobility, while the shuffling of the nobility through the various governing offices in the south provided the royal court with extra assets for controlling that nobility.

Thus the Abyssinian state, here viewed broadly as a form of class rule, revealed striking continuity and growth during the 19th century, in spite of dramatic changes in the fate of its symbolically central institution, the monarchy. The Abyssinian nobility aggrandized itself at the expense of its traditionally subject peasantry and succeeded in finding new objects of exploitation in the peoples of the south. In so doing the Abyssinian nobility created a social formation with some striking resemblances to a feudal mode of production. This social formation, as late as 1974, formed the framework of the Ethiopian revolution.

NOTES

1. Markakis and Nega (1978) is written from the perspective of the Ethiopian People's Revolutionary Party. Dan Connell has reported the views of the Eritrean People's Liberation Front in the *Guardian* (New York) and the *Observer* (London). The Ethiopian Democratic Union is the only substantial political organization not to have made use of Marxist-Leninist rhetoric.

2. The most ambitious attempt is by Addis Hiwet (1975).

3. Cliffe (1974) strays in this direction, although his remarks are directed to the last days of the *ancien régime*.

4. For a discussion of these factors as general characteristics of precapitalist societies, see Hindess and Hirst (1975, 1977).

5. Apart from Levine, very little has been done on ideology in Ethiopia.

6. This seems to be one major characteristic of what Marx intended by the Asiatic mode of production, a concept which in its totality suffers from incoherence (Marx, 1965; Hindess and Hirst, 1975; Anderson, 1974: Note B). French Marxists have been more sympathetic to the Asiatic mode of production.

7. The changes of which we have record are comparatively minor: Ali Zamach Marēt in Yajju, Amorā Tabāqi in Dambeyā, Webē's *tazkār* in Tegrē. For the two former see, Gebre-Wold (1962: 317, 320) and for the last see Parkyns (1868: 97–98).

8. See, for example, Gwoshu's investiture as *rās* in 1848: Conti Rossini (1947: 395) and charters No. 66–100 in Huntingford (1965), some of

which have royal sanction. The Huntingford charters are particularly significant in this regard since they emanate from Aksum in Tegrē while the emperors were generally resident in Gondar, a considerable distance away, under the control of rivals of the rulers of Tegrē.

9. But contrast with the case of the Gamo, discussed by Abélès (in this volume).

10. These figures should not be taken as very sound since they rest on problematic surveys conducted in the 1960s by the old Imperial Ethiopian government's Ministry of Land Reform (Cohen and Weintraub, 1975: 51, Table 11).

REFERENCES

ABIR, M. (1968) Ethiopia. The Era of the Princes. The challenge of Islam and the reunification of the Christian empire 1769–1855. London: Longman.

ADDIS HIWET (1975) Ethiopia from autocracy to revolution. London: Review of African Political Economy.

ANDERSON, P. (1974) Lineages of the absolutist state. London: Longman.

BEKE, C. T. (n.d.) A diary written during a journey in Abessinia in the years 1840, 1841, 1842, and 1843. London: British Library, Add. Mss. 30250A, 30251, 30252.

BRUCE, James (1790) Travels to discover the source of the Nile (5 vols.). Edinburgh: n.p.

BRUCE, John (1976) "Land reform planning and indigenous communal tenures: A case study of the tenure 'chigurafgwoses' in Tigray, Ethiopia." S.J.D. dissertation, University of Wisconsin—Madison.

CAULK, R. (1966). "The origins and development of the foreign policy of Menelik II, 1865–1896." Ph.D. dissertation, University of London.

_____ (1972) "Firearms and princely power in Ethiopia in the nineteenth century." Journal of African History 13: 609–630.

_____ (1978) "Armies as predators: Soldiers and peasants in Ethiopia c. 1850–1935." International Journal of African Historical Studies 11: 457–493.

_____ (forthcoming) "Dependence and reformism," in A. D. Roberts (ed.), The Cambridge History of Africa (vol. 7). Cambridge, England: Cambridge University Press.

_____ (n.d.) "Menilek II and the diplomacy of commerce, prelude to an imperial foreign policy." Addis Ababa: n.p.

CLIFFE, L. (1974) "Capitalism or feudalism? The famine in Ethiopia." Review of African Political Economy 1: 34–40.

COHEN, J. (1973) "Ethiopia after Haile Selassie: The government land factor." African Affairs 72: 365–382.

_____ and WEINTRAUB, D. (1975) Land and peasants in imperial Ethiopia: The social background to a revolution. Atlantic Highlands, NJ: Humanities Press.

CONTI ROSSINI, C. (1947) "Nuovi documenti per la storia d'Abissinia nel secolo XIX." Atti della Accademia Nazionale dei Lincei, Series 8, 2: 357–416.

CRUMMEY, D. (1969) "Tewodros as reformer and modernizer." Journal of African History 10: 457–469.

_____ (1972) Priests and politicians: Protestant and Catholic missions in Orthodox Ethiopia 1830–1868. Oxford, England: Clarendon Press.

_____ (1975) "Society and ethnicity in the politics of Christian Ethiopia during the Zamana Masāfent." International Journal of African Historical Studies 8: 266–278.

_____ (1978) "Orthodoxy and imperial reconstruction in Ethiopia 1854–1878." Journal of Theological Studies, New Series, 29.

___ (1979) "Abyssinian feudalism." Past and Present No. 89.

d'ABBADIE, A. (1868) Douze ans dans la haute-Ethiopie. Paris: n.p.

DORESSE, J. (n.d.) La vie quotidienne des éthiopiens chrétiens aux XVII et XVIII siècles. Paris: Hachette.

Ethiopia, Provisional Military Administrative Council (1975) The Ethiopian revolution. First anniversary of the Ethiopian revolution. Addis Ababa: Author.

_____ (1976) The Ethiopian revolution: Second anniversary. Addis Ababa: Author.

FANTAHUN BERHANE (1973) "Gojjam 1800–1855." B.A. dissertation, Addis Ababa University.

GABRA SELLASE (1930) Tārika Zamana ZaDāgmāwi Menilek Negusa Nagast Zaltyopya. Translated into French as Chronique du règne de Ménélik II Roi des Rois d'Ethiopie (2 vols.) Paris: Coppet.

GARRETSON, P. (1974) "A history of Addis Ababa from its foundation in 1886 to 1910." Ph.D. dissertation, University of London.

GEBRE MEDHIN KIDANE (1972) "Yohānis IV: Religious aspect of his internal policy." B.A. dissertation, Addis Ababa University.

GEBRE-WOLD, I. W. (1962) "Ethiopia's traditional system of land tenure and taxation." Ethiopia Observer 5: 302–339.

GETACHEW KELEMU (1970) "Internal history of the Aleta Sidanchos." B.A dissertation, Addis Ababa University.

GILKES, P. (1975) The dying lion: Feudalism and modernization in Ethiopia. London: Julian Friedman.

GRIAULE, M. (1934) "Un camp militaire abyssin." Journal de la Société des Africanistes 4: 117–122. Cited in A. Hoben, "Land tenure and social mobility among the Damot Amhara," *Proceedings of the Third International Conference of Ethiopian Studies, Addis Ababa, 1966* (Addis Ababa: 3 vols., 1970), III, 69–88.

GUIDI, I. (1912) Annales Regum Iyāsu II et Iyo'as. Rome: n.p.

HINDESS, B., and HIRST, P. (1975) Precapitalist modes of production. London: n.p.

———— (1977) Mode of production and social formation: An autocritique of precapitalist modes of production. London: n.p.

HOBEN, A. (1973) Land tenure among the Amhara of Ethiopia: The dynamics of cognatic descent. Chicago: University of Chicago Press.

HOBSBAWM, E. (1971). In I. Mészáros (ed.) Aspects of history and class consciousness. London: n.p.

HUNTINGFORD, G. W. B. (1965) The land charters of northern Ethiopia. Addis Ababa and Nairobi: n.p.

KEA, R. (1979) "Land, overlords and cultivators in the seventeenth century Gold Coast." (unpublished)

LEFEBVRE, T. (1845) Voyage en Abyssinie éxécuté pendant les années 1839, 1840, 1841, 1842, 1842 (6 vols.). Paris: n.p.

LEVINE, D. (1974) Greater Ethiopia: The evolution of a multiethnic society. Chicago: University of Chicago Press.

LITTMANN, E. (1902) The chronicle of King Theodore of Abyssinia. Princeton, NJ: Princeton University Press.

MARCUS, H. G. (1975) The life and times of Menelik II: Ethiopia 1844–1913. Oxford, England: Clarendon Press.

MARKAKIS, J. (1968) "An interpretation of political tradition in Ethiopia." Présence Africaine 66: 79–97.

———— (1974) Ethiopia: The anatomy of a polity. Oxford, England: Clarendon Press.

MARKAKIS, J., and NEGA, A. (1978) Class and revolution in Ethiopia. London: n.p.

MARX, K. (1908) Capital (vol. 3). Chicago: Chicago University Press.

———— (1965) Precapitalist economic formations. New York: Random House.

McLELLAN, C. (1976) "Perspectives on the naftanya-gabbar system: Darrasa." Presented at the annual meeting of the African Studies Association, Boston.

ORENT, A. (1968) "From the 'Good King' to the 'Good Chief': The evolution of micro politics in Kafa, Ethiopia." Presented at the annual meeting of the African Studies Association, Los Angeles.

OTTAWAY, M. and OTTAWAY, D. (1978) Ethiopia: Empire in revolution. New York: Africana.

PANKHURST, R. (1964) "Misoneism and innovation in Ethiopian history." Ethiopia Observer 8.

———— (1966) State and land in Ethiopian history. Addis Ababa: n.p.

PARKYNS, M. (1868) Life in Abyssinia. London: n.p.

PERHAM, M. (1948) The government of Ethiopia. London: n.p.

RICCI, L. (1968) "The organization of the state and social structures in Ethiopia," pp. 205–210 in P. McEwan (ed.) Twentieth century Africa. London: n.p.

ROSEN, C. B. (1974) "Warring with words: Patterns of political activity in a northern Ethiopian town." Ph.D. dissertation, University of Chicago.

ROSENFELD, C. P. (1978) The medical history of Menilek II, emperor of Ethiopia (1844–1913): A case of medical diplomacy. Pasadena: n.p.

RUBENSON, S. (1966) King of Kings: Tewodros of Ethiopia. Addis Ababa and Nairobi: n.p.

———— (1976) The survival of Ethiopian independence. London: Heinemann.

SIMONE, E. (1975) "The Amhara military expeditions against the Shawa Galla (1800–1850): A reappraisal," pp. 35–45 in H. G. Marcus (ed.) Proceedings of the first United States conference on Ethiopian studies, 1973. East Lansing: Michigan State University.

TADDESSE TAMRAT (1972) Church and state in Ethiopia 1270–1527. Oxford, England: Clarendon Press.

TSEHAI BERHANESELLASSIE (1969) "Menilek II: Conquest and consolidation of the southern provinces." B.A. dissertation, Addis Ababa University.

WEISSLEDER, W. (1965) "The political ecology of Amhara domination." Ph.D. dissertation, University of Chicago.

WELD BLUNDELL, H. (1922) The royal chronicle of Abyssinia, 1769–1840. Cambridge, England: Cambridge University Press.

ZEWDE GABRE-SELLASSIE (1975) Yohannes IV of Ethiopia: A political biography. Oxford, England: Clarendon Press.

Index